Mendel & Me

Mendel & Me

LIFE WITH CONGRESSMAN L. MENDEL RIVERS

Margaret Middleton Rivers,
with Margaret M.R. Eastman & L. Mendel Rivers Jr.

Charleston · London

History
PRESS

Published by The History Press
Charleston, SC 29403
www.historypress.net

Copyright © 2007 by Margaret Middleton Rivers, Margaret M.R. Eastman and L. Mendel Rivers Jr.

First published 2007

Manufactured in the United Kingdom

ISBN 978.1.59629.288.8

Library of Congress CIP data applied for.

Notice: The information in this book is true and complete to the best of our knowledge. It is offered without guarantee on the part of the authors or The History Press. The authors and The History Press disclaim all liability in connection with the use of this book.

To Mendel and Marwee
and
To those who have served in the United States Armed Forces,
past, present and future.

Contents

In Memoriam

In 1995 Marion Rivers Ravenel, daughter of L. Mendel Rivers, published a biography of our father entitled *Rivers Delivers*, a hard-bound volume that contains invaluable historical information and family lore.

In 2000 Margaret Rivers (widow)—better known as Marwee—Margaret Rivers Eastman (daughter) and L. Mendel Rivers Jr. (son) published a collection of their memoirs entitled *Mendel*. Marwee was then eighty-six, and she wanted to leave her progeny anecdotes about our colorful patriarch. The books were published with a plastic-spine "cookbook" binding. It was a modest effort indeed.

Margaret Rivers died in 2004. She had been a prolific chronicler. After her death, we discovered even more of her memoirs. We agreed to republish *Mendel*, but this time in a traditional form and with proper attention to Mendel's better half.

We had to decide how to approach the manuscript. *Mendel* consisted of Margaret Rivers's memoirs, plus commentary by Margaret Eastman and Mendel Rivers Jr. It was disjointed and rather hastily edited. In this version, we let Marwee tell her story from start to finish, seamlessly combining *Mendel* with the unpublished works. Most of the additions are Marwee's; however, we have taken a few liberties. Where the words are ours, if they are not exactly what Marwee said, well, they are what we hope she would have said if she had been given another chance to publish. We have used the lexicon of the mid-twentieth century instead of language that is considered "politically correct" today. The purist is invited to solve any authorship mysteries by reviewing the L. Mendel Rivers papers at the College of Charleston Special Collections Library.

We have attempted to explore more fully Mendel Rivers's background, his family life and his approach to politics, and to explain how a man with human failings could accomplish great deeds and be adored by so many. We hope to show that Marwee was his equal, his superior and his foil, as he was hers. We tried to be objective and attempted to put our parents in the context of the times in which they lived.

Thirty-six years after his death, people still enjoy recounting their Mendel Rivers stories and how he helped them and their families. Many who served in the armed forces during the turbulent days of Vietnam declare that Chairman Rivers has never been replaced as their strongest Congressional advocate. Marwee continues to be remembered for her gentility, kindness, patriotism and generosity.

Margaret M.R. Eastman and L. Mendel Rivers Jr.

February 6, 2007

Acknowledgements

Our deepest gratitude to:

John White and Marie Ferrara at the College of Charleston Special Collections Library, who have catalogued the remainder of the Rivers papers and memorabilia. John White wrote his master's thesis on Mendel Rivers's segregationist stance in the changing times before desegregation; he has edited this volume twice. Anne Bennett processed the Rivers photograph collection.

The College of Charleston Special Collections Library for permission to reproduce pictures from the Rivers photograph collection.

Dorothy Anderson, who spent countless hours providing new insights, clarifying events and trying to ensure this volume portrayed her sister's personality and outlook on life.

Robert Eastman and Edward Eastman, the Rivers grandsons who served in the U.S. Marine Corps, whose anecdotes confirm the esteem with which the military regarded Mendel Rivers long after his untimely death.

Beverly A. Rivers, who helped make sure comments reflected Marwee's style and character.

Marion Rivers (Ravenel) Cato, for *Rivers Delivers*, which has been a much appreciated source of verification when our memories fail since we no longer have Marwee to consult.

Captain Rusty Pickett, who provided the nautical terms for this volume, and the other captains of the *L. Mendel Rivers*, who have given friendship in countless ways: Roderic Wolfe, Ray Jones, Frank Jordan, Hollis Holden, Mario Bagaglio, Carl Mauney, Brad McDonald, George Petro and David Portner. *Rivers* crewmembers are equally dear.

Ted Stern, distinguished College of Charleston President, who generously shared his recollections.

Timothy S. McCay, a cousin we met through our research, who wrote a McCay genealogy and helped us resurrect the accomplished C.G. McCay and his sensational murder near McClellanville, South Carolina.

Vice Admiral H.G. Rickover, whose analysis of Mendel Rivers's contributions to history is incorporated into this volume.

Frank Jameson, Eddie Hébert and Russ Blanford, for insights into how Mendel Rivers maneuvered politically and the subterfuges he sometimes used to accomplish his goals.

The City of St. Stephen and Libba Carroll, who have preserved the Rivers heritage, including the Episcopal church graveyard where the Rivers family is buried.

Charleston Southern University L. Mendel Rivers Library staff and the university personnel who continue to honor Mendel Rivers.

North Charleston Mayor Keith Summey and Ed Fava, Chairman of the Greater Charleston Navy Memorial Park, and their committee, whose leadership has recognized Mendel Rivers's contributions to the naval base.

Charleston County Council for preserving the memory of L. Mendel Rivers through maintaining the monuments that bear his name.

Our special appreciation and thanks to others who contributed: Deborah Carver, Patricia Rivers Chaplin, Joseph R. (Bubber) Cockrell Jr., Mendel Davis, Gilly Dotterer, Lisa Pringle Farmer, David and Nancy Fortiere, Julie Foster, Carol Furtwangler, Trez Hane, Marshall Hudson, Arla Holroyd, Langhorne Howard, H.C. (Hop) Howlett, John Rivers Hope, Sandra Hughes, Jenny Kaemmerlen, Bill Kinard, Michael Kinard, Abbott Middleton, Charles Mitchell, George Palmer, Katie Parry, Lesleigh Patton, Lisa Reynolds, Charla Springer, Robert Stockton, Peggy Reeves, J.H. "Jack" Rudloff Jr., John H. Rudloff III, Jim Sawers, Tony Von Kolnitz, Robert J. Walker, Mary B. Wilson, Kathy Worthington, Larry Zelner and "the General."

Berkeley County Gentry

In 1968, after thirty years of marriage to a dynamo who was adored by millions of hero-worshipers, sniped at continually by a hostile media, who frequently amazed, amused, or exasperated me, I decided to learn more and write about his exceptional life. One of the most important questions I asked him was, "Do you mind if I write you up as you truly are?" His answer was emphatic, "No! Tell it like it is." I was glad to record personal glimpses of a powerful, creative, loveable man who was also a collection of contradictions. He became an astute statesman who worked hard to strengthen his country in turbulent times.

Excerpts from Marwee's preface to *Mendel*

This is a love story—a story about love of country, love of the principles upon which it stands and love for those who have fought to preserve them. It is the story of a man who was larger than life, passionate, brilliant, forceful, brash, generous and above all someone who had an amazing ability to recover from defeats, both personal and public. Nothing came easily to this man; he was obliged to make his own way by his own abilities and intelligence. There was no soft road of wealth or patronage for this man. His essence typifies the American ideals of honor, patriotism, dedication, hard work and success. He was a realist, and never wavered when he felt he was right. He tried to ensure that our country had a national defense second to none. Through the strength of his own character, he earned the respect of his colleagues and his people, and thus he was able to accomplish some wonderful things for a constituency that ultimately became the United States military around the whole world

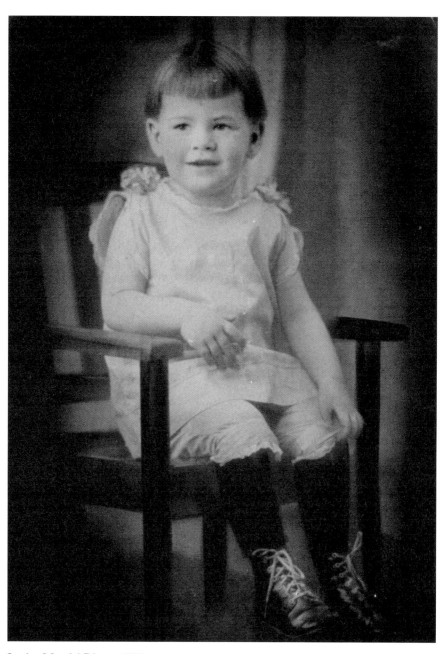

Lucius Mendel Rivers, 1907.

during the most unpopular war in U.S. history. He lived as he died, a "man's man" in every sense of the word.

Lucius Mendel Rivers was born on September 28, 1905, in Gumville, near Hell Hole Swamp,* Berkeley County, South Carolina, a location that never failed to amuse his biographers. Always the nonconformist, when the media asked him where he was from, he delighted in replying, "I'm from Gumville. It's near Hell Hole Swamp. If you don't know where it is, look it up." It didn't really matter that the place was not on any map.

His father, Lucius Hampton Rivers, was born in 1864 in Sumter, South Carolina. L.H. Rivers, as he was called, was orphaned early in life and was adopted by an aunt and uncle. But he was ambitious. He worked with his adopted father in the lumber and turpentine business and in his early thirties decided to go into business for himself. He was a Baptist, a teetotaler and a patient, careful man.

L.H. was also a good businessman. He began to acquire land. Soon his eye fell upon one of the belles of the region, Henrietta Marion McCay. She was a direct descendant of Gabriel Marion, brother of the legendary Swamp Fox of the American Revolution, and another Revolutionary War hero, General William Conway. She was also the daughter of Thomas A. McCay and granddaughter of Charles Greenland McCay. That was L.H.'s mistake.

Known as C.G., Charles Greenland McCay cast a long shadow over his descendants. He was strong and determined, and he was, by any family's standards, highly successful and a tough act to follow. C.G. was born in 1809, the eldest son of Charles McCay.

The McCays had apparently been in South Carolina for generations. There are records of McCays involved in trading between Carolina and Virginia as far back as the 1730s. The elder Charles was not poor. In 1825 he filed a tax return claiming ownership of 2,100 acres of land and four slaves. These holdings would have represented one or more working plantations. He died around 1831, and the young C.G. was his executor. He no doubt inherited much, if not most, of his father's estate. In 1832 C.G. "stole" Frances Causey from her father and married her on horseback.

C.G. then set out to acquire land, which he accomplished amazingly well. His holdings just grew and grew. By 1850 he owned 10,000 acres and livestock valued at over $10,000, an immense sum in those days. By 1860

---

* In the mid-twentieth century, Hell Hole Swamp produced numerous prominent South Carolina politicians, including Governor Robert McNair, Congressman L. Mendel Rivers, State Senator Rembert Dennis and Columbia Mayor Lester Bates. Hell Hole Swamp was a remote area consisting of approximately twenty square miles and was known for its lawlessness during Reconstruction after the plantation system collapsed. No one knows for sure how it got its name.

he owned 20,000 acres and $40,000 worth of livestock. By 1879, the year of his death, he owned land estimated to be between 26,100 and 40,000 acres, spread out over as many as seventeen plantations. They had lovely, picturesque names: Sugar Loaf, Bull Head, DuPree, Ball, Fell Corner, Barnet Island, Greenland, Fidda, Hickory Ridge, Manigault and Poplar Grove. His cash crops included rice, cotton, wool, butter and vegetables. He owned three thousand head of cattle, of which one thousand were dairy cattle. Before the war he owned seventy-four slaves and fifteen slave houses. He even owned a race horse, the ultimate token of country gentility.

It would be a romantic and untrue fancy to imagine C.G. McCay buying up the plantations of impoverished aristocrats after the Civil War at sheriffs' sales. It would be even more romantic to imagine that his untimely end in 1879 was somehow connected to his opportunistic purchases. In fact, C.G. began his acquisitions long before the hostilities began. As for the plight of the aristocrats, C.G. probably thought of himself as one of them, different only in that he was able to prosper both before and after the "Great War."

He took part in local politics. In 1849 he was appointed to a vigilance committee, whose job was to "intercept and destroy all publications having a tendency to injure local interests"—that is to say, all publications from those pesky Northern abolitionists. After the war, he helped organize the "colored Democrats" prior to the Presidential election of 1876.

He was still going strong in his seventieth year, when he was felled with a single shotgun blast and robbed on April Fools' Day 1879 while overseeing repairs to Palmer's Bridge, seven miles north of McClellanville, South Carolina. C.G. had had premonitions of his death and had written his will less than two months before his dastardly murder.

A suspect was eventually charged. He was an ordinary white man described as a "cracker." A sympathetic newspaper reporter wrote that if the accused were indicted, he was to be defended by his erstwhile Confederate commander, General B.H. Rutledge. One wonders if the former comrades in arms closed ranks once again, for there are no further known publications about a trial or conviction, despite compelling circumstantial evidence against the accused, including owing money to the victim, altercations about his debt with the victim and the presence of C.G.'s bloodstained knife and a large sum of cash in the accused's house.

C.G. left a widow and six children who survived to adulthood. C.G. parceled out his holdings among his children in his will. After his death, time, tide and the Panic of 1893 took their toll. The family fortune began to disappear. It is strange to contemplate how C.G. and his father before him had the skills to acquire and to make things grow. It was in their nature. His sons after him and their sons could only spend. Court records are ample evidence of the heirs' continuing disputes over his property. Thomas and his siblings lacked their father's knack for business and acquisition. They incurred debts and redeemed them by conveying away land. They sold land to pay the taxes on the land. They sold the timber and turpentine rights.

C.G.'s vast holdings disappeared by 1940. What C.G.'s father began in the eighteenth century was gone by the twentieth. It took fifty years to create. It took fifty years to dissipate. Family tradition has always held that the McCays owned most of what later became the Francis Marion National Forest, there being some dark suggestion that the evil federal government marched in and took the family's cherished holdings through eminent domain or other intimidation. But the feds didn't steal it. The McCays lost their inheritance on their own, through the same impersonal forces that caused them to acquire it.

Evidently, Thomas A. McCay felt he was country gentry. He inherited Sugar Loaf Plantation, his father's flagship holding, and he supported himself by working his inherited land and selling off parcels when he needed money.

He had major plans for his daughter, Henrietta, or Etta as she was called. In an era where few women were educated, Thomas sent Etta to Greenville College for Women, later a part of Furman University, where she graduated in the mid-1890s. She was an educated "young lady," and he encouraged her betrothal to an appropriate, in his mind, suitor—one Mendel L. Smith, a prominent attorney in Camden, South Carolina. They were engaged. Enter Lucius Hampton Rivers.

L.H. and Etta fell in love. Thomas forbade the union. Their love grew deeper. He forbade his daughter to see L.H. at all. Their love grew deeper still, and Etta was determined to elope with her true love. One night in 1896, she climbed out of a window, down to a waiting wagon L.H. had placed beneath it. The couple dashed off, at the speed of two horses, and promptly married.

Thomas reportedly waved goodbye to Etta from his porch and then disowned her shortly thereafter. He didn't simply disown Etta. He assassinated her—or tried to. Thomas removed his favored daughter from the line of those who might enjoy all that C.G. had accumulated. He sent her a letter, and what a letter it was! Perhaps his poison epistle was typical of those melodramatic, maudlin Victorian times. Perhaps every family has such a letter swirling between the skeletons in its closets. Yet I cannot read his letter without wanting to cry.

Mrs. L.H. Rivers; I suppose.
    How I loved you once, as well as a Father could love a child; now nothing would relieve me quicker than to see you dead, or to know that you were dead.

You have stuck yourself in that damn buzzards nest, now father, the redhead raven, and mother, the she-buzzard. Now you have started a nest to raise dirt daubers; now never Father me nor Mother Maggie while you draw breath, nor brother Charles nor sister, none of your sisters, for you have disgraced them and all of the family. My God, how do you feel perched up in those bug dens and among such people, that is not how you were raised.

You said in a note that you were going to leave this country; I think the sooner you leave the better, and Africa is the only place that would be fit for you, among those people, as you are as black and low!

I never want to see you again while we live, for the way I feel now, I would not mind wearing the black cap.

Thos. A. McCay

Even the Victorian preoccupation with death can't explain away the depth of Thomas's anger. Was this a battle of wills in a time when domineering fathers ruled the household, or was something even more ominous behind the falling out? We will never know, for Etta rarely spoke of the McCays. Yet she kept her father's terrible letter. With no explanation, it exists in faded and tattered form, an open wound, to this day.

Thomas and Etta never reconciled. He died in 1905, the year L. Mendel Rivers was born.

Ironically, Etta's young husband had much in common with Thomas's father, C.G., whose success had provided Thomas with his airs. Both were prudent businessmen who carefully purchased land and made it pay. Both understood the value of patient acquisition. Both understood money. Both became county road commissioners and were struck down while in the performance of their official duties. And both eloped with their brides, over the objections of their future fathers-in-law.

L.H.'s family had pretensions of its own. He told his wife, and anyone else who would listen, that he was descended from English aristocracy. He could trace his family back to the beginnings of the colony of Carolina, and he counted among his ancestors the long-dead Lord Mayor of London. Many of his Rivers cousins were prominent in Charleston society.

It must have rankled L.H. to be called lower class and not good enough to marry a McCay, but there is no mention in the family lore that he ever publicly complained of the injustice. He devoted himself to hard work and to proving to the McCays just how wrong they were.

L.H. immediately built for his bride a typical four-room "starter" home: two large crossed beams, wood framing and a porch stretched across the front. In later times, such structures would become the classic symbol of grinding rural poverty. In L.H.'s time, it was home.

He began acquiring land near the town of St. Stephen. In 1907 he moved his growing family to a spacious eight-room house he built himself of heart pine timbers, with an airy breezeway, a canopy to protect ladies from the elements and a fireplace in every room. There his family enjoyed a privileged existence. Their house was large, and they invited many people over for various social events. They gave their children piano lessons and stylish clothes. One child, Blanche, would speak nostalgically in her later years of her twenty-seven dresses, her tassel-trimmed shoes and her pony.

By 1915 L.H. owned a sawmill that cut the timber for the new home, a general store, a turpentine still, a cotton gin and extensive timberlands as well as the second automobile in Berkeley County. He was on his way. He became a notary public. He might well have run for political office, or perhaps parlayed his modest assets into major enterprises that might have shaped the world. We shall never know.

The Rivers family lost L.H. in 1915. The family never really recovered.

One morning in November 1915, as County Roads Commissioner, L.H. set out on horseback to inspect roads in a far-flung section of Berkeley County. That afternoon, an unexpected thunderstorm burst. L.H. rode home through the storm and arrived safely, but he was thoroughly drenched and developed a cough. The cough turned into a bad cold, which developed into pneumonia. He went to bed. His condition became serious.

Fifteen years before the discovery of penicillin, pneumonia was still "the old man's friend." There was no effective treatment for pneumonia in 1915. Many doctors, unwilling to do nothing at all, recommended strong doses of alcohol. Family lore has it that L.H.'s family doctor recommended corn whiskey or brandy, but L.H. adamantly refused. He was a Baptist-turned-Episcopalian but still a teetotaler, and he took sobriety seriously. He was content to die, if that was the Lord's will. He began to slip away.

Why was L.H. Rivers so adamant? Why did he refuse even a drop of alcohol to relieve a pain-wracked body and perhaps save his life? I have long suspected that he was wary of alcohol either from his own family experiences or from the stories his wife told him about Thomas McCay's drinking escapades. I have no direct proof that Thomas McCay was an alcoholic, but the malady runs in the family. Family members always seem to pass on this information.

His children, among them L. Mendel Rivers, age ten, had to watch their father, the powerful figure of their lives, die before them. After a ten-day struggle, Lucius Hampton Rivers died. He was fifty-one years old. His children began a slow reversal of fortune that would color their lives and their attitudes forever.

L. Mendel Rivers, 1935.

Mendel's Coming of Age

Etta Rivers attempted to maintain the genteel lifestyle that both her father and her husband had provided. She expected her eldest son Earle to pick up where his father had left off and to maintain the farm, the store and the going businesses of ginning cotton and distilling turpentine. Mendel, the only other male, was far too young, and women just weren't considered management material—not in 1915, and certainly not in rural South Carolina.

But Earle was really only a child himself, eighteen years old. He married one of the local gentry, Alma Jernigan. Running his father's various enterprises was beyond his age and his skills. His mother hired a farm manager to help him. Neither man could make the farm profitable, as L.H. had so nimbly done, but they kept trying.

During these years of struggle, a cousin persuaded Etta to move with her five unmarried children to a tiny hamlet just north of Charleston, later to be called North Charleston, but then simply known as the North Area. With the remains of her savings she purchased a home on the streetcar line and began to take in boarders. She sent her two oldest daughters to live with relatives, and, along with Mendel and the two remaining girls, she squeezed into far smaller quarters.

It was a long, painful way down. Etta was forced to sell many of her most cherished belongings. A family in St. Stephen now proudly displays her fancy Sears, Roebuck sewing machine. Young Mendel remembered until the day he died, with perfect clarity, the smell, taste, color and texture of the ripe red tomatoes his mother would carefully prepare and serve, not to him, but to hungry boarders, who would engorge themselves upon the food he craved and felt he deserved. No more new ponies and tasseled shoes!

The final indignity arrived in 1922, when the entire farm was lost, foreclosed upon to satisfy a relatively tiny debt of a few thousand dollars for fertilizer.

It was classic tragedy. The season before, Earle had mortgaged the property to purchase fertilizer. Of course, Earle didn't own the land; his mother did. So he forged her name to a note and mortgage. When the note came due, prices were low, and Earle missed his payments. The lender foreclosed. Etta could have defended against the mortgage foreclosure successfully by denying that she had ever signed the documents. The lender knew this and threatened to prosecute Earle for fraud if Etta denied the validity of the mortgage. She chose her son's freedom over her farm, of course. What mother wouldn't? But she never really recovered. Forty years later, when she would tell the story, her eyes would cloud over. Earle had broken her heart. The dream of returning to St. Stephen and the prosperous country life they had once known was over.*

The tragedy may have destroyed Earle as well. He was divorced at least twice (in an age when divorce was nearly unheard of among respectable people), became a severe alcoholic and lost his relationship with his only child, who never liked him because of his drinking. He had talent. He became chief troubleshooter, or wrecking master, for the Atlantic Coast Line Railroad, a coveted job. Even when he was drinking, he was given credit for being the best wrecking master ACL ever had. Earle Rivers died at fifty-two.

To Etta's credit, she bore her vicissitudes stoically and did not become a complaining, angry old woman. Her strong character provided an example for her younger son, in whom she now placed all her hopes. He returned her loyalty.

Young Mendel Rivers was transformed from a rich man's son with servants to a widow's kid with a daily chore schedule. Losing his father at a young age and losing so suddenly the status of being a wealthy man's son did something to young Mendel Rivers. It took something precious out of him his faith in the inherent rightness of things. It put something

---

* The house subsequently passed through various owners. In 1972 several of Mendel's admirers in Berkeley County purchased the house plus a one-acre square upon which it sat, with the intention of restoring it. Their efforts were, to say the least, deliberate, and little was done until 1989, when Hurricane Hugo blew off most of the roof and created terrible damage. As the damaged building continued to deteriorate, young Mendel and others tried in vain to raise the funds to restore it. They were unsuccessful, and the house was demolished in 1996. Today a lone tree marks the location of the once-proud home.

powerful into him: a determination to depend upon himself and himself only, to never again be dependent upon another—even a loving parent—to provide what he needed. It transformed his outlook on life. He no longer saw himself as the child of privilege, looking out. Now he was the child of misfortune, looking in. It hardened him, as it made him stronger. Certainly, it was the great adversity that would follow him all his life. Like all great men, he measured all of his later life's challenges against that one watershed event.

It may also have affected his politics. Mendel Rivers came into this world believing it to be a comfortable, predictable place. At age ten, that certainty was shattered. As an older man, he looked back upon his life prior to age ten with the golden hue of nostalgia, a sort of paradise lost, impossible to reclaim. It had been so perfect, and then something bad happened and ruined it. In like measure, as he aged, he liked to ruminate upon the fate of his country with the same sense of irretrievable loss: "Marguerite [or Son, or whoever the listener might be], this country is not going to hell. This country has gone to hell."

The North Area had little to offer a young man. The aristocrats of the community were known as the "Car-line Crackers," as they enjoyed the distinction of living by the trolley tracks. Most people worked in the asbestos factory or the lumber mill. The only church was Cousin Robert Lebby's Union Sunday school, held in the railway depot. Political discussions at Colie Morse's soft drink stand provided further entertainment. Radios and television were still in the future. The closest high school, library, theater and movie house were miles away in Charleston. Baseball, the chief recreation of the community, was not permitted on Sunday.

During the sweltering heat of a South Carolina summer, young Mendel took his first real job at the port terminals transporting a heavy, sloshing water bucket to thirsty Jamaican laborers as they loaded ships bound for the war effort overseas. Only a skinny boy of eleven, he never forgot their half-friendly, half-threatening refrain, "Water, Jack! Water, Jack! You oughta be there and halfway back!"

It was 1917. The feverish activity of construction and commerce gave the youngster a glimpse of widening horizons. It made him determine that his future would hold brighter prospects than a daily ride on a converted cattle car to a job that yielded fifteen cents an hour for eleven hours a day, six days a week.

Mendel delivered newspapers, and before leaving for the two-teacher school, he also chopped wood, milked the cow and staked her in an empty lot. In summer he always held a job, but sometimes he managed to sneak away from the wood chopping at home for a game of sandlot baseball or a swim in the creek. Sometimes he worked in a grocery store. Grocery clerks had to be versatile in those days. Besides taking orders, assembling and delivering groceries, they had to cut meat, weigh and compute prices (without the help of modern scales), stock the shelves and clean the store after closing hours. For an eighteen-hour day, he received $2.50. He worked hard, and his boss liked him. On Saturday afternoons, he gave Mendel three hours off to play baseball.

Mendel played baseball all his life. He started on sandlots. The General Asbestos and Rubber Company, better known as GARCO, was the primary employer in North Charleston, and it fielded a team early in the twentieth century. Mendel got a summer job with GARCO so that he could play on the team. He was apprenticed in the weaving room, paint shop and machine shop, but his love was baseball. GARCO would buy the equipment, and every day after work until darkness forced them off the field, Mendel and his team of stalwarts would practice on a diamond in GARCO Village, the little neighborhood of company houses that surrounded the plant. They were semi-professional baseball players. They were paid two, sometimes three dollars a game.

Mendel could play almost any position. One story he liked to tell about himself involved his days as a player/coach. Among other things, player/coaches substitute players, including themselves, as the game progresses. On

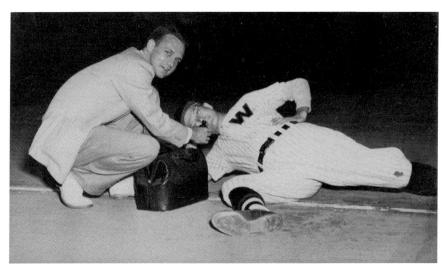

In the old days Mendel's batting average was well over .300. He also got numerous runs in the Congressional baseball games until they were discontinued. This picture hung in his Washington office throughout his career.

one particular evening, player/coach Rivers assigned one of his best friends to play center field. Several innings later, while the friend was playing center field as assigned, he missed a routine fly ball. Coach Rivers was furious. When the inning ended, he jerked his friend out of the game and assigned himself to play center field. The very next inning, while he was playing the position, Player Rivers missed a routine fly ball to center field. When that inning finally ended, Rivers trotted into the dugout with the rest of the players. They all gathered around him, waiting for his apology to his friend, now sitting the game out and looking expectant. Instead, Rivers walked straight up to his friend and shouted, "You son of a bitch! Now look what you've done! You got center field so fucked up, *nobody* can play it!" Classic, vintage Mendel Rivers.

When asked if he had ever had any dates, Mendel replied, "Oh, yes, some on Friday nights. There wasn't anywhere to go. My mother had a car, but kids didn't get cars in those days. After the churches came to North Charleston, we went to church socials mostly." Then he went on: "But it was education that mattered. Education was something I figured I was going to get. I knew that would take care of the future." He was already beginning to develop his credo, "Think big."

As an awkward teenager, young Mendel attended Charleston High School, a forty-five-minute trolley ride away. There was no high school in North Charleston or in any of the other suburbs. Charleston High was the one and only high school for white young men in the Charleston area. It was not an easy place to grow into manhood. Fights between students were common, and even the teachers feared certain students. Bullies sailed pin-equipped paper missiles at their victims and backed up the torment with their fists. No hero in those days, Mendel later freely acknowledged that he was cowed by the bullies who ruled those turbulent classrooms, a fact that surprised many of his admirers, who knew him only as the self-assured man he would become. At the same time, he was snubbed by many downtown Charleston sons of privilege, who simply looked down in general upon anyone from North Charleston, regardless of their Berkeley County pedigree. He remembered those slights well. He found them especially painful.

Mendel's most vivid memory of his high school years was the day his English teacher, Hervey Allen, an accomplished author of fiction (the bestsellers *Anthony Adverse* and *Israfel*), climbed up on his desk at the front of the room to illustrate the difference between transitive and intransitive verbs. Allen was an unusual man who favored Western boots and cowboy buckles when no one else in stuffy Charleston understood or appreciated them. He was a large man. Wearing his heavy Western boots, he ferociously jumped up and down on his desk. Cowboy Allen, as everyone called him, then yelled out to his astonished class, "You think I'm crazy, don't you, boys?"

"Oh, no sir, Mr. Allen!"

"You'll remember this day, won't you, boys?"

"Oh, yes sir, Mr. Allen!"

"Well, remember this, too: The verb 'to be' never takes an object!"

Hervey Allen eventually left Charleston under suspicious circumstances that suggested he, shall we say, failed to appreciate proper boundaries between students and teachers. But perhaps it was from him that Mendel acquired his love of poetry. Certainly, he read and quoted liberally from the great masters, earning the sobriquet "silver-tongued orator from South Carolina." He particularly loved Robert Burns and Thomas Gray's "Elegy in a Country Churchyard." In later years Mendel's speeches often included poetry.

He was not much of a student, but his study habits improved when one of the boarders helped him string an exposed electric light bulb over his bed. In those days a student had to pass every subject before he could be promoted. Mendel had to repeat his first year because he received a 69 instead of 70 in math. It took him six years to finish high school. He was almost twenty-one when he was awarded his graduation certificate, the only diploma he ever achieved.

He attended the College of Charleston. In college, he began to develop the people skills that would become his trademark. Those who remembered him in college recalled a cheerful young man with plans for himself. He learned English syntax through his study of Latin and Spanish. He attempted to weed out from his speech some of the awkward participles that were acceptable in North Charleston and in sandlot baseball. He also decided to improve his posture. After three years at the College of Charleston, Mendel was ready. He applied for and was accepted at the state law school.

He was less than impressive as a law student. "Nobody would have bet a plugged nickel on me then," he would chuckle. "Even when I knew the assignment, I'd freeze with stage fright. It was all I could do to say 'Pass me, Professor.'"

At the end of his second year, the Dean of the School of Law asked the aspiring lawyer to come into his office. He gave young Rivers a fatherly lecture, concluding with, "Son, I understand that your father was a farmer in Berkeley County and a good one. Why don't you go back there and become a farmer? You'll never make a lawyer."

"And you, Dean Friarson, will never make a Dean," Mendel retorted. Or so he said he retorted, when he told the story years later.

Mendel left the law school in Columbia and returned to North Charleston. There he read the law, which was permitted in those days in lieu of a law degree, and later he took the state bar examination. He needed two attorneys' recommendations in order to take the bar exam and had to struggle just to locate two who would vouch for him. He was not a hot prospect.

In June 1932, Mendel was at his mother's house in the backyard, chopping wood, when she casually came to the porch and announced, "Here's a letter for you." Mendel saw a two-cent stamp on the envelope (he later had it framed and hung it in his office) and the return address of Laneau and Lide, a law firm in Marion, South Carolina. Senator Lide was Chairman of the Board of Bar Examiners. It was the results of the bar exam. Mendel took the envelope, but his hands began to shake—a little at first, and then more and more violently. He tried to open the envelope but could only fumble and nearly ripped it apart. He decided he would destroy it before he could even read it, so he handed the envelope back to his mother. He was sure he had failed, for the exam was so long that no one ever finished it. In order to have a strong beginning and ending, he had started answering questions at the top, then skipped to the end.

But he didn't fail. He had passed the bar examination. He was a lawyer now, a man of twenty-seven with a future. He had no idea what life held for him, but he saw it spread out before him, and he knew his life would be different from his North Charleston peers. Let them stay in North Charleston and settle for that "dream job" in the grocery store or at one of the mills. Mendel was headed elsewhere.

He sought employment with the local Broad Street law firms, then, as now, the most prestigious attorneys in Charleston. He knew that through his father he was kin to, and rather closely, many of the aristocratic downtown Charleston attorneys. He was family. He asked them to hire him.

Every firm refused him utterly, including those of his cousins. In fact, when he mentioned that he was related to them, several of them politely denied any kinship. He remembered that snub all of his life. His mother even swallowed her pride and went downtown to the same law firms and asked them to hire her son. She was a McCay, she would say, but her son was a Rivers, one of you. Please help my boy. She was no more successful. It was the Depression, and besides, blood is only thicker than water when we want it to be.

Mendel began to practice law on his own. His first cases were small cases in the Magistrate's Court. He had many Negro clients, some of whom were uneducated and quite poor. He couldn't always be sure they would get to court without his help, so he picked many of them up in his car and drove them to court. He laboriously did his own stenographic work at home or used a typewriter at the high school. His first professional effort produced a deed full of errors.

Eventually, Mendel found office space with a former City of Charleston Magistrate, Joseph Fromberg. Joe insisted that everyone call him "Judge" although he had never been judge of a court of record, but rather the Magistrate's Court, sometimes known as traffic court or police court. A term on the Magistrate's Court was considered a way station along the career path for ambitious lawyers. (The Judge had many noteworthy accomplishments: He graduated from the University of South Carolina School of Law in 1910 at the age of twenty. It required a special act of the South Carolina General Assembly so that he could take the bar examination and become an attorney. He was a highly intelligent man. He had courage, too. He had risked his own professional standing by vigorously challenging the slack efforts of lawyers appointed to represent Negroes in criminal cases. The South Carolina Supreme Court, instead of criticizing the slack lawyers, criticized him. But he never backed down.)

I do not know why or when Mendel decided to become a politician. I know that he developed a taste for state politics in the summer of 1930 when he helped Ed Pritchard run against Russell McGowan. Ed was defeated. Mendel was hooked.

Mendel's friends in North Charleston saw something in him. He saw something in himself. Politics may well have been the only avenue he saw open. In 1932 he decided to run for the state legislature. In those days, all candidates were elected at large from the entire county, not from individual districts within the county. Mendel's first stop was to seek the blessings of the most important local political figure—Hizzoner the Mayor of the City of Charleston, Burnet R. Maybank.

He didn't get it, not in that election, nor in the elections to come. He never really did achieve full acceptance among the City of Charleston politicians. It bothered him at first. In time, he simply went around them, and eventually, over the years, they all came to him.

He lost his first election effort in 1932, but was elected a year later in a special election when the incumbent resigned. His campaign slogan was the catchy, irresistible "Give the Northern End of the County Representation." One shudders to think what the loser's slogan was.

Mendel thrived in the legislature. When he ran for reelection in 1934, he led the ticket, meaning he received more votes than anyone else running for the office (usually upward of twenty candidates for twelve seats) and was elected by his peers as chairman of his county's delegation. He served on the Judiciary and Education Committees and enjoyed learning the fine points of the legislative process. He increased his activities in the Young Democrats, becoming its state president in 1935. He was elected a delegate to the Democratic National Convention of 1936.

He never could give any satisfactory explanation of how he broke through his timidity. In his sixties, he opined, "Those things sort of develop. I knew I was smarter than most people, and I wanted to get ahead."

He was ambitious. Word got around. The newspaper reported that Mendel Rivers had requested from the secretary of the State Democratic Party an entry form to file for office in 1936, an ominous sign that perhaps he was planning to file for U.S. Congress against the incumbent, Tom McMillan.

Mendel and Joe Fromberg even met with Tom, just as friends, of course, pretending to discuss the upcoming 1936 elections in general. No doubt Tom wanted to size Mendel up, as Mendel wanted to size him up. Tom wisely bought Mendel off. He offered him a job as "Special Assistant to the Attorney General of the United States," with the chance to go to Washington, do important work and earn a handsome salary to boot—$3,200 per year. Real money, at last. Mendel accepted. Tom wasn't going to live forever. (Once he started working for the Justice Department, Mendel discovered that he had been misled. He was one of hundreds of lawyers, all of whom were Special Assistants to the Attorney General of the United States.)

He worked in Washington, New Orleans, Atlanta and many other places around the South. He was assigned to collection of unpaid criminal fines and forfeited bail bonds. It was the Depression. Jackson Love, an investigator with the Department of Justice who worked with him, recalled years later that he tried to be compassionate while doing his job. Mendel knew what it was like to be poor. Dot Lucas Corcoran told me that once when Mendel was giving her a ride from New Orleans, he realized he had been overpaid two dollars by a service station attendant. He turned around and drove back ten miles to return the money. In Depression days, two dollars was a huge amount.

Like his father, L. Mendel Rivers had become established by his early thirties. Like his father, he was ready now, and only now, to marry. Like his father, he sought upward mobility through marriage.

Aristocratic Charleston

My background was vastly different from Mendel's. I was a Charlestonian and Charleston marked her own. Our accent seems to have been influenced by coastal fogs, Negro dialect and settlers from the area of Newcastle, England. We like it. It always amazes me to hear a Charlestonian who has managed to eradicate its distinctive cadences and who actually wants to talk like an outsider. Getting rid of a Charleston accent is a most difficult undertaking. Our attitude, too, is unusual. Charleston was intended to be an aristocracy from its earliest days; we are as caste conscious as any Brahmin.

Carolina was presented to eight English Lords by Charles II in 1665. (The Spaniards and French had already made tragic attempts to colonize our coasts.) The Merry Monarch was extremely generous with his grant; he gave his friends both the Carolinas and Georgia and set the western boundaries at the Pacific Ocean. With such vast holdings, the Lords Proprietors had an opportunity to establish a model colony in the new world. Their idea of a model state was, of course, aristocratic. They had no idea of setting up a government ruled by a "too numerous democracy." Their vivid recollections of Cromwell and his cohorts prevented any such foolishness.

The earliest Carolina arrivals were given an opportunity to become titled landholders. All they needed was enough money to purchase the land. Depending upon one's pocketbook, one might become a baron, cacique or landgrave. (I was always impressed when I heard that someone was a descendant of Landgrave Smith, the most fruitful and renowned of those early American noblemen. I didn't find out that important item about the ready cash until I was fifty, while studying a course for tourist guides.) A thriving aristocracy was soon established, for land could be grabbed up for a penny an acre.

Charlestonians of later generations appreciated the efforts of those early pioneers. Our first settlers pushed their trading posts as far as the Mississippi River a hundred years before Daniel Boone explored Kentucky. A high quality of European culture was transplanted to our soil in the late seventeenth century; many bona fide members of English and French aristocracy joined the newly made Carolina ones. As merchants and artisans prospered, they too bought lands and became part of the ruling agrarian class. Charleston gradually became the center of a prosperous and highly refined civilization.

Charleston's wealthy sons were usually educated abroad. They played a major part in establishing the government of the United States. Our beautiful city flourished for two centuries, cultivating the arts and establishing a vast empire built on agriculture, slavery and commerce. Eventually, Charleston set the pattern for the antebellum South, a region where romance and chivalry were idealized, if not achieved. The aristocratic ideal, established by Lord Anthony Ashley Cooper, that indefatigable Earl of Shaftsbury, continued to flourish. Even the terrible upheavals of the War Between the States (many Charlestonians call it the Southern War) and the worse exigencies of Reconstruction failed to alter the reverence for the order desired by those eight cavaliers. If anything, Charleston became more caste conscious after "The War."

By the time I arrived, the past had been exalted to a high degree. It was often said that Charlestonians resembled the Chinese, who also ate rice and worshiped their ancestors.[*] Charlestonians struggled valiantly to maintain an air of splendor in our battered town, battered not only by bombardment and enemy occupation, but also by devastating fires, a severe earthquake, hurricanes and half a century of poverty. Brass knockers gleamed on weather-beaten doors; oleanders, roses and jessamine graced gardens that had once been formally and expensively planted. Many elegant homes had been defaced by crude wooden stairs that gave access to the apartments of noisy white tenants. Some architectural gems suffered the worse fate of being turned over to large, impoverished colored families that frequently occupied but one room. In those neglected dwellings, axe blows were rained on carved mantels and wide-beamed floors.

Charleston's aristocracy, which had little left but its birthright of superiority, had gradually reestablished itself by the time of my birth in 1913 in the lower end of our peninsular city, deserting neighborhoods to the north that had

---

[*] This quotation is generally attributed to William Watts Ball, editor of the Charleston *News and Courier*.

once been fashionable. Although slums still festered in some of our downtown streets, it was generally conceded that living below Broad Street was mandatory for social acceptability. Bluebloods might cling to their lovely homes in the hinterlands of Uptown, but unless they were attractive and gregarious, they had a hard time keeping in good standing with the Downtowners. We were caustically known by some as SOBs (South of Broad).

I lived in our Eden between two rivers for many years before I realized I had been thrice blessed: I was born into the Upper Crust; I lived below Broad; and I was christened in St. Michael's Episcopal Church, where I had the privilege of learning about man and God, in that order. For me, the fear of man superseded the fear of God.

St. Michael's was intimidating to many another Charlie Brown. It was a mecca for tourists and a Gibraltar for our aristocracy. In those days, individuals and families rented their pews. Heaven defend any innocent visitor who found a seat for himself when the ushers were busy on a crowded Easter! (The pew tenants would not ask the offender to leave. Instead, they would make him feel isolated, unwelcome and most uncomfortable, trusting that they received the message to never repeat the offense.) There were parishioners who attended only annually, usually at Easter, and yet considered themselves absolutely entitled to the exclusive use of their pews after having rented—and ignored—them for a whole year. We called them Easter Lilies.

In 1938 a tornado blew a hole in the roof of St. Michael's. An irreverent Charlestonian declared it an act of God because, he said, "God had been trying to get into St. Michael's for two hundred years, and He had finally decided to see what it looked like inside."

A family friend told us that her son wanted to attend our Sunday school. "But Tat," she protested, "you go to a nice Sunday school."

"Mother, you don't understand," Tat replied. "At our Sunday school, all we hear about is God and Jesus and the Bible. At St. Michael's, it's different. They *never* talk about those things."

If St. Michael's and St. Philip's were Gibraltars for our gentry, the St. Cecilia Society was our Alcazar, an inner fortress to be held fast even unto death, no matter how strong the siege. The St. Cecilia Society is one of the most exclusive in the world. Some young eligibles have to wait for a member to die before they are admitted. At St. Cecilia balls, tradition has the autonomy of the laws of the Medes and Persians, which altereth not. No gentleman smokes; only sherry is served on the dance floor. Debutantes sit with their chaperones; no lady may leave the floor until the glittering assemblage descends from the ballroom in a grand cotillion, led by the president and the Bride of the Ball. The lavish supper is followed by more card dances.

In my youth, no one could be a debutante unless she was presented by her parents at the St. Cecilia balls. Sometimes, aspiring newcomers to Charleston tried to get into the St. Cecilia with less than Machiavellian skill; they were summarily rebuffed. They had to content themselves with presenting their luckless daughters in Washington, New York or Philadelphia. Ineligible Charlestonians knew better than to risk such a public disgrace. They presented only excellent qualifications before they risked the ignominy of receiving a black ball when their names came up for membership in the society.

I am grateful to my grandfather, Fanfan, who made the grade. He was a parvenu. His family only came to Charleston in the 1830s. He got us into the sanctum sanctorum despite his handicap of having the same name as one of the most illustrious families of our city. Thanks to providence and to him, our family of Middletons, who weren't "The Middletons," inherited what amounted to Salvation by Grace—the privilege of attending the balls of the St. Cecilia Society. Fanfan had eleven granddaughters. Nine of them married themselves out of the St. Cecilia. Fortunately, he had nine grandsons.

Attending the St. Cecilia was so important that one of our family anecdotes was about a relative who died unexpectedly. When talking about his untimely death, one of the relatives commented that "George never could get into St. Cecilia. I have been thinking that now that he has gone, probably his brother can take George's daughter to the Ball. And if Eleanor can go to the St. Cecilia, I'm sure that George would have been glad to die."

I attempted to capture this elitism in a satirical verse entitled "Serene Highness."

Thanks to forebears whose desires sired me,
Providing éclat and a fine pedigree.
Framed coats-of-arms all discretely proclaim
Proof of my ancestors' prestige and fame.
Grateful that noble blood elevates me,
I can relax in my family tree.
In shady comfort I cling like a sloth,
Knowing I need not go venturing forth.
Glad that the Cosmos revolves in accord;
For I am Elect, and I'm loved by the Lord.

Such was Charleston, circa 1930.

Marwee, 1933.

Marwee

Characteristically, I hung back when I was given my first chance to make an effective entrance. This exasperated a great many relatives, all of whom were interested in the first arrival in a new generation. The nation had just celebrated its birthday, but my exhausted parents didn't feel much like celebrating when I finally arrived a day later on another hot, humid Charleston summer day. Nobody even bothered to conceal the general disappointment that a baby girl had caused them; everyone knows that a first child should be a boy!

Father, who was the eldest of five sons, rallied sufficiently to commemorate the event with beautiful lettering on the large windowpane of the nursery. With Mother's diamond, he inscribed, "Margaret Middleton, July 5, 1913." I was the third generation of Margarets in our family. My father did not think girls should be given multiple names; he felt that they should use their family name as their middle name after they married. So I was just plain Margaret.

My earliest recollection was when I was permitted to view the wonderful baby brother that had joined our household. My enthusiasm for a new plaything rapidly degenerated into a case of chronic loathing, however, as Charlie was responsive, uncomplaining, adaptable, enthusiastic and blessed with a sense of humor. I had none of those admirable traits.

We lived in the shadow of our paternal grandparents' house. My grandfather Fanfan gave each of his children a house, but I was too young to appreciate his generosity. My grandparents' spacious antebellum brick home dwarfed our ugly little two-story wooden one. Our yard was so narrow I could always call for permission to visit my aunt Eunice next door who was six years my senior; I loved to follow her and her friends. Although I knew that I'd probably be teased by older girls, it was always a treat to be given permission to visit 10 Limehouse Street.*

Once I'd managed to push open the enormous street door, I'd run up the short flight of stairs that led to the piazza (Charlestonese for porch). With the prospect of visiting, it was not hard for me to bypass the charms of the joggling board,** the standard equipment of the long, wide porches that run the length of Charleston houses. There was an impressive and dangerous curving staircase in the entrance hall. Through archways, I could view the two enormous parlors, one on my left and one on my right. Ten Limehouse Street always seemed palatial to me, after leaving the dark, jerrybuilt interior of 8½. And it was the affectionate welcome from my grandparents that made their home a haven for even the most timid of granddaughters. Fanfan and Nanan are still known by the names I gave them.

Fanfan's eyes were piercing and blue. They could be frightening, but they usually twinkled. His personality was so commanding that it never occurred to me that he was not a giant physically as well as spiritually. I was about eighteen when I realized that our benevolent patriarch was short, heavy and lamed by sciatica. Fanfan will always be a giant among the great people I have been privileged to know. (He often said, "Make them do as *you* say," a precept useful for a born leader, but not for a reticent granddaughter. I never dreamed that I would later marry another charismatic, brilliant man who delighted in making people do as he said.)

Fanfan's father, the first in a line of Charles Francis Middletons, was the son of Philip Francis Middleton, who arrived circa 1834. (There were eventually five Charles Francis Middletons.) Fanfan's father was the chief engineer of the Civil War blockade runner, the celebrated *Mary Celestia*, and another, the *Lelia*, which pulled apart on its maiden voyage from Liverpool. Blockade running was dangerous business. The ships had to hug

---

* My grandmother Nanan had set her sights on a handsome Federal house located several blocks away at 21 Legare Street. She cried with disappointment when Fanfan surprised her with the keys to number 10, one of the two most imposing residences on Limehouse Street. The house is three stories high and stretches back to Greenhill Alley. With so many children and so many flights of stairs, the Middleton household was "read out" in the Negro churches, their way of blacklisting employers.

** A joggling board was Charleston's ingenious adaptation of the classic front porch bench. It consisted of three pieces: a long, flexible board about twelve to fourteen feet long, suspended between two stands mounted on rockers. Joggling boards were usually painted the ubiquitous Charleston green. Children loved to jump and bounce as the joggling board swayed back and forth; young couples would rock more sedately as they courted.

the coastline, where the shoals were, to avoid the pursuers of the U.S. Navy. Both ships eventually ran aground. Fanfan's father survived the first mishap but not the latter, dying in December 1864. He left behind a widow and two small sons, the older of which was Fanfan, age five. (Poignant letters of his adventures were later published by my sister.)

After "The War," my great-grandmother, Fanfan's mother, struggled to support her family by opening a millinery shop with her last asset, six hundred gold dollars her husband had left her. She scraped by and supported her family, including her sister. Some family members were scandalized that a lady in our family would "go into trade." She was one of the many resourceful and courageous women in our family. I am proud of her.

Fanfan began his business career at the age of fifteen, when he left Dr. Porter's school to help support his widowed mother, her sister and his younger brother. He wrote a polished letter, which landed him his first job as office boy. His charm, intelligence and diligence helped him throughout the long years when he struggled to make a livelihood in a prostrated community. He was so poor that he would chew tobacco instead of taking a lunch to work.

By the time he was twenty-four, Fanfan had done so well he decided to take a wife. He courted Miss Lucile Johnson. One fateful day, he took a ferry for Mount Pleasant. Miss Lucile was staying on Sullivan's Island, and there he intended to propose marriage. On the long ride in the horse cars that carried the ferry passengers to the island, he decided to visit some friends. Fanfan got off at another station before he reached Miss Lucile's home, and there, at Grandma Walter's boardinghouse, he beheld Lois Hazlehurst.

She was a beautiful young girl, with red-gold hair, finely chiseled features and smooth white skin. Young Mr. Middleton was smitten, even though Miss Hazlehurst was barefoot. He wanted to buy her some shoes, he told us later. (She probably had only one pair.) At any rate, Miss Lucile was immediately forgotten, and Fanfan, with characteristic energy, began courtship of a much more interesting young lady. They were married in the little Episcopal church on Sullivan's Island. Nanan was barely sixteen. It was four years before their first child, my aunt Hazel, was born. Nanan had twelve children, eight of whom lived. She always referred to Fanfan as "Mr. Middleton."

Nanan enjoyed all festivities. She was always ready to give a party or celebrate an anniversary. Her Christmas trees were as monumental as her generosity. She was a delightful mimic; her laughter was joyously contagious. She was faithful in remembering grandchildren's birthdays and in entertaining the old ladies of the family.

Nanan had an unusual gift for prescience. If she dreamed of a white horse, it portended the death of someone in her family. After a miscarriage, my mother was given up for dead by her exhausted doctor. Only the entreaties of her nurse made him remount the stairs of the hospital and, as a last gesture of resuscitation, put salt water into her veins. Mother regained consciousness. She later told us of having the sensation of floating in pulsating, beautiful, peaceful navy blue, and of saying to herself over and over, "This is the real me; now I am really beginning to live." She did not want to return to her body. (Nanan had dreamed of a white horse, grazing by a river with a white foal.)

Ours was an affectionate clan. Nanan's brother, Uncle Ed, lived on our block. The Middletons and Hazlehursts were constant companions. We had tea with Nanan every Sunday evening. It was a joy to help her prepare the sandwiches and cakes, and to help her serve. We were a kissing crowd. Each new arrival kissed most of the assembled relatives; his sons always kissed Fanfan. Uncle Willoughby, the brainiest of the family (a magna cum laude at Harvard Law School) always carried a handkerchief, which he used unobtrusively between his dutiful busses.

It was Nanan who gave us Middletons our illustrious heritage. One of her forebears was Dr. Henry Woodward, who was one of the most fascinating pioneers our country has produced. He went on an exploratory voyage sent out by the Lords Proprietors; he volunteered to stay with the Indians of Carolina in 1666, four years before Charles Towne was founded. The Red Man taught him the lore of the virgin wilderness and later saved the colony from starvation. Dr. Woodward was imprisoned by the Spaniards at St. Augustine and was rescued when the British sacked that town. It was he who established trading routes as far west as the Mississippi. Woodward married the daughter of Colonel John Godfrey, a gentleman who led a party of settlers from Barbados. Among their descendants are many prominent Charlestonians.

The great-grandmother who intrigues me most was Lois Mathewes Hall, whose husband, George Abbott Hall, was highly commended by George Washington. President Washington appointed him the first collector of the port of Charleston after the Revolution. The Halls paid dearly for their patriotism. George Abbott Hall was one of the thirty-three men of Charles Town who were roused from their beds by British soldiers during the enemy's occupation. They were sent to St. Augustine aboard a prison ship. One of his fellow prisoners was George Hall's brother-in-law, Thomas Heyward Jr., an impetuous young man who had recently signed his name to a declaration of independence from their mother country, much to his father's indignation. (The elder Heyward soon changed his opinion of the British.)

The two sisters and their children remained in Charles Town in a house that is now a museum; it was to become famous for President Washington's visit there. The British commander of Charles Town ordered its citizens to illuminate their homes in honor of the defeat of the Continentals. Elizabeth Heyward and Lois Hall stoutly refused although they knew the horrors of the provost, a dungeon where criminal and political prisoners were herded together in a foul state of neglect. When they barricaded their windows instead of displaying the prescribed candles, the turncoat rabble of Charles Town bombarded their home with rubbish and invective. Within a few days, Lois Hall died in childbirth, leaving several small children in the care of her sister and her eldest daughter, also named Lois. (The Heyward-Washington House is reputed to have a ghost that I like to fancy is the spirit of the ill-fated Lois Hall.)

Somewhat later, when the family went to Philadelphia, they attended a victory ball. President Washington selected Mrs. Heyward as the Queen of Love and Beauty. It was in Philadelphia that young Lois Hall met her future husband, Robert Hazlehurst, whose signature may be seen on currency issued by the Continental Congress.

John Geddes was another of Nanan's ancestors. He married Harriet Chalmers and was elected Governor of South Carolina in 1818. He entertained President James Monroe in grand style when the President visited Charleston. Governor Geddes personally bore much of the costs of a weeklong celebration, which considerably depleted his private fortune. He sold his house, which is now the Confederate Home on Broad Street. In 1831 after his death, the South Carolina General Assembly appropriated $3,000 to reimburse his heirs.

It is surprising to me that my mother never told us about her forbears. She was an avid student of South Carolina history. Possibly she was bored by older relatives who had nothing to bolster their morale but their ancestors. She was born just thirty years after "The War." She must have had to absorb and divert a great deal of bitterness. She told us, sensibly, that ancestors were a good springboard but not a crutch.

Mother was a One-M Simons. Mother accepted her status and prestige matter-of-factly, although she often said she wondered why their standing was so exalted in our community. (On his last tour of America, Lafayette visited their ancestral plantation, Middleburg, on the Cooper River and signed his name with a diamond on a living room windowpane.) We laughed with her at relatives who practically deified their Swinton pedigree. After all, Mother said, the original Swinton had been a mere swineherd who had the presence of mind to save the life of a king.

Mother was amused, but Father wasn't, when she discovered that his cherished great-grandfather Governor Gibbes had been elected to his office under extremely unbecoming and suspicious circumstances. (The Lords Proprietors withheld his salary as Governor when it was learned that he had resorted to bribery, force of arms and possibly poison to ensure his election.)

Mother's modesty about our families had the effect of increasing my Charlie Brownishness. I associated with people whose names were revered—Rhetts, Heywards, Pinckneys, Rutledges—and all I knew was that our Middletons were not The Middletons. Embarrassed by my poverty of pedigree, I remember passing our jewel-like Huguenot church and wishing that I could claim such brave Frenchmen as my ancestors. I had no notion that I had more Huguenots in my background than most of the members of its defunct congregation. (Sometimes ignorance isn't blissful. When I joined the Huguenot Society, my aunt and godmother, who was its secretary, kindly entered into my application for membership all claims of membership. When those French names were rolled off at my first meeting, I was at first pleased, then amused, then embarrassed. I felt ostentatious, for most of the other new members had entered but one Huguenot ancestor.)

Mother's parents lacked the aura that Fanfan and Nanan wore in my eyes, although ancestor-wise, their background was impeccable. Their home was Uptown (north of Broad), at 1 Pitt Street, a substantial Federal residence of dark brown bricks. At her request, my grandmother was known as Old Lady, the name she'd called the grandmother who reared her, Jane Margaret Adams, wife of Governor James Hopkins Adams. My mother was her namesake.

Governor Adams was my great-great-grandfather. He married Jane Margaret Scott, the daughter of Samuel Scott and Margaret Dudley, a lineal descendant of Governor Dudley of North Carolina. Their union linked the two wealthiest families in Richland County. According to family tradition, Mrs. Adams was a remarkable woman in her own right who provided her husband with useful counsel in his political career.

James Hopkins Adams was the outstanding figure in the entire Adams family. He was a member of the South Carolina legislature when only twenty-two, a state senator in 1850 and Governor in 1854. He believed passionately in the institution of slavery for the continued prosperity of South Carolina. As Governor, he prevented a professor whom he regarded as insufficiently pro-slavery from becoming President of the South Carolina College, the precursor to the University of South Carolina. He urged the South Carolina Congressional delegation to attempt to repeal the federal law banning the importation of slaves and thus reopen the slave trade. He further urged every white family to acquire at least one slave, believing that the surest road to prosperity for South Carolinians was acquiring property, and the best property was slaves. To that end, he proposed exempting from taxation the first slave to be purchased, both as a means of encouraging wealth creation and to help preserve the institution.

My great-great-grandfather, like my husband, thought big. It is painful today to revisit his grand vision. He wanted to open Africa up to the wholesale transportation of Africans as slaves to North America, where they could acquire the inestimable benefits of proximity to a superior race. They would learn important skills; they could acquire refinement by copying the behavior of whites; and most important of all, they could become Christian and save their souls. The whites could expand cotton production all the way to the Pacific Ocean using slave labor, turning the entire Southern United States into a prosperous sea where King Cotton could unfurl his sails to its fullest glory and profit. To be fair, my great-great-grandfather cared about public education, taxes and agriculture. But slavery was his passion. The consequences of that passion are the legacy he left us.

My maternal grandmother had grown up on Live Oak Plantation, near Columbia, in somewhat luxurious circumstances for a Southern girl of her generation. Great-great-grandmother Adams received a fortune of $100,000 after a hundred bales of her cotton got through the federal blockade (purchased for a gold dollar a pound in England). Sherman's army plundered the plantation during The War, but the house survived until it burned down in the twentieth century. The land was later sold to the U.S. government; the site of the plantation house was near the back south gate of McEntire Air National Guard Base. My grandmother applied her share of the sale of the plantation to the purchase of 1 Pitt Street.

Governor Adams died in 1861 and the elder Old Lady assumed the responsibilities of running the household. She was strict with her numerous children and with her granddaughter, my grandmother, who had been left in Old Lady's care after her daughter Laura died in childbirth. The infant's widowed father had left the baby on the plantation and moved to New York, where he was credited with making and losing several fortunes. (He was a Hanahan, which we pronounce "Hanny-han," and lost a leg in the war.) My grandmother was not permitted to wear many of the clothes that her father sent her each season. When the barrels from Lord & Taylor were opened, the more frivolous garments were sent to her city cousins in Columbia. My grandmother suffered the added indignity of seeing her finery again when the cousins visited Live Oak. When I knew Old Lady, she could have afforded Lord & Taylor clothes, but she dressed simply. Her home and her garden were her chief delights and both were cared for with unremitting zeal. She seldom visited; a host of friends stopped by to enjoy her unassuming welcome.

Grandpa Simons was somewhat remote. He had started to work at twelve, taking on the support of his widowed mother and several dependents. He was a lanky, quiet man, with many resemblances to Abraham Lincoln. (It's lucky that Old Lady didn't live to hear such a damning association. She wouldn't display the American flag during World War I, and the family feared that she might be arrested because of her numerous loud, anti-U.S. government tirades as she paced back and forth on her piazza.) They had achieved a comfortable environment after many years of struggle.

Grandpa Simons sometimes told of his privations as a boy on war-ravaged Edisto Island. He remembered breakfasts that consisted of but one biscuit for each person. Although his grandfather had been a multimillionaire, Grandpa Simons knew the value of a penny. He'd pounded brickbats into powder, which he put into matchboxes and peddled to the housewives of Edisto Island for a penny apiece. The moistened dust was used to beautify smoke-darkened fireplaces.

When he went courting in Charleston, Grandpa Simons had bought a fine green coat with brass buttons. He was such a bumpkin, he said, that he didn't realize that the Jewish merchant had sold him a coachman's coat until he heard the snickers as he escorted a young lady to Holy Communion Church. He was superintendent for Planter's Fertilizer Mill. I was always a little chagrined by his inelegant job, comparing it unfavorably with Fanfan's offices and enormous bustling wharf on Concord Street with its compress that compacted the cotton bales and the noisy, burly stevedores loading the waiting ships.

(The Middleton and Company office building was located at the corner of Hasell and Concord Streets. Across the street was their huge warehouse and attached wharf beyond it. During the Depression, the income from storing "government cotton" in the warehouse carried the entire Middleton family. Business was still sluggish when the Second World War began, and my brother Charlie tried to preserve the wharf before he joined the Marine Corps. After my cousin Abbott joined the Naval Air Force in September 1941 and Charlie's untimely death a few years later, the elder Middletons were overwhelmed by the enormity of struggling to keep a business going without a younger generation to help with the many new challenges they faced. The business was sold to Cheshire Sullivan around 1944.)

Mother was one of six children. They were so poor that a new dress was a special event. When the Depression hit our country in the late twenties, Mother's comment was, "Well, at last this country is getting back to what I call normal." It certainly had not always been thus. Mother's paternal grandmother was Susan Caroline Baynard. Our family tradition is that she was raised at Prospect Hill on Edisto Island and was outrageously spoiled. Supposedly, her father would bribe her to behave. She never learned to dress herself. After the Civil War, when her slaves had departed, she required her children to dress her.

When I was six, Father went to Liverpool, where he planned to open a branch of Middleton and Company. The little yellow house at $8\frac{1}{2}$ Limehouse Street was sold, much to Charlie's regret. Father left us in Little Switzerland, North Carolina, for the summer. It was Mother's first sight of mountains. She was twenty-eight; she had only ever been to New York, Savannah and Valdosta, Georgia. We stayed at a large boardinghouse. We had wonderful times that summer. We gathered the tiny wild strawberries; we discovered varieties of moss and wildflowers. There were charades in the evening. There I indulged in my cacoethes scribendi for the first time, scrawling meaningless symbols, and then pretending to read the stories I'd composed.

When we returned to Charleston, we moved around the corner instead of to Liverpool, a fact for which I was not sufficiently thankful until I saw that dreary town several decades later. Our New Street house was imposing. It had been built by a scalawag named Mackey who had served in the Reconstruction government as a sheriff; such people were despised as collaborators. I was told that his wife was a mulatto with the illustrious name of Rutledge. The house had once been a showplace, although no respectable person ever entered it until it was turned into a boardinghouse after his death. There were large gold leaf mirrors over the mantels, gilt cornices and an upstairs ballroom. There were all sorts of fascinating cupboards, passageways and a large backyard to be explored. We had a lovely playroom in the pigeon roost, the upper story of a spacious chicken house.

My sister Dorothy was born when we'd been on New Street about a year. Her name was well chosen, for it means "gift of God." She has been a blessing to us all. Dorothy was named for Fanfan's and Nanan's last child who died young from rheumatoid heart problems. Nanan mourned deeply after her death. When my sister Dorothy came home from the hospital, Charlie, aged five, peeked at the infant and said, "What a boo-stal baby." From that time on Dorothy was affectionately known as Boo. As she grew up, she and Charlie established a rapport, which I didn't share; their childish games exasperated me. I wanted to live in a Neverland, somewhere between the Land of Oz and the Little Colonel's Kentucky. I was terribly shy.

One summer I refused to help Mother and Charlie when they appeared to be drowning just off the beach at Sullivan's Island. Mother, who couldn't swim, had unwisely waded out with little Charlie, who was merrily floating on a large inflated bolster case. She went out too far, and the water rose quickly around her and her precious, helpless charge. Suddenly, she found herself, as many do, dangerously far out in the water, which was now up to her nose.

Margaret Middleton with Boo, Charlie and Marwee in their parlor at 24 New Street, 1921.

"Get those men, Marwee," Mother gasped, thinking that those might be her last words, and pointed desperately to a Coast Guard lifesaving crew that was practicing rescue tactics a few hundred yards down the beach.

"I can't," I wailed, agonized but unbudging.

"Go on, Marwee!" was all Mother was able to say, as Charlie started drifting away from her.

"I don't know what to say!" I shouted, paralyzed by my shyness. Fortunately, the tide was coming in, and Mother and Charlie were floated in toward the shore by the waves.

My first six years of schooling were received at Miss Prioleau's school. They were pleasant ones on the whole. Literature, dramatics and French received most of our attention. Apparently, addition and subtraction were painful to Miss Prioleau, although she drilled us to perfection in multiplication tables and Roman numerals. Arithmetic has bothered me ever since. Arabic numerals produce a Pavlovian reaction in me. I still become paralyzed with dismay when numbers have to be added, subtracted or divided.

Our commencements were memorable. Our little class, which was the last to be graduated, was sent its way with much celebration. One of the festivities was the *Courtship of Miles Standish*. I starred as Pricilla, the Puritan maiden. Despite the fact that my opening song was received with subdued giggles, I managed the rest of my role quite well. I was convinced that I was going to become a famous actress. However, I had been typed. Subsequent stage appearances, usually in tableaux, were always my portrayals of angels or old-fashioned girls.

How I hated to look like an angel or an old-fashioned girl! Father insisted that I wear my hair long. All the other girls imitated modish flappers who had their hair shingled in Felder's Barber Shop. By the time I was eleven, I had grown taller than all my contemporaries. I was further handicapped by bulging muscles, unfashionable, embarrassing curves and long blond tresses that might have inspired poems in another era.

I wailed when I learned that I was going to have to attend a public school, but enter it I did. It was a big adjustment for one of Miss Prioleau's star pupils. The stern teachers terrified me, especially when I discovered that I knew practically nothing about arithmetic or geography. Worst of all, I was awed by the presence of so many boys. Even at eleven, I wanted to be popular, with dozens of boys asking me for dates. No one would ever have guessed it, however, for I was a demure creature who froze whenever a young man indicated the slightest interest in me. That situation got much worse before it began to get better. I was fated to be a late bloomer, but in those early teens I was sure that I was doomed to chronic, incurable blight. I could conceive of no fate worse than unpopularity, and I endured it for many years.

To lessen my chances of meeting young men, fate, in the form of the Charleston School Board, soon removed them to the Charleston High School. Boys seemed to become as remote as the Himalayas and almost as beautiful and unapproachable as those heights. I did, occasionally, have a blind date with a cadet at The Citadel. But those I liked didn't return the compliment, and the others seemed so countrified I would never have dated them.

Memminger High School was a prison, physically and spiritually. We were severely restricted behind its high gray walls. I knew a girl who was suspended for waving to a boy over the wall. With few exceptions, our teachers were tired, aged maidens who dared not let us stray from dull texts. I liked literature, French and art despite the poor quality of teachers. (Law prohibited married women from teaching.) Natural curiosity was discouraged. It was impertinent to ask, "What happened then?" The most galling feature of Memminger was the extra year that was tacked onto our curriculum. Boys attended school twelve years; we had to attend thirteen. It had originally been a "normal" school for training teachers, and with Charleston's conservatism, it had not been modernized.

In spite of my deplorable lack of dates, I had friends who tolerated my company. I finally got invited to a Citadel Hop when I was fifteen. I was with a group of girls at a friend's home when the cadet telephoned me. My heart pounded, and I hesitated. The girls listened in, crowding around me. "Go on, say yes," they hissed in loud whispers. After more prodding, and some surprised urging from the cadet, I summoned the courage to accept his invitation. I felt that I had been pushed into a dreadful situation. "Suppose I get stuck," I kept worrying. ("Getting stuck" meant being forced to dance with the same person for longer than was fashionable and was considered a social disaster.) I rushed home sick with apprehension. "Mother, come quick," I called as soon as I reached our downstairs hall. Mother's alarmed face appeared in the upstairs hall. "Oh, Mother, something terrible has happened. It's awful. I've been asked to go to the Senior Hop."

It was a last-minute invitation, so I was spared the misery of prolonged apprehension. We went to see Eunie immediately and borrowed a long blue taffeta dress with a red sash. There was a spot on it, so we took it to a dry cleaner who assured us that he would have it ready by the next day and that it would not smell like cleaning fluid. When my date called the next evening, I was ready. I tried to seem like a poised person who went to Citadel dances all the time. Mother made a terrible faux pas, I thought. Trying to be pleasant to the young man, she said, "It's so nice of you to take Marwee to the dance." Horrors! Didn't Mother know that I was supposed to be doing him a big favor in letting him take me to the hop?

When we got to the dance, I joined the girls in the dressing room. We crowded around the mirrors. It was bad form to seem to be too anxious to go back to the dance floor. All the popular girls I'd been envying were chattering one universal theme: I'm scared. Are you scared? I am so scared I don't know how I will ever go out on that floor! Reassured, my stage fright diminished considerably. I went out to the dance floor and faced the ordeal calmly. Naturally, I didn't get broken in on as much as did the most popular girls, but thanks to my date and his hardworking friends, I met a lot of stags and went through the evening without the humiliation of getting stuck.

One of my less successful experiences at that time was when I was greatly smitten by another cadet, Herbie H., a tall, handsome freshman. Although his grammar was shaky, he looked like a young viking. We had a blind date. I tried hard to be charming as we rode around in the rumble seat of another cadet's car. We rode around the Battery, the Boulevard, the Point, Hampton Park; we had some refreshments at a drugstore; we rode around some more. It was exhausting as well as exhilarating. I hoped that Herbie was as greatly impressed by my charms as I was by his. He wasn't. I haunted the house near the phone, but he never called me. He called Betty Rhett, however. She was distressed when I learned through accident that he asked her to attend the next mess hall dance. I managed to accept my defeat without too much bitterness. I was used to defeats. I even composed the following verses:

Relief!
Of loving you in vain,
I've found this out: It never pays.
I won't fall soon again.
I was so very silly, for ["For" and "saw" are perfect rhymes]
I knew you weren't sincere.
And yet, the less of you I saw
The more I seemed to care.
But now, be gone! A fond farewell!
You're all right in your way.
But darling, if you went to hell,
I wouldn't care today.

In 1948 I met Herbie again. Our meetings provided a contrast. On the second occasion, I was traveling in a special private plane; our pilot was the foremost stunt flier of this country, Beverly Howard. I was dressed in my finest clothes, and I was in impressive company. My husband had been in Congress for eight years, and we were with a candidate for President of the United States—our Governor, Strom Thurmond, and his wife. As a publicity gimmick, we flew to Edgefield, where photographers took pictures of our arrival and of Governor Thurmond casting a vote in his home ballot box. On the steps of the courthouse, people crowded up to shake our hands. A seedy-looking man approached me. He was gray, balding, unkempt and his teeth needed attention.

"Hello, Margaret," he said, obviously pleased that he could be calling me by my first name.

During Strom Thurmond's 1948 Dixiecrat Presidential candidacy, Jean Thurmond, a former beauty queen, greets Marwee in front of ace pilot Beverly Howard's plane in Edgefield.

"Why, hello," I replied, puzzled as to his identity.

"Don't you remember me?"

"Why, uh…" I am no campaigner.

"I'm Herbie H. Don't you remember when we used to go together when I was at The Citadel?" I got the impression that Herbie had probably told his friends that he had taken me to several mess hall dances.

When we finally graduated from Memminger, I delighted Mother by winning the Mitchell Medal, the annual essay prize. She had competed for it also. My tongue-in-cheek essay had pleased the judges. I'd described the celebration of Charleston's first two hundred years in grandiloquent terms, written mostly in ire, for I'd had an earache during the celebration; my essay was a fulsome paraphrase of John of Gaunt's tribute to England. After days of dreaded anticipation, I read my essay with aplomb at our graduation exercises.

It's a wonder our classmates didn't hate Betty Rhett and me. We thought that our graduation should be different. We did our best to dominate that large class. Caps and gowns were tacky, we said; the rest of them voted for caps and gowns. We thought that Class Night festivities were silly; again we were overwhelmingly outvoted. We didn't think we should have a yearbook, but the rest of the class did. Only in the class prophecy did we have our way. We wrote insulting verses about each graduate. We thought they were hilarious; the girls were kind enough to accept them with good humor.

During those early teens, my parents must have despaired of ever molding me into a sweet little lady. I blew off a lot of steam at home; slamming doors was one of my specialties. (I cracked the transom of one.) I groaned over my piano lessons and used to speculate upon how long my disagreeable old music teacher could possibly live. (Fanfan later gave Boo the grand piano that had once been played by the great Polish statesman and pianist Ignacy Jan Paderewski, when he visited Charleston. His hands were so powerful that he broke the sounding board, and the owner put the piano up for sale cheap. Our family always did like a bargain.)

At seventeen, I felt the sudden smile of fortune. My first real beau appeared. I was metamorphosed into a creature who was acceptable to the other girls. I was asked to join the Question Mark Club, an exclusive group of young ladies whose dances were limited to the most acceptable young people in town. Suddenly, my horizons were greatly widened, and I had the weekend excitement of dances, picnics and beach parties. My beau was a senior at The Citadel. I even served as a Citadel sponsor complete with my picture in their yearbook, an honor that had seemed unattainable only a few short months before.

Fortune continued to smile, for Fanfan came to live with us. He had stayed with various of his children after Nanan's death four years earlier. His interest and affection gave my slender ego another puff of inflation. His presence added quite an air to our household. He was generous in sharing his Buick and his colored chauffeur with us. The chauffeur also served our meals. Fanfan often gave me checks for trips and dresses. Fanfan also tried to teach me to hold myself well; Mother never stressed posture.

I went to the College of Charleston because I didn't know what else to do. My parents did not feel they could afford to send me away to an expensive Ivy League college, but tuition at "The College" was a mere $300 a year in those Depression days. Even my parents could afford such a reasonable sum. I probably would have married my beau if times hadn't been so hard. That was lucky, for within a month's time, I'd decided that my suitor was a bore.

At the College, I joined the prestigious Tri Delta sorority. I was suddenly discovered by the Charleston boys. I was even voted the most popular girl in the sophomore class! (The honor didn't please me; I disdained all politics, even campus ones.) I should admit that I was not popular with my sorority sisters. I did not share their lofty attitude toward the lesser Greeks and barbarians on campus. I was indiscreet in repeating the remarks of another nonconformist about the rituals in which we stressed sisterly love before we sat down to tear each other to pieces at our meetings. I learned something in that sorority: some girls were admitted only after deathlike struggles among the membership. Once in, they never showed the least indication of humility or appreciation. They quickly attached themselves to catty cliques and turned their malice upon us dull sisters who had been willing to give them a break.

I was a debutante during my college years. Fanfan gave me my gown; it cost thirty-five dollars and was especially ordered by Mrs. Chisholm, who had the best shop in town. I tried on a peach gown in her store and ordered one like it in white; she volunteered the promise that she wouldn't sell the peach one to anyone from Charleston. I felt very elegant in my exclusive, expensive white dress. Then to my horror, one of the debutantes came down the receiving line in that same peach dress. She was from Kingstree, about fifty miles away.

Our tea dance was a great success. Mother and her friends made the sandwiches; she bought the cakes and wafers. Father made fruit punch, spiked with the corn liquor that he'd aged in oak kegs in our bedroom closets. The whole affair cost about $300. My escort for the St. Cecilia ball was a tall young cousin, whose membership papers got through just in time. His mother used a clean bedsheet to line the shabby upholstery of his coupe. We were duly impressed by the elegance and formality of that splendid affair. (I went to two other balls with another beau in later years. Thus ended my career in society.)

We were the class of 1935. Graduation was beautiful. My homemade white organdy gown was favorably mentioned in a gossip column. A beau sent me a bouquet of peonies, the first I'd seen. I had the honor of dancing in the ballroom scene of *Romeo and Juliet* with Emmett Robinson, the genius of our class. The production highlighted our graduation exercises.

My teaching career wasn't successful. Betty Rhett's brother-in-law offered me a job as a music teacher in Sumter County. I told Jimmy that I couldn't play the piano and tried to prove it to him. I played "Sweet and Low" and "The Minstrel Boy." He said I did well enough. I got a book of simplified tunes and practiced them all summer. Mother and I went to Sumter, where we found a room in a teachery. Plump, motherly Mrs. Parrot charged a dollar a day for half a pleasant room and delicious meals. My salary was seventy-five dollars a month. I think I could have made out on that if it hadn't been held up occasionally when the county couldn't collect delinquent taxes. My piano playing was so inadequate that after my first attempt, I was hastily transferred to another school. Only Fanfan complained. He was from the "old school" and was horrified that his granddaughter had a paying job after graduating from college; he thought that a lady should live at home with her parents until she had a husband to care for her.

My first grade had few pupils who were capable of learning. Most of them were kept in school so that we could have a minimum enrollment of seventy-five children. Among my charges was an unfortunate young man of fifteen who had been in first grade for many years and seemed to me incapable of learning. He should never have been in that class. His presence was a disruptive influence that was certainly not healthy for the other children, and I feared for my own safety. I tried hard, but I never did teach those pathetic little children how to read. However, one of those repeaters showed me that I couldn't spell either. I wrote examples about "nickles," and she pointed out to me that I should have written "nickels."

That Christmas was difficult for me. Earlier in December, for reasons I cannot remember, I had decided to chew on a feather that I had pulled from a quilt while Boo and I were laughing about something on our bed. The feather evidently had some bacteria on it. The bacteria entered my system. My throat began to swell, and the swelling would not stop. Eventually, I acquired a huge, unsightly, grotesque "second throat," just beneath my first. My parents put me in the hospital. While I was awaiting my operation, and feeling very sorry for myself, my brother Charlie came to visit me. There I was, hideous and in pain. He took one look at me and burst into uncontrollable laughter. He doubled over. He could not stop laughing. I remember that laughter even better than the operation itself. The surgeon removed over a cup of thick black fluid from my throat, and I had a long convalescence.

I enjoyed the holiday from school, and the attentions of family and friends. Only my super-conscientiousness made me return the next fall. By that time, I hated the school, the city of Sumter and most of all, myself for having agreed to return. At least I began to teach myself to type. I also taught myself some bad typing habits.

I got another job that second Christmas working on the society page of the Charleston newspaper. It was like a miracle. Jobless people roamed the streets of every town that year of 1937. I secured a position I liked in a congenial atmosphere and in close association with one of the most attractive people I knew, Selma Tharin. I think that Selma must have wanted me to be her assistant, for my interview with the editor of the paper couldn't have landed the job.

"Can you write?" he asked, eyeing me seriously.

"I honestly don't know, Mr. Emerson. My teachers have said I can. I won a medal for an essay once."

I was hired.

Selma and I shared a small office. She was beautiful, talented and generous. When our work for the society page was slack, she'd sometimes tell me of her experiences as a hoofer, when she'd aspired to become a dancing star. We shared an enthusiasm for the Footlight Players, a struggling group that had hired Emmett Robinson to be its youthful director. Selma was an artist, poet and a tactful boss. How lucky could I get?

For the first time I felt rich. My fifteen dollars a week was ample for the miniscule board that Mother accepted (and put into a bank account for me). Clothes were cheap and my mode of life was simple. I dated several young men and went to parties occasionally, but I had no need for an elaborate wardrobe. Mother thought that my beach outfit of cape, hat and swimsuit was extravagant. (It had cost eleven dollars.)

Life was pleasant. My hardest task was writing under pressure when I had to produce a review after a play or concert. I knew little about music; local musicians sometimes resented my remarks. I didn't know that I was soon to get a new and more important role. I was quite pleased with my life.

Marwee, 1938.

Mendel & Me

In 1938, when Mendel Rivers, like Lochinvar, came riding out of the West, I didn't suspect that my life would soon be greatly altered. I'd been at the newspaper for about eighteen months when he came to Charleston from New Orleans. We had known each other slightly from Kanuga, the Episcopal church camp near Hendersonville, North Carolina, and I had had a not-so-successful date with him once while I was at the College. He surprised me with his sudden and intensive courtship.

I was impressed by his self-assurance and his good looks. I didn't even realize that he was interested in politics, although I vaguely remembered that he'd served in our legislature for a few years. At the time I was confident Mendel was very important because he was a Special Assistant to the Attorney General. I was sure the Attorney General himself had gone out on a search to find the best lawyers anywhere, and he wanted Mendel to work specially for him. (Only later did I learn that every lawyer at the Justice Department has the title "Special Assistant." After he started working, Mendel had felt deceived, but not so deceived that he passed on to me just how un-special "special" was.)

He was unorthodox in his courtship. He'd appear with a peck of fresh corn, a puppy and a carton of cigarettes that he tossed at me saying, "Marguerite, here are some cigarettes. I hope you'll quit smoking." I never could understand why Mendel called me Marguerite instead of the more intimate Marwee of my family and close friends. He was a most interesting beau. I was as surprised as anyone else when I found myself wearing his diamond. We became engaged on June 28, the anniversary of Charleston's most famous battle, when General William Moultrie defeated the British fleet off of the coast of Sullivan's Island in 1776.

Poor Mendel! He didn't realize that I was completely indifferent to most of the things he enjoyed—baseball, politics and forms of entertainment that I considered corny. I began to have misgivings. Mendel was the country kin of many Charlestonians who tried to keep him in his place by snubbing him. He had grown up in North Charleston, a community that in no way resembled our Holy City. His mother had supported her lively brood by taking in boarders after the death of her husband and the loss of their thriving farm. His mother had joined the Daughters of the American Revolution, an organization that Selma and I had written off in the newspaper with amused condescension. His sisters were friendly, but I overheard one of them call me "Miss Priss." They made no effort to overcome the slipshod grammar of their environment.

Mother had never defended my other beaux, but she championed Mendel's suit. Perhaps her fear of having an old maid on her hands reinforced her admiration.

I learned a little about political campaigning that summer, for my fiancé made political speeches for our local congressman who had suffered a heart attack. I thought it very noble that a Special Assistant to our Attorney General should campaign on behalf of a sick congressman. I didn't know that our congressman had secured a decent job for Mendel in order to keep his promising rival out of the field.

We planned to be married after the Democratic primaries and to live in New Orleans. I was delighted with the Creole cookbook and the New Orleans apron that were given me at trousseau showers. We planned to live in the Old Quarter. (It was twenty-seven years before I saw New Orleans. Our visit differed from our original plans: we were met by distinguished citizens; we had a police escort to part the traffic before us; we were housed in the presidential suite; we were showered with gifts, adulation and hospitality. Mendel made a speech that rated nationwide headlines; even I was called to the podium to make the briefest speech in New Orleans history. Such are the interesting quirks of Fate.)

At least our wedding looked cool, that hot, muggy September noon. Boo and my other attendants all wore green organdy; we carried white flowers. Everything went smoothly until Mendel and I started to make our first trip together—the long walk back down the aisle of St. Michael's. He gave me the first of his Mendelian surprises.

Naturally, I expected him to look down at me adoringly, oblivious to the crowded pews. I was quickly disenchanted. Mendel recognized guests, smiled and greeted them cordially as we progressed to the rear of the church. I had no alternative but to look around, too. In the crowded vestibule, Mendel discovered a special acquaintance. He walked over to a most unpretentious-looking man and shook his hand. "Hello, John," he said. "Glad to see you. Meet Mrs. Rivers."

Our wedding trip was an appropriate beginning for our life together; both have been marked by constant change of scenery and many surprises. After the crowded reception at New Street, we drove to Myrtle Beach, where we'd planned to stay at the large Ocean Front Hotel. It was in darkness. A man with a flashlight informed us that it had closed for the season that morning. We found a room in a much less impressive hostelry down the beach. There, for the first time in my life, I had the anticipation of opening a beautifully packed suitcase; my bridesmaids had labored with pins and tissue paper for hours. I opened the bag upside-down, and my finery landed in a tumbled heap on the dusty floor.

That enormous new suitcase continued to have a baleful influence on our trip. When we got to Little Switzerland, that hotel was closed also. Mendel had to unload our bags and drag that accursed bag up a steep path. His back was wrenched badly; it continued to get worse during the rest of our trip. We had a few peaceful days at Blowing Rock, where we found a good hotel, finally. Continuing to move, we visited Mendel's friends, John and Dot Neff, at their home in the Shenandoah Valley. It was my first trip to that lovely region, and I declared that I could think of no pleasanter place to live. (I was to regret those words.)

In Washington, Mendel's back finally forced him to stay in bed for the only festivity of our vacation. Reluctantly, I went alone in a taxi to a Dutch-treat party given by some of his office friends. The orchestra played the Wedding March and turned the spotlight on me while I was dancing with a strange man. I was thankful to get back to Mendel and find him somewhat improved.

We went to Atlanta instead of New Orleans. We ranged all over Georgia and Tennessee that fall and winter. I wrote notes acknowledging our wedding presents while I waited for Mendel to examine records in hot, dusty little towns. I discovered things that I'd never suspected before. There was something called the World Series, and Mendel wanted to listen to it over the radio all day long. He liked Fibber McGee and Mollie, instead of symphonies and dramas. He called Charlestonians "Broken-Down Aristocrats." He liked to window shop, especially for men's shoes. One night I got another Mendelian shock. He pointed to a huge, overstuffed platform rocker; it was upholstered in dark green brocade. "That looks good," he said. "I'd like to have one like it."

I wanted to scream. I wept inwardly. What a tragedy, I groaned in silent misery. I have married a man who has no taste. I wanted to board a train for Charleston and forget all about him. It was distressingly apparent that our marriage was a clash of cultures that almost certainly would never be reconciled. Mendel's unfortunate background had prevented him from cultivating things that were compatible with what I considered my more refined pursuits. As usual, I eventually transferred my frustrations into rhyme:

> *Gone are the days*
> *Beyond recall*
> *When I have tried*
> *To like football…*
>
> *Shrieks of aged*
> *Adolescents*
> *Bring me ennui*
> *In its essence.*
>
> *Football games*
> *Now top my list*
> *Of all the things*
> *I'm glad I've missed.*

We stayed in Atlanta until June. By that time I looked horribly pregnant. Tactless people wouldn't believe that there was just *one* baby expected in September. We drove to Washington where Mendel was now to work. We had been there for about a month and picked out an apartment in a Virginia development when my doctor advised me to stay wherever I wanted the baby to be born. This time, I did board a train for Charleston but with utmost reluctance. It was my twenty-sixth birthday.

My family was very sweet to me, but the heat and the waiting seemed interminable. I gained forty pounds that summer. Mendel finally joined us, but the stork hovered in the distance. Mendel woke me up on our first anniversary to listen to the reports of Hitler's invasion of Poland.

The baby, a girl, finally arrived on September 23. We named her Margaret Simons, after my mother. She was the oldest daughter and the fourth generation to be named Margaret. To avoid confusion, we decided to call our daughter Peggy. Once we moved to Washington, I had Peggy's name changed from Margaret Simons to Margaret Middleton because the war was raging on and the future was uncertain. I wished to ensure against any possibility of problems in Washington with the anti-Semitic Nazis and their sympathizers who might have thought Simons was a Jewish name. In

Mendel and Marwee at
24 New Street, 1939.

Charleston, the One-M "Sim-muns" may have been elite, but I did not want
confusion about Peggy's origins once we moved away.

Peggy received a rousing welcome from family, friends and the nurses
who petted and congratulated me. She was a beautiful child. I was very
happy.

Mendel and Judge Fromberg came to see me when Peggy was six days
old. I was still in the hospital convalescing (women giving birth stayed in
hospitals far longer back then), breastfeeding my newborn and happily
planning to take her to New Street the next day. Mendel and his friend
didn't pay much attention to my small talk.

Then Mendel dropped his blockbuster.

"Marguerite, Tom McMillan died today. I'm going to run for
Congress."

"Oh, No! That would be terrible, Mendel."

The Judge agreed. He looked grim.

"Mendel won't have a chance," he said.

"Well, I'm running."

Mendel was deaf to my protests and entreaties. The news upset me so
much I was literally curdled. Peggy had to be put on a bottle. I stayed in
the hospital another ten days, full of pain, fever and self-pity. I couldn't
understand how Mendel would run for Congress whether I liked it or not.

Judge Fromberg did not help during the primary, strongly advising
Mendel not to quit his secure job with the Justice Department. Fromberg

probably knew what an uphill battle it would be for Mendel to fight the established Charleston County Democratic Party machine without any financial backing.

After Mendel won the election and was assured a handsome living of $10,000 a year, Fromberg immediately left his job in Washington, assuming that they would practice law together. He rented a spacious office at Broad and Church Streets, relegating Mendel's desk to a small back corner of the room. He hung out his shingle and liked to brag, "Mendel is my boy." He assumed that I would continue on as his secretary since I had filled that role during the primary. I resented his presumptions at the time because I felt that he took advantage of my husband. The Judge always said that I disliked him because he was Jewish. That was untrue.

Politics and More Politics

Mark Twain claimed there was no distinctly American native criminal class except Congress. Mendel Rivers claimed the Congress was the only insane asylum in the country run by the inmates. Historically, it has been an exclusive male-dominated fraternity. But the men in charge of Congress have also historically permitted the widows of politicians to complete their husbands' terms when they unexpectedly die in office, with the unspoken expectation that they will not seek the seat at the next general election.

Congressman Thomas S. McMillan died in Charleston on September 29, 1939. In a special election held on November 7, his widow, Clara McMillan, was elected to complete her husband's unexpired term. She, of course, chose not to seek reelection in the next Democratic Primary election, scheduled for August 27, 1940.

Mendel was required by law to give up his government job when he ran in the primary. In February of 1940, Mendel resigned his job with the Justice Department and returned to Charleston to "practice law." His return to the city prompted the Charleston *News and Courier* to speculate that he intended to seek McMillan's old Congressional seat.

It took a lot of courage for Mendel to quit his job with the added responsibility of a new family and no political support. He opened an office on the second floor of 29 Broad Street, but he had few clients. I worked there in order to save the expense of a stenographer. We stayed at New Street with my parents for over a year. We had a wonderful nurse for Peggy, Lottie Wright. We gave her five dollars a week. A stenographer would have cost seven. Sometimes I wonder how I ever typed out those long legal sheets without any mistakes. I had to go very slowly. Most of the work was for Mendel's campaign. It was a strenuous summer for both of us.

In 1940 South Carolina's First District consisted of nine counties: Allendale, Beaufort, Berkeley, Charleston, Clarendon, Colleton, Dorchester, Hampton and Jasper. Two-lane country roads wove their way through large tracts of practically unpopulated timber land and farms where wooden houses with peeling paint, rusting roofs, drab yards and erosion were continuing reminders of economic depression. What prosperity existed was confined to the urban areas, and most of those people were still struggling from the ravages of both the Civil War and the Great Depression. Poverty clung to the air like an unpleasant, cloying perfume. Education even for the whites was minimal.

The post-Reconstruction legacy was a one-party system where every "respectable" citizen voted Democratic. For years the rural areas had been dominated by the City of Charleston political machine. That phrase "political machine" is often overused. Many "political machines" are merely the good will created by a successful politician, good will that dies with him. Not so with the City of Charleston political machine. Charleston's version of Tammany Hall could bring as many voters to the polls, including dead ones and/or more voters than were registered, as might be needed to win any given election. It could guarantee "the right vote count" on election night. It could send out the Charleston Police Department to harass and bully opposition candidates. It knew how to win. It was used to winning.

The City of Charleston machine was run by the Mayor of the City of Charleston, His Honor Henry W. "Tunka" Lockwood. Tunka enjoyed his power. He selected candidates for office and made certain they won. Hizzoner once drank too much alcohol at a wedding reception in Beaufort, South Carolina, the second largest city in the First Congressional District behind Charleston. "You need to be more like Charleston," he bragged to the Mayor of Beaufort. "Back home, I've got a magic wand right behind my desk. I bring it out every election and wave it over the ballot box, and the votes always come out right." It was meant to be very, very funny. Mendel Rivers happened to be present.

When Congressman Tom McMillan died, Tunka selected an apolitical friend, decorated veteran and loyal ally, Alfred H. "Fritz" Von Kolnitz, as his congressional candidate. As a favor to Tunka Lockwood, Fritz agreed to run. He immediately became the man to beat. With the Mayor's backing, Fritz seemed unstoppable.

To be fair, Fritz was an impressive choice. His resume was strong. He had received a law degree the day after he turned twenty-one, although he never practiced law and chose business (real estate and insurance) instead. At the University of South Carolina, he was captain of the football team and a member of the varsity baseball team. He went on to play Major League baseball with the Cincinnati Reds and the Chicago White Sox. He departed the White Sox to join the U.S. Army and was promoted to major in the infantry at age twenty-five. (After his failed run for Congress, Von Kolnitz was called back into the service, serving as senior intelligence officer for the 322nd Bomber Group during World War II.)

Von Kolnitz had written magazine articles and delivered lectures, and he proclaimed himself, in his campaign pamphlet, "an authority on national defense, historical research, and wild life conservation." His father was a former state senator and present Judge of the Charleston County Domestic Relations Court. His grandfather had served with the legendary Wade Hampton in the Fifth South Carolina Cavalry during the Civil War.*

But Von Kolnitz had never run for office. Though he claimed to be an accomplished public speaker, Fritz was uncomfortable with crowds. He was a nice man. He was not a born politician. He could not, like Mendel, "roll with the punches" (one of Mendel's favorite expressions) and change tactics and strategy as the campaign evolved. He had only one speech; it was memorized. He did not tailor his remarks to the audience before him. Perhaps he felt it unnecessary. People outside of Charleston soon found that stilted speech uninspiring, if not downright boring.

And suddenly, here came Mendel Rivers in a flashy red Chrysler, a color new to the auto world and certainly conspicuous in the conservative First District. When the muffler developed a hole, the car made a fearful racket as it roared along the country roads, announcing Mendel's impending arrival. It sounded almost like thunder. Family members asked him to have it fixed because it was embarrassing. And his reaction was typical.

"Hell no. I want people to say, 'Here comes Rivers and his blitzkrieg.'" Mendel thought it was wonderful publicity.

Mendel couldn't wait to speak to anyone he could. He could discuss any topic and would by instinct shape his message to fit his audience. The opposite of Von Kolnitz, Mendel had a flair for impromptu speeches. He could improvise a different speech for every occasion if need be.

* Hampton was a Confederate general who later led the movement to eradicate the postwar Reconstruction government and replace it with "Bourbon" rule. My grandfather Fanfan rode with Hampton and his famous "Red Shirts." Having no money to purchase uniforms, supporters wore red shirts, thereby gaining the nickname they appropriated from Giuseppe Garibaldi's "Red Shirt" volunteers.

Fritz Von Kolnitz had been drafted to run for Congress. He was stiff and formal. Mendel Rivers wanted the job. And Mendel was a natural.

Fritz had accepted the honorary position of Chairman of the Board of Parks and Playgrounds of the City of Charleston and had evidently enjoyed it, since he had served for seventeen years by the year of the election. Among many other things, his agency had responsibility for the city zoo. Mendel would use that against him.

It was an ugly campaign. The Mayor wanted his own man in the congressional seat, and he was used to winning. He sent officers of the City of Charleston Police Department out into the counties to drum up votes for Von Kolnitz. Emblazoned with posters of their candidate, Fritz Von Kolnitz and the Charleston Police Band attended many hustings. Some policemen were issued rakes to tear down Rivers posters from the roadsides.

Mendel knew the Mayor planned not only to try to influence votes against him but would also steal votes from him in Charleston. He planned on losing the City of Charleston but felt he could still win the election with a strong showing in the rest of Charleston County outside of the city and with the other eight counties of the First Congressional District.

But he knew he must minimize his losses in the City of Charleston, or the other areas wouldn't be able to carry him. So he attacked the Mayor at every opportunity and successfully made "Lockwoodism," which he likened to totalitarianism, a major campaign issue. In a political advertisement, he wrote:

> *Many people recall the story of the camel who first pushed his head into the Arab's tent and then by degrees put his whole body there and ousted his master. Few people realized at the time how Hitler was forming an "Empire" absorbing weak and unsuspecting countries. It seems to us that the present Charleston administration is hoping to expand its political "Empire" by taking in adjoining counties, so that nearby "Political possessions" will have to come to Charleston, for political patronage—the "Crumbs", as it were, from Charleston's abundant table.*

He suggested vote fraud was coming. "This is a federal election," he stated during one stump speech, "and that ought to be sufficient to certain ears in this community. State law permits any citizen to witness the count of ballots, provided order is preserved. All we want is a fair election. A square election and you know I am your congressman."

Mendel even challenged the legal authority of the Chairman of the Democratic Executive Committee (a Charleston alderman and ally of Lockwood) to conduct the election, on the grounds that he had moved his residence and was required by law to resign.

In his final radio broadcast before the primary, Mendel was explicit:

My opponent says he does not wish to lower the dignity of the campaign. Neither do I. Does my opponent consider it dignified to have the taxpayers' dollars spent in the furtherance of his campaign? Does my opponent consider it dignified to have his support solicited by the Police Force of this city? Does my opponent consider it dignified to have representatives of the Charleston underworld distribute his literature all over the District? Does my opponent consider it dignified to have his henchmen pull down my posters with rakes and ladders, so that the torn fragments cover the First Congressional District like confetti? And finally, does he consider it dignified when the Mayor of Charleston stated in the early spring at the 25th wedding anniversary of the Honorable Bert Rogers, Clerk of Court of Beaufort, in the presence of the Mayor of Beaufort and other prominent persons, and in my presence, that in Charleston a magic wand can be waved over the ballot boxes so that the votes could come out as desired?

Von Kolnitz was forced to respond. In his own paid campaign literature, he (ostensibly a group of concerned citizens) repeated Mendel's charges and then wrote, "From every stump and platform, and now through the press, L. Mendel Rivers has left no stone unturned to defame the good name of Charleston and her citizens, especially the Mayor, and members of his administration…A vote for L. Mendel Rivers is a vote for Charleston's openly avowed enemy!"

Mendel challenged, and Fritz responded. He allowed Mendel to frame the terms of the debate. But Von Kolnitz attacked where he could. He quibbled with Mendel's claims of being Special Assistant to the Attorney General. At one stump, he quoted from a letter from "an assistant attorney general" to the effect that Mendel's title while with the Department of Justice was "associate attorney" and "special attorney," that he was not an Assistant to the Attorney General and that about one thousand other persons were employed in the same capacity as Mendel Rivers.

True, but scarcely a body blow. It was a fine point probably lost on most of the audience.

Von Kolnitz had an affected accent. It was my impression that he had either studied at Harvard or wanted people to think he had. His accent, wherever it came from, was something well beyond the "old Charleston" accent of my parents and their contemporaries. It didn't sound "old Charleston." It sounded almost foreign, perhaps even German. After all, Von Kolnitz was certainly a German name.

It was unfortunate (for Von Kolnitz) that Hitler had just invaded Poland. The uneducated country folk thought that Von Kolnitz had a German accent and had difficulty pronouncing his name. They called him "von Collins."

I well remember one rural voter approaching me at one of the many stump meetings we attended: "Mrs. Rivers," he began slowly, "this here von Collins fella, why, he ain't even lost his German accent!" Perhaps I should have corrected him and told him that Von Kolnitz was a war hero who had fought the Germans and whose family had been in South Carolina for generations. I didn't.

Mendel capitalized on Von Kolnitz's name, calling him "Von Kolnitski," and ridiculed his accent. Mendel would skillfully sneer the name in such a manner that it implied that he was almost a Nazi sympathizer.

He likewise dismissed Von Kolnitz's qualifications, trying to suggest he didn't have any. In his last radio address, he offered:

> *I will now depart from a discussion of my opponent, for I believe that the people of the First Congressional District already know that he has not had one day of legislative experience; that his ability in that field is still an unknown quantity; that his temperament in that position is questionable, and that his public service has principally been confined to the perfunctory pastime of maintaining the upkeep of the playgrounds of the city, and overseeing the general welfare of the monkeys and other curiosities confined in the cages at Hampton Park.*

Mendel was never one to do things in a small way. When asked how he could presume to run against such odds, he retorted, "Well, I intend to campaign. If I talk to one person, it will be a conversation. If I meet two people, I will make it a speech." And campaign he did through that sweltering summer. There were few days when Mendel did not make several speeches and return home for a rally or a radio address in the evening. His efforts received almost no press coverage from the local paper.

Unlike Von Kolnitz, Mendel Rivers spoke the language of the "little people." "The only banker I knew was the one who foreclosed the mortgage on my mama's farm after my daddy died," Mendel would shout as he campaigned. He knew the right way to butcher a cow and how to approach a fly ball in center field. He had been poor as a youngster. It certainly didn't matter to the impoverished country folk that I had only one outfit to wear during that campaign summer. Mother made my seersucker dress. It had to be rinsed out every evening to be fresh for the next day's appearance.

A Charleston policeman stopped me as I drove the office jalopy on the Battery one afternoon. "Get that Rivers sign off your car, see?" he told me. He had no idea that I was the wife of the candidate. My heart was pounding furiously as I enquired why. "Because it is the wrong sign, see?" I summoned all the courage I could muster. "Well," I said without too much emphasis, "I think it's the right sign." The policeman replied, "I'll let you off this time, lady. But don't use it no more, see?"

One night Mendel received a threatening phone call from the City of Charleston Chief of Police. "Get out of the race," he told Mendel, whose response was so vituperative that I was sure he would be ambushed on his next trip out of town. Mendel launched into a tirade of filthy words, mostly about the race and parentage of the chief. "You half-caste son of a bitch! I know all about you!" he shouted. "You come near me, and I'll kill you!"

I was horrified. The chief was from Berkeley County. He was a "brass ankle," a member of an ostensibly white family that was rumored to contain some African blood. In brass ankle families, Negro features would suddenly appear in a newborn. Such families were whispered about and were considered lower class. They were also believed to be vindictive and violent. No one called them brass ankles to their faces, of course. That is to say, no one but Mendel Rivers. I was very, very frightened, and I told Mendel so. "Why did you talk to him like that? How could you?" I fussed. I honestly feared that Mendel would be murdered on some lonely road, or worse. "You let me handle this, Marguerite," was all he said.

I underestimated Mendel. It wasn't the first time nor was it the last. The following morning he rode out as usual, conspicuous in his earsplitting red Chrysler. No more was heard from the bullying caller.

Ironically, my father had been elected a city councilman during Mayor Lockwood's administration. The Mayor had appointed him the City of Charleston Police Commissioner. Although it was a strictly honorary position, my father was proud of the honor. He attended ceremonies, talked to policemen and felt he was making his city safer. He instructed the police force to remain neutral in the upcoming primary election. Initially, he just could not believe Mendel's reports about the dirty tricks that Lockwood's men were committing, but as the police tactics became more blatant and were personally directed at both me and Mendel, my father began to realize that his honor was at stake. He had been duped by someone he had trusted and regarded as a friend. He called on Mayor Lockwood personally and protested about the Charleston police being involved in partisan politics. There was an exchange of letters. Once the correspondence was published in the local newspaper, the "neutral" police force limited its activism to raking down Rivers campaign signs and harassing motorists in the weeks just before the election. (It was long after the furor of the election before I appreciated how difficult this situation had been for my gentlemanly, honorable father.)

In fairness, some of Mendel's supporters retaliated by raking down Von Kolnitz's signs. Palmer Gaillard, later Mayor of Charleston, was a friend of my cousin, Sammy Hasell; they thought it was a lark to go out in the country and tear down Von Kolnitz signs. Even Mendel was not above raking down Von Kolnitz's signs he saw posted on trees growing beside deserted country roads.

It was a long, hot summer. When Election Day finally arrived, some of Mendel's poll watchers were evicted from the polls, while opposing watchers were told how many votes to allow Rivers in each ward. Back then ballots were on paper and were counted manually. Mendel stressed throughout the campaign that anyone could watch the counting.

In the late afternoon of Election Day, my sister Boo and I took a voter to Ward 12 at Burke High School, a very rough precinct. As we approached, Mendel's watcher, Gedney Howe, was being helped away from the polling place by two men. We thought he was drunk, but learned afterward that he had been kicked in the groin by the opposition. Since Gedney was incapacitated, Boo called a muscular Citadel friend to protect us as we sat at either end of the table watching the vote count. We observed votes being stolen as piles of votes for Rivers were placed on the bottom of a pile and a single Von Kolnitz vote was put on top. My parents watched the tallying of another precinct also located at Burke. They rushed to the school when they heard the rumor that Mendel had been shot and Marwee was standing over his body.

A Democratic Party official's wife tried to evict me from the poll tallying. She snarled, "Why don't you get the hell out of here?"

I replied, "I have a perfect right to be in this room as long as I do not create a commotion."

The woman hissed, "I could just spit in your eye."

About a month after Mendel won the election, I was crossing the intersection at Wentworth and King Streets, and the same woman approached me, gushing, "Oh, Margaret, I am so glad to see you! My husband and I are having a party Saturday, and you and Mendel must come!" (I always wished I had replied, "You counted us out in the primary, and you can count us out from now on.")

Mendel won, just as he had predicted, by winning the outlying counties. He lost the City of Charleston by a margin of three to one. Tired of the Charleston machine's arrogance, rural district voters piled up a plurality of 3,700 votes for Mendel Rivers, despite the strong-arm tactics.

In a surprising show of childish pique, Hizzoner proudly proclaimed his own losing status on election night: "I am proud that the City of Charleston voted as I did and voted three to one for Von Kolnitz." He forgot to congratulate the winner.

The primary election night victory celebration was held in Mendel's second-story office. It was hot, crowded and we were all in high spirits. At some point the French doors were opened for ventilation. Unfortunately, there was no balcony or grillwork to protect people from falling into the courtyard below. One of Mendel's supporters had been drinking. He stepped into the void and suddenly disappeared. No one seemed concerned about his plight. The only person who noticed was Palmer Gaillard, who vaguely wondered how the man escaped from an enclosure that was surrounded by three walls and a tall building.

Human nature is endlessly interesting. I learned a lot that summer. I learned that I had married a man who could turn a disadvantage into an advantage. He knew how to use his flair for repartee, his gift for sensing the mood of a crowd and his ability to inject a touch of humor at the right moment. And I learned that he had extraordinary courage. He won the election. He lost thirty-four pounds.

Mendel subsequently appeared at the meeting of the State Democratic Committee and formally protested the dishonest conduct of the election. Although he was ignored at the time, his complaints were legitimate and important. Voting machines and other improvements have since vindicated his concerns.

Von Kolnitz had not participated in the dirty tricks of the Charleston political machine. According to his nephew, he was so disgusted with the ugliness of the campaign that he refused to leave his home in Mount Pleasant the last two weeks before the election. Several years later, Von Kolnitz wrote Mendel a kind letter telling him how much he approved of Mendel's job performance in Congress. Mendel cherished that letter and appreciated Fritz's gesture of friendship.

After 1940, no strong opponent challenged Mendel. In 1950 Arthur J. Clement Jr. ran against Mendel in the Democratic Primary. He was an insurance salesman, civil rights advocate and the first Negro in the First District since Reconstruction to seek the office as a regular Democrat. It was no contest. Poll taxes and white control over the voter registration process virtually excluded blacks from the political process. Clement's candidacy unnerved some white segregationists, but Mendel won handily 42,000 to 7,000. In another primary in the 1960s, Mendel's opponent received only one vote, presumably his own. Mendel loved to laugh at the results and say not even his opponent's wife would vote for him.

But we got a scare in 1968. That was a difficult, frightening year. President Johnson announced he would not run for reelection, Martin

Luther King and Robert Kennedy had been murdered and cities across the country burned.

George A. Payton Jr. was a Negro attorney practicing law in Charleston. Maybe he thought those troubled times would cause voters to want to break with the old and elect someone completely different. Maybe he wanted to advertise his business as an attorney. (Attorneys couldn't advertise back then, so many of them would run for public office as a way of advertising their practices.)

When Payton announced his intentions to run for Mendel's seat in Congress, I had never heard of him. But I did hear this: Payton was a pawn. He was a stalking horse for substantial "Kennedy money," and more—paid staff, volunteers from out of state, advisors, technical support and goodness knows what else—all poised to be poured into the First Congressional District, to defeat Mendel.

Mendel wouldn't comment on the rumors of Kennedy money lining Payton's coffers. All he would say was, "I'm not scared. I'm concerned. I'm damned concerned."

Looking back on it, I can see that the Kennedys had no interest in defeating Mendel. He liked them, and they knew it. He admired Jack Kennedy, and he was prepared to work with Bobby and Teddy. He never shared my distaste for them.

But Mendel ran like he had never run before since the election of 1940. It was the only real election campaign he ever had after the election of 1940.

The Mendel Rivers of 1968 was a far cry from the gangly thirty-four-year-old who challenged Tunka Lockwood's machine. By 1968 Mendel had been reelected thirteen times and had doled out favors all over the First District. He was fast becoming an institution, and he was the powerful Chairman of the House Armed Services Committee. He had friends in high places. The Mayor of the City of Charleston loved him. All the mayors loved him. They, and congressional colleagues, generals, defense contractors and lobbyists, to name a few. He was owed some favors. He called them in.

In 1968 Mendel raised three times the campaign money he ordinarily raised. He put up billboards all over the First Congressional District. He made radio commercials and stated,

> *Now, I know you want to vote for me. I know you want to return me to Washington to continue to work for you. You know what I have done for you. But did you know that you can only vote for me if you vote in the Democratic Primary? Anyone can vote in the Democratic Primary, even people who don't consider themselves Democrats. So don't forget to vote in the Democratic Primary, so you can vote for me.*

Campaign billboard.

He was concerned about a Republican primary, which would be a competing primary that would siphon off his supporters, many of whom more and more often called themselves Republicans. (If only one party held a primary, then voters of either party could vote in it. But if both parties held primaries, then their supporters would vote only in their own primary.) Mendel feared being isolated in a Democratic primary against a black man, with most whites voting in a Republican primary and unable to vote for him.

So he persuaded the local Republicans not to hold a primary that year. He actually did it. They agreed to nominate their candidates by convention, and they did it to save Mendel Rivers. By 1968 he was that powerful. That was the year a local Republican leader stated, "Mendel Rivers is our best natural resource."

He ran a wonderful TV ad: A man appears facing the camera, looking comfortable and pleasant. He smiles and says, "Hello. My name is Bob Edwards, Member of Congress from the state of California. I'm the

Chairman of the Republican House Congressional Campaign Committee. It's my job to elect Republicans. [Pause, for effect] But if I lived in Charleston, South Carolina, I'd vote for Mendel Rivers."

Edwards smiles again. Fade. End of commercial.

Ten days before the primary election date, Mendel arranged to have fifteen members of the House Armed Services Committee inspect the local Polaris Missile Facility (which he had brought to Charleston), along with Vice Admiral Hyman Rickover, Father of the Nuclear Navy, to make certain they understood what they saw. All present sang the praises of their Chairman and host extravagantly.

Mendel set up a campaign headquarters in the Francis Marion Hotel and kept phone banks manned. He asked for volunteers and got them. He could afford paid staff now, and he hired several people, as I recall. Even young Mendel came down from Georgetown University and volunteered to campaign for his beleaguered father. Then he arranged for his roommate, his girlfriend and his roommate's girlfriend to visit—never a good sign. I think he partied as much as he sought votes for his dad. Marion also volunteered. I know Peggy would have, but she had two small children and lived far away. We had plenty of help.

The Kennedy money never arrived, but we didn't know that. Payton had no "media blitz" at any point in the campaign. In fact, he seemed rather quiet. We heard rumors he was "operating in the black churches." Was there a conspiracy of silence? Were all the black ministers railing against Mendel, and we didn't even know it? We heard rumors of dark involvement by the NAACP, which might organize vast legions of voters before we could mobilize our own supporters.

Payton's campaign theme was "Time for a Change." He criticized Mendel as a "warmonger and superhawk," rhetoric he thought might resonate with black voters, I guess. What resonated with black voters was good jobs and a better future, and Mendel Rivers had already shown he could deliver those. Payton talked about a higher minimum wage, expanded Social Security and federal housing programs. Mendel delivered higher wages, helped his voters feel more secure and helped them afford better housing.

Mendel's tone during the campaign was condescending to Payton. He seldom criticized Payton, who was busy criticizing him at every turn. His ads suggested he was already the voter's choice. The question was, "Are you going to the polls to keep me?"

I never met George Payton. The only time I ever saw his face was the day before the election, when he aired a poorly done black-and-white TV commercial, consisting of himself speaking to the camera about Mendel and the need for change. He said he had no money and couldn't compete with all that Mendel had spent. He didn't sound radical or crazy. He was educated. He was courteous when he mentioned Mendel. I wasn't quite sure what we had been so frightened about.

Election Day was cool (for June) and rainy. But we liked the initial news; the lines to vote in North Charleston and at the military bases were long, all day. Everybody in town was voting.

We heard touching stories of Negroes who walked miles in the rain to cast their ballots "for Mendel" and stories of elderly white Republicans who crossed party lines to vote for Mendel in the Democratic primary. We heard the white wards were voting strongly, but so were the black wards. We worried, even though we had done all we could.

Then the first returns came in, from predominately black Daufuskie Island, in Beaufort County. We (young Mendel, Marion, Trez Hane and others of Mendel's staff) were sitting around our den, watching the early returns with Mendel Davis, who was Mendel's aide at the time. It was tense. The announcer seemed to take forever:

"Let's see, now. Yes, we have the first returns in the race for U.S. Congress, from Daufuskie Island. Let's see…Yes…I think that's right…Yes…It's Rivers, 14. Payton, 2."

Everyone cheered except Mendel Davis. He paused for dramatic effect, stroked his chin and solemnly intoned: "Don't worry, everybody. We're gonna find those two sons of bitches!"

Mendel won everywhere. He won hugely in every white ward. But he won hugely in the black wards as well, winning by a margin as high as three to one in black wards. The final tally was 65,842 for Rivers, 18,883 for Payton. The Republicans didn't offer a candidate for Congress that year.

George Payton was assassinated in his law office ten years later by a professional hit man who scheduled an appointment, calmly waited to see him and then pulled out a pistol with a silencer as soon as he walked into his office. The man shot George's brains out and then calmly walked out of his law office and into the noise of the city. He was never seen again. Motive and suspects unknown.

Mr. Congressman

After the election, moving from conservative Charleston to cosmopolitan Washington was an adjustment for both Mendel and me. I had been used to being part of the upper social echelons and was not worried about my role because I had been a debutante. How little I understood Washington etiquette. Suddenly, I found myself in an environment of rigid social protocols that were considerably more complex than the more relaxed social life of provincial Charleston. I soon discovered that I had a lot to learn.

The wife of a junior congressman was required to perform certain duties, which demanded handsome clothes, Emily Post manners and lots of time. During the struggles of that ghastly primary, I had not thought much about what it would be like living in Washington. The wife of another South Carolina congressman (also named McMillan) who had already served one term considered herself to be a veteran and kindly took me under her wing. She introduced me to the custom of the obligatory social calls a junior congressman's wife was expected to make. We started at the White House and moved on to pay calls to the wives at the embassies and the homes of senior government officials.

When Margaret McMillan decided that I had mastered the technique, she informed me that it was my turn to make the customary inquiries. I quickly made a fool of myself when I timidly asked an embassy doorman, "Is the Mad-am in?" instead of the correct, "Is Ma-dam in?" I still shudder with embarrassment as I recall the ugly stare, as the doorman replied coldly, "There is no Mad-am here," and then quickly shut the door. To this day

I wonder if he actually thought the two stylishly dressed young women in front of him were applying for employment as ladies of the night.

Mendel's mother visited us when he was sworn in. She had encouraged him through the lean years and was fiercely proud of his accomplishments. It was the realization of her dream that he would someday be in Congress. She envisioned this as an opportunity for Mendel to resurrect some of the lost family fortunes. She and Mendel posed by a statue of Wade Hampton and were interviewed by the correspondent for our home paper. I am ashamed to say that I was furious when the reporter misquoted me as having said that I'd dreamed of his becoming a congressman. I should have been more supportive, but I did not adapt well to being a political wife and the demands it placed upon me.

Mendel's first Washington office in 1941 was a modest single room for the congressman and his staff of one, an aged lady secretary he'd inherited from his predecessor. Although the previous Congressional Session had lasted about three months, after Pearl Harbor Congress remained in session almost continually. Mendel earned the impressive salary of $10,000 a year. This seemed like such a fortune to my mother that she was afraid that our infant daughter would be kidnapped for ransom just like the Lindbergh baby.

Mendel's predecessor apparently had very lax office practices. When the inherited secretary finally retired, I took over some of her duties. At her desk, hidden away under an ink blotter and wedged next to the wall, I found a large envelope containing her private "stash" of dozens of letters from constituents (now our constituents) that she had found inconvenient to answer. So she simply stuck them in an envelope, hid the envelope and went on with her day. In addition, Mrs. McMillan had carelessly left behind some correspondence she had had with the Charleston political machine during the recent primary. It was an inauspicious beginning.

But Mendel could turn a lemon into lemonade. Every congressman, upon being sworn in, is assigned to a particular committee. When he first entered Congress, Mendel requested that he be assigned to the Agriculture Committee. It seemed a natural fit. The First District was largely rural. The country folk had elected him, over the City of Charleston machine. He wanted to help his farming constituents. The Agriculture Committee was full. Mendel was denied his committee preference. The Committee on Committees assigned him to the Naval Affairs Committee. He was severely disappointed.

As he told the story, he fumed and fussed to anyone who would listen, until a wiser, more experienced colleague took him aside.

"Mendel," the colleague asked, "don't you have a naval base and a naval shipyard in your district?"

Mendel replied almost petulantly, "So what?"

"Well, there's a war. We need ports for the war, and upgraded air bases, army posts and naval bases. Your naval base and navy yard might need the help of a congressman on the right committee. Seems to me, you're in a position to really help your district."

"You don't say!"

Mendel understood the message: Use your position to advantage. Bring the American military to Charleston. Be a breadwinner for your people. The Naval Affairs Committee was later incorporated into the Armed Services Committee.

In May 1945, Mendel's position on the committee enabled me to be asked to sponsor a submarine named the *Serago*. When I christened the boat, I was determined to break the champagne bottle on the first try because it is considered bad luck to fail. I had a plan! I imagined that the bottle was Hitler's head. My mental trick enabled me not to embarrass myself or harm the good reputation of the boat. I smashed the bottle so well that the champagne sprayed everywhere. The whole experience was exhilarating; the military brass and distinguished guests were ever so cordial. I still cherish my association with the *Serago*. (Years later, in 1971, it gave me great pleasure to let my daughters share such an experience, for Admiral Rickover and I

Marwee imagined the bow of the *Serago* was Hitler's head when she smashed the champagne bottle.

decided that they should be invited to sponsor the *L. Mendel Rivers* submarine instead of me, as would have normally occurred.)

Born leaders can insult people and somehow make those very people love them. Being elected to Congress scarcely caused Mendel to bridle his tongue. If anything, it made him bolder. In 1941 Mendel was a member of the U.S. delegation sent to the British West Indies to discuss the Lend-Lease Program, a major United States military aid program, which formed a key part of the British national defense system during the war. This was early in the war. Lend-lease was a matter of national security to both countries, and Mendel was a mere freshman congressman. He had yet to make his name.

Following one of the sessions, a British envoy who had met Mendel before approached him. His manner was snooty and, to Mendel's mind, extraordinarily condescending.

"I say, I am most dreadfully sorry, but I cahn't seem to remembah your name," he began. Clearly, Mendel's name had been insufficiently important to remember when they were introduced.

But Mendel had been snubbed by Charleston's best. He was not the least intimidated by the arrant elitism that confounded less stalwart souls. His reply was classic Mendelian, "Why don't you just call me 'Mr. Lend-Lease'? You can remember that, can't you?"

Another time when he was in his fourth or so term in Congress, around 1948, he had occasion to attend a football game at Stoney Field. As he was patiently working his way through the turnstiles, a constituent, Leo Livingstain, came up out of nowhere, pulled on his sleeve and excitedly asked Mendel, "What's my name?"

Mendel recognized the man. He had stopped at his hardware store several times. Mendel's mother and stepfather were good customers. He probably couldn't remember his name and was embarrassed at being put on the spot in front of a crowd. He stared at the man.

As for Leo, we later learned he had made a bet with a friend that the amazing Mendel Rivers always remembered everybody's name. Leo actually had money on the line!

"Well, then," Leo asked, holding up the other fans that were crowding the gate, "what's my name?"

Mendel exploded. "You goddamned fool! You come to me, and you don't even know your own name, and you expect me to remember it for you? Well I'll tell you what: I'll get a dog tag, and we'll hang it around your neck. Maybe that will help you remember your name."

Leo stepped off briskly without another word. He later became one of Mendel's greatest admirers. Mendel reciprocated the admiration and boasted of his friendship with Leo Livingstain.

Reminiscing about the outlandish things Mendel said, a colleague recalled the time Armed Services Committee Chairman Carl Vinson assigned Mendel to a special subcommittee with Overton Brooks, another flamboyant congressman. His friend recalled, "Mendel told the Chairman, 'You've got to take me off that committee.' When Vinson asked why, Mendel replied, 'You can't have two crazy men on the same committee.'"

Wartime housing was scarce in Washington. We rented a row house on Adams Mill Road overlooking the Washington Zoo. Peggy's nurse, Lottie, accompanied us. She spoiled us all and charmed us with her cooking and conversation. She often told me, "You is duh luckiest white woman I ever did see! Mr. Rivers sho' is a good prowider, yuh?"

After our lease expired, we rented a duplex in a housing development in southeast Washington called Fairfax Village. It proved to be a mistake. A patrol reprimanded any tenant who had opened the window, even when it was stifling inside. In addition, the owners took advantage of wartime rationing and skimped on fuel. Furnaces were fired up in early mornings when the husbands were at home. Our apartments gradually cooled off until it was time for them to return. I kept Peggy as warm as possible. The second winter when the situation became worse, I had a built-in heater, for Marion was born the following May.

We parted with Lottie shortly after our move. She had made a friend in Washington, a "Miss Cohens," who had altered Lottie's attitude toward us. (Miss Cohens gave Lottie manicures and pedicures and loaned her a fur coat.) Lottie visited the Cohens on her days off. Loyal, lovable Lottie became glum and critical. She corrected Peggy's grammar badly. When Peggy once told a visitor, "Oh, thank you for visiting Lottie and me," Lottie reprimanded her, in front of the visitor and with great pride: "Now Peggy, you must say, 'Thank you for visiting Lottie and I.'" One day I dumped out our trash and discovered a postcard Lottie had started to her daughter. I deciphered it, pleased to see that she had learned to write. I read: "I don thin I comen bac mis rivers geten to sicnen." (I don't think I coming back. Mrs. Rivers getting too sickening.)

Three-year-old Peggy read my mind and sensed my moods on numerous occasions. She would frequently embarrass me with her remarks, a trait she seemed to have inherited from her father. One afternoon as I watched her play in the sandbox at Fairfax Village, she bit one of her playmates. The mother was furious. I was appalled. In my most disciplined voice I asked, "Peggy, how could you do such a thing?!" I expected her to be properly contrite. How little I knew that child of mine! She replied, "Easy! Like this," and she grabbed the child's hand and bit her again.

One Sunday afternoon my brother Charlie visited me in our drab apartment. He had volunteered for the Marine Corps, although he had a wife and a young son and another child on the way. He had completed his boot training at Parris Island and was attending the Officers Training School at Quantico. Charlie's calloused hands told me a lot about the rigorous training he'd received. He was not quite twenty-eight; he looked lean and strained; he was balding rapidly. I was glad I had learned to cook after I got married and gave him a hearty meal.

Mendel and I went to Quantico when Charlie received his bars as second lieutenant. I was awed by the high-ranking officers and cabinet members we met there. I felt tongue-tied and inadequate. We were relieved when Charlie told us that he would be stationed at Quantico instead of being ordered overseas immediately.

That was the last time we saw him. A few months later, he was lost on the Potomac on a freezing night. Characteristically, he had volunteered to go in order to improve his officership. He had had little sleep the previous night. Someone saw him on deck at the stern of the training craft before midnight, just before the company sought warmth below decks. He was missing when they reached the farther bank.

It was a terrible winter for our family. Mother, who had been stricken with encephalitis the previous summer and still wore a patch over one eye, had just begun to recuperate from the disease when we received the news of Charlie's disappearance on February 1, 1944. For six weeks we didn't know what had happened to him. Well-meaning people offered all sorts of conjectures: that he had been picked up by a U-boat, that he was being nursed in the cottage of some illiterate fisherman. His body was finally discovered after the icy waters relinquished their hold on his remains. The Marines called Mendel, who had the unpleasant task of confirming his identity. Mendel recognized Charlie's Clemson ring. His second son, Philip, was born a week after he was lost.

The one happy event that year was a wedding. Boo and Mac Anderson had been sweethearts for years. Mac had finished medical college and was being called to active duty. They wanted to be together and married in September, which overlapped another Rivers family return to Charleston.

Trying to escape the infections that plagued the children in our wretched Washington housing development, we returned to New Street and crowded into my parents' basement rooms. Later we relocated to Mother's rental property at 24 Queen Street, a tall row house designed in 1804. Originally it had had an upper residence and a street-level store. The high ceilings and delicate mantels gave it an elegant air, but it was not readily adaptable to our needs. The stairs had been worn uneven, and using them was a frequent and dangerous necessity. The store area had been converted into a garage and a room with a maid's toilet and furnace; we lived on the upper floors. The tall windows were difficult to darken during the nighttime air raid warnings.

Twenty-four Queen was two blocks above Broad Street, in a fairly tough ward, so Mendel had consented to stay there. It was also two blocks from the docks where merchant mariners disembarked when they came ashore to carouse. I was concerned about those rough sailors and forbade Peggy to go beyond Philadelphia Alley and the Footlight Players theater.

A few maids moved in and out of our hectic existence. One of them took all the family's presents with her just a few days before Christmas. Another, simple-minded Blossom, was wafted our way on an ill wind; she couldn't do anything right, and we quickly replaced her with another. Anna, the best, was a scary young girl who lived in "Ryan's Jail," the colored tenement across the street. The neighboring Negroes kept chickens, and every morning we were awakened by their cheery cock-a-doodle-doos.

As Mendel had no office in Charleston, our living room was used for the visits of his constituents. The dining room became a waiting room. The most compelling feature of that room was a superb panorama of St. Philip's steeple and the tiled rooftops of nearby historic buildings. Frequently our visitors would have to sit and contemplate the remains of our breakfast of hominy (grits) and eggs while I answered the telephone or attended to the little girls. I doubt they appreciated our extraordinary view.

In that first campaign Mendel had promised the voters he could come back every year to hear their problems, and he kept that promise. The district trips were a series of meetings in the county seats where Congressman Rivers would see people who had problems with the government. An aide took notes. Anything from Social Security to military assignments was handled back in Washington. One writer described those annual trips as "pure Americana."

One of Mendel's earliest successes in Congress was getting the federal tax on oleo margarine repealed. Oleo was made of the oil from cotton seeds and soybeans, both crops native to the First District. But sales were sluggish, and oleo was unable to gain a foothold as an alternative to dairy butter because, among other reasons, it was heavily taxed by the federal government. The dairy farmers, located primarily in the Midwest, enjoyed a powerful bloc in Congress and strongly defended the tax on oleo.

Mendel attacked the tax with gusto. He made so many speeches that he earned the name "Oleo" Rivers. "Butter will kill you deader than Job's turkey, but eat a little margarine and you will look like a million dollars," he told his colleagues.

He challenged the old alliance between Southern Democrats and Midwest Republicans. This is how one Washington columnist described the situation in 1949 under the heading "Oleo and Old Lace": "The one issue that parts those dear friends in Congress, the southern conservatives and right-wing Republicans, is oleo. It's a blunt economic conflict between the rural North and the cotton South. The argument has almost bristled into fisticuffs." The column goes on to describe a scene in the House of Representatives where an angry Mendel Rivers of South Carolina refuses, "acidly, to yield any further time to a certain Midwestern Republican with whom he is ordinarily arm in arm comrades." Other columns of the day describe Mendel happily taking on as many Midwestern dairy-bloc congressmen as wished to join the fray. He had a cause.

When the tax was eventually repealed, Mendel proclaimed immodestly, "This is one of the greatest pieces of legislation ever struck off by the hand of man." Margarine could now compete with butter. In gratitude, several brands of margarine sent us complimentary boxes of oleo until the day Mendel died.

As a consumer, I shared the opinion of many a housewife that being able to purchase an inexpensive imitation butter spread was a godsend. Only the wealthy purchased the beautiful uniform sticks of yellow butter; it was considered a luxury item, almost a status symbol. Most of the people I knew ate oleo.

Before Mendel got the tax repealed, oleo margarine was sold either in solid white one-pound blocks that looked like lard or alternately was sealed in plastic packaging that contained a capsule of yellow dye. If a housewife wanted to make the effort, she could painstakingly hold the capsule while it was still sealed in with the white lump of margarine; when the heat of her hands melted the capsule, the yellow coloring was kneaded into the softened mass. The process took a long time. The yellowed oleo was then removed from the package, shaped and refrigerated. Housewives hated being forced to spend so much time preparing this butter substitute. Mendel had actually performed a great service for the American masses.

Recently, I ran across two interesting letters from 1952. In the first, the lobbyist for the National Association of Margarine Manufacturers writes to Mendel asking him to help get authorization for the U.S. Navy to use margarine. In the second, not only does Mendel agree to help, but he also asks for more margarine! "When I return to Washington, my icebox will be empty so I know we will have to have some more margarine." His nice little sentence is so innocent, almost childlike. Today, his request would be a crime.

Mendel truly enjoyed the prerogatives of his position. His godson, namesake and successor, Mendel Davis, recounted how South Carolina finally issued congressional license plates. When the state decided to give special tags to certain elected officials, it could not decide how to number the plates of the congressional delegation. Using seniority was considered, but Mendel, realizing how long it would take him to acquire the seniority of some incumbents, suggested numbering the plates according to the number of the representative's district. His, of course, was the "First District," and Mendel took full advantage of that wonderful number one.

Mendel certainly had his quirks. Most of the time, like any general, he just barked orders when he wanted something. He was proud of his ability to make people jump. He once made a bet with a visitor to his Washington office that he could clear his staff out of the office within two minutes. I was a witness. He issued orders to everyone in sight, watched them leave and then sat back and laughed heartily with his guest.

Mendel had no fear of inconsistent behavior. As a young man, he smoked Chesterfields, like everyone else. In fact, as a first-term congressman, he used his habit to his advantage. President Franklin D. Roosevelt visited Charleston in 1942 to attend a ceremony at the Charleston Naval Base. Mendel, as the U.S. Representative representing Charleston, was of course on hand to greet the distinguished visitor. He probably expected to be ushered by some protocol officer into the great man's presence. Whatever he expected, he quickly learned it didn't work that way. Nobody cared if a mere first-term congressman ever saw the President.

At the main event, Mendel found himself entirely shut out from the President by a tight band of senior legislators, senior state officials, senior military officers and self-important local officials who had all managed to crowd their way into the President's little circle. There was essentially a wall—or worse, a Gordian knot—of dozens of men, strong, egotistical men, between Mendel and Franklin Roosevelt. Another man would have accepted his position and decided to see the next President, after he had acquired some more seniority.

Not Mendel Rivers. He took it as a personal challenge: those men were in his way. His task was to move them. He muscled, elbowed, bullied, shoved, pushed, excuse-me'd, cajoled, joked and threatened his way through the entire phalanx. At one point, he became so aggressive, he was afraid he'd be mistaken for an assassin and arrested, or worse, by the Secret Service. He didn't care. He continued to shove and elbow, smile and keep moving.

And then he was there, next to the Great Man himself, the President of the United States. Roosevelt, of course, was seated, in his wheelchair. He heard Mendel's commotion. He turned to look at the brash young congressman and stared. Mendel Rivers stared back. What was he going to say, now that he had worked so hard to speak to the leader of the nation?

"Mr. President, I'm Mendel Rivers. I'm the congressman from this district. I'd like to welcome you to Charleston."

"How do you do, Mendel?" responded the President affably. "What can I do for you?"

"Can I borrow a cigarette?" It was all he could think of to say. He smoked a Chesterfield with the President.

In his later years, Mendel grew to despise tobacco. When he quit, he expected the world to quit with him and to hate tobacco as much as he now did. He was as actively anti-tobacco as he had once been pro-, and he saw no reason to contain his strong feelings. In those years, an admirer once gave him a splendid ashtray. I was in his office, when Mendel phoned to thank him: "I want you to know how much I admire that beautiful ashtray you sent me. I am looking at it right now. It makes my desk look like a million dollars. I really appreciate it. Of course, I don't smoke, you know, but if some damned fool wants to kill himself smoking in my office, I'll see that he does it First Class!"

Mendel prided himself on his pronunciation of the words "filthy, stinking, nasty," which he dragged out with a heavy sneer, every time he mentioned the word "tobacco." He never uttered the one without the others. And yet whenever I thought I had it figured out, he would do the unexpected. Sometimes it was very successful.

Young Mendel's godfather offered him $1,000 if he would not smoke before his twenty-first birthday. He refused the offer. Like most young people, he preferred to go along with his peers. But he never smoked in front of his father. In fact, young Mendel was terrified of his father's strong negative reaction to cigarettes (not enough to quit smoking, of course). One summer day, young Mendel bought two packs of cigarettes, Lucky Strikes and Salems. He hid them under a blanket in his closet, the remotest place imaginable on a summer night, unless there is a sudden cold snap in the South, which almost never happens. But it happened that night. Solicitous of his son's comfort, Mendel tiptoed up to his son's room, reached into the closet for a blanket and was nearly knocked over by falling packs of cigarettes and matches. He left the evidence of the crime on the closet shelf, covered his son with the blanket and never mentioned the incident.

Mendel did much the same with Peggy. She started sneaking cigarettes from me and would try to smoke with a friend in her upstairs bedroom. She was so naive that she did not realize that the pungent smell quickly drifted downstairs and permeated the entire house. Mendel just happened to be home one day when Peggy was experimenting and went upstairs to investigate the odor. The girls heard his steps and quickly slid the still-lit cigarettes and ashtray into a bureau drawer. By the time Mendel opened the door, smoke was billowing out of the chest. The girls were terrified at how Mendel would react. He mildly said, "I see you girls are smoking." He left the room and never mentioned the incident again. Peggy didn't try another cigarette for years.

I, too, continued to sneak cigarettes until I embarrassed myself by bumming one from a plumber and decided that it was time for me to quit.

Throughout his tenure in Congress, Mendel wanted his family around for important occasions. During the Truman administration, Mendel took Peggy and me to a State of the Union address. It was at night, and we were all dressed up for the occasion. I headed for the gallery, where family members watched the proceedings from afar. As I reached for Peggy's hand, Mendel suddenly grabbed it and took her along with him. They walked through sturdy mahogany doors that clearly stated "Representatives Only" and went into the House chamber. Peggy was the only child there. She was told to sit down in one of the aisle seats midway up the Democratic side and to stay there. Peggy was scared and knew that she did not belong once the Representatives started filing in and leaned up against the walls when all the seats were taken. Her chief recollection of the President's speech was the fear that she would be evicted from her seat, so she sat miserably through it all. The next morning we looked at the newspaper. There in the front page photograph was Peggy's little head among the crowd of legislators. Suddenly, she felt better about the whole experience. The next year we looked at similar pictures, but there was no child's head to be seen.

In the ensuing years Mendel would make arrangements for the family to attend functions given in his honor, and he expected them to come. San Diego, New York, Charleston, the Hampton County Watermelon Festival. It never mattered. He wanted all of his family to be there and share his life.

Once Jack Dempsey, the prizefighter, and Air Force General Curtis LeMay attended some event at The Citadel. Mendel made arrangements for Peggy and our infant-in-arms grandson, Robert, to fly from Detroit to Charleston in a private plane. The weather was sufficiently foul to close the Charleston airport, and the plane was diverted to Savannah. So Mendel called South Carolina Highway Patrol and arranged for them to be driven back to Charleston in highway patrol cars. Babe in arms, Peggy had to transfer into a different vehicle each time they entered a new county jurisdiction. They arrived exhausted, but just in time for the festivities. This type of thing couldn't happen today, but life was vastly different then.

Mendel's commitment to the First District went far beyond expanding the military presence that had existed when he took office in 1941. Realizing how important industry was to the area's economic stability, Mendel used his considerable influence as he rose in seniority on the Armed Services

Mendel trades imaginary punches with boxer Jack Dempsey at a Citadel function.

Committee to get defense contractors to build facilities in the Lowcountry, among them General Dynamics and Avco Lycoming. Avco announced its closing almost immediately after Chairman Rivers died, but the General Dynamics facility remained for years. This farsighted awareness was long before state legislatures would offer generous, sometimes ridiculously costly tax incentives to induce manufacturers to locate in their states.

Our beautiful town has lost so many wonderful old buildings, foolishly demolished by shortsighted opportunists who chose to replace lovely historic buildings with ugly modern ones, or worse, parking lots and filling stations. In the early 1900s Charleston had no Preservation Society or Board of Architectural Review to protect its outstanding architectural gems. Charleston's little old ladies joined forces to protect their heritage. My mother helped save the Heyward-Washington House and the Glebe House. She was President of the Society for the Preservation of Old Dwellings. On several occasions, Mendel was also instrumental in saving local landmarks.

In the 1950s, the demolition of the lovely Greek Revival U.S. Customs House was proposed, and fortunately, the idea was eventually scrapped. Although he had discussed his successful intervention with young Mendel, it was years before I learned of Mendel's role in protecting the building. My good friend, the celebrated Charleston tour guide Liz Young, told me

Mendel at the Charleston Veterans' Hospital groundbreaking ceremony.

about it. (The newspaper had attributed this effort to Fritz Hollings, but as a state politician, he would have needed the federal support Mendel would have provided.) Today that treasured landmark with its Corinthian columns stands a still-proud monument to Charleston's commerce. Middleton Wharf was located on Concord Street nearby until it was destroyed in July 1951.

In 1961 the navy announced that it planned to enlarge the navy yard dry dock facilities to accommodate larger ships and Polaris submarines. The site selected was where the navy yard commandant lived. The house, called Marshlands, was a handsome 1810 mansion built by John Ball, a Cooper River rice planter. The Preservation Society asked Mendel to help save the building. As it was government property, it could not be conveyed to the many private individuals who wished to acquire it. Through a lot of political maneuvering, the City of Charleston arranged for the College of Charleston to move the house at their expense to Fort Johnson on James Island. It was an impressive accomplishment wherein Mendel, Mayor Palmer Gaillard, College President George Grice and Navy Yard Commandant Admiral McManus all joined forces. The newspapers had full details about floating the house down the Cooper River to James Island on two barges, where it stands to this day.

Mendel's constituents appreciated his efforts, and he received countless honors in his lifetime. In 1948 a section of Highway 52—the only four-lane road in North Charleston—from the Five-Mile Viaduct to the Berkeley County Line, was named "Rivers Avenue." In 1965 a bronze bust of Mendel was placed in front of the library on Rivers Avenue across the street from the naval hospital. North Charleston had a Rivers Annex Post Office, and a hunting and fishing lodge on Goat Island near Summerton had a Rivers Room in its restaurant. There is a Mendel Rivers Road in St. Stephen.

The Baptist College at Charleston (now Charleston Southern University) has a L. Mendel Rivers Library. The now-defunct Shelton College in Florida named its auditorium after Mendel Rivers. Scores of groups gave him tributes and plaques. He received honorary doctorate degrees from The Citadel (1959), Clemson University (1965) and the College of Charleston (1968).

In 1964 the federal government erected an office building across from Marion Square in Charleston to house various federal offices. It was named the L. Mendel Rivers Federal Building. Mendel received one of the nicest office suites. Finally, after all the years of suffering through cramped quarters on Broad Street, he had a decent office in Charleston.

Joseph P. Riley Jr., longtime Mayor of Charleston, was the son of Mendel's campaign manager. His recollections of Mendel:

> *He once mentioned to me that my father was a big thinker. I have often thought of that remark because that is exactly what Mendel Rivers himself was. He did not harbor small thoughts or ideas, and that is the way he approached life and public service…He could speak to a street sweeper and make him feel like a million dollars. He was at ease and in command when dealing with the most powerful and prominent people in the world. He loved public service and helping people.*

Almost everyone called him Mendel, and he liked it that way. Many considered him their personal friend. Although many public honors were heaped upon him in the First District and elsewhere, one particularly kind gesture was private. A friend and admirer from Ridgeland, South Carolina, Josie Rivers (no relation), knew the financial burden of a congressman who was raising a family while being forced to maintain two residences, one in Charleston and another in Washington. She and a group of loyal supporters raised enough money to pay off the Wappoo Heights mortgage so that Mendel could have not only a secure retirement in the future but also less financial strain in the present. The contributors wanted absolutely nothing for their generosity. I don't know that such a thing would happen nowadays. Congressmen tend to be wealthy, and their constituents often think of them as crooks who haven't been indicted yet.

States' Rights and Segregation

As every Southern lady has said, "Our ancestors were good to our slaves." My father always insisted that slaves had been regarded as valued property whose health and welfare were important. I believed him. Field slaves may have suffered at the hands of cruel overseers, but that was far removed from my generation.

In my time, education for Negroes was not considered particularly important because they were still valued primarily for cheap labor. Many white households had servants they loved and treated almost as family, but there was an invisible line and nobody crossed it. In those days, people from nice homes called black people "colored" or "Negroes." Children were forbidden to call someone a "nigger" because it would hurt the servants' feelings, and ladies never said that word.

Nobody told me about the stench of the punishment house on Logan Street in the second block above Broad where hapless Negro slaves had been beaten until the odor of their decaying sores stank up the street. That was a mere three blocks from my condo on lower Logan Street. It took one of our own (a renegade member of the Ball family, no less) to expose some of the finer points of slave control.

Before the Civil War much of South Carolina's wealth came from the slave trade and forced labor. The population was 65 percent black. After the war there were twelve harsh years of Reconstruction Republican government enforced by United States soldiers. With the plantation system destroyed and a hostile government in place, there was much resentment and want. In 1877 the federal troops finally departed, and white males took political power back when Wade Hampton became our governor in a hotly contested election. While the state struggled to recover from the collapse of its economy, the problem of a huge underclass of uneducated eligible voters remained.

By the 1890s, states all across the South began passing laws that required that the white and black races be separated in public accommodations such as schools, restaurants and passenger terminals. These laws were known as the Jim Crow laws. In South Carolina, Governor Benjamin Ryan Tillman, known as "Pitchfork" Ben Tillman, and his cronies passed our state's version of the Jim Crow laws.

The Jim Crow laws may have stated that facilities for whites and blacks were "separate but equal," but they never were equal. The Jim Crow laws had but one purpose: to ensure that the Negro population would never again enjoy the power and privileges they had known when occupying troops forced their leadership upon the defeated. And poll taxes and reading tests effectively disenfranchised black voters.

The system was obviously unstable. Pressure to deal with the segregation issue grew enormously after World War II, when colored soldiers served prominently in a segregated army and the injustices became well publicized. Then Vice President Harry Truman became President in 1945. That's when our troubles began!

Although he was a Democrat, Truman was not from the Deep South, but rather from a border state. He ordered that the U.S. Army be integrated. He spoke approvingly of new federal voter-rights and anti-lynching laws.

Mendel was raised in the rural South and was typical of his day. He was a Democrat who supported states' rights, and he was a vocal segregationist. As congressman, some of his vehemence was no doubt hometown rhetoric. He made strong statements, and he was certainly opposed to racial integration, but he made certain he did nothing to impede the flow of federal funds pouring into his district.

Mendel reacted strongly to the "class treason" of Federal Judge Julius Waties Waring. The judge was from one of Charleston's oldest and most respected families. The Warings were highly accomplished lawyers, educators and journalists. Waties served as attorney for the City of Charleston and handled himself well. He was a quiet man who paid attention to detail. He had the qualities people associate with a judge. When he was nominated to the federal bench, his nomination was supported by all who knew him. He was considered a logical choice. He was easily confirmed by the U.S. Senate and became our local federal judge, doing his job just as we all expected.

Then he met Elizabeth Hoffman.

It is the stuff of modern legend: The conventional, formal Southern judge and dignified wife meet the wealthy Detroit businessman and headstrong wife. They play bridge. Judge and other man's wife fall in love. They have a torrid affair. They leave their spouses and marry. The judge believes he can simply tell his former wife to go, and all will be well. She does, but the town hates him for it. The judge and his new wife continue to live in the same town—even in the same house at 61 Meeting Street, where the judge had lived with his first wife—but as pariahs.

Elizabeth Hoffman changed Waties Waring. Exactly how, we do not know. He issued rulings declaring the whites-only Democratic primary to be unconstitutional and required that blacks be allowed to vote in the primary. He issued rulings declaring the segregated Clarendon County public schools to be unconstitutional. He encouraged the U.S. attorney's office to prosecute white officials accused of injuring black men.

Elizabeth, meanwhile, gave a speech at the Charleston YWCA in which she proclaimed that we were (and these are her words) "degenerate." She said that we were prejudiced and backward and must learn to accept the Negro into our schools, our hearts and our lives, as equals.

Before her speech, Mendel had already hated Elizabeth Waring. Now he was furious. He turned up the heat on her husband as much as he could. He wrote to the Chief Justice of the United States, Fred Vinson, and asked him to initiate an investigation against Judge Waring, with a view toward discipline. Vinson declined, stating there needed to be a formal complaint, and some grounds, to commence an investigation. Mendel likewise tried to have Waring impeached. He ran into the same problem. Waring hadn't committed any crime or any ethical breach. He had simply issued terrible, terrible orders.

Mendel could do little to stop the civil rights juggernaut. He made speeches on the Floor of the House criticizing both of the Warings. He called Elizabeth names and laughed at Waties. But he could not change the course of history. Waties was no traitor; he was merely the agent of change.

As for Waties and Elizabeth, they remained in Charleston, shunned by their former friends and perhaps fearful for their own safety. Their only friends were Negroes. Someone even threw a brick in the window of their downtown home. There were lots of rumors. The Warings continued to live on Meeting Street until the judge retired. Then they moved to New York City and seldom returned to Charleston.

Mendel was no fan of President Truman because of his support for civil rights, especially in the U.S. military. Truman had already ordered the racial integration of the military in 1948. Mendel was outspoken in his condemnations, calling Truman among other things a "dead chicken," a "bankrupt politician" and a "traitor."

Mendel even had attempted to have his name removed from the regular Democratic (Truman) ticket in 1948, supporting Strom Thurmond's Dixiecrat ticket in a calculated move designed to shake up the national Democratic Party and move it away from its left-leaning civil rights policies. The "Solid South's" intention in 1948 was to deny both major candidates a majority and to cast the election into the House of Representatives. The ploy failed, and Mendel lost his patronage privileges. He was fortunate that he was not also stripped of his committee status.

Mendel's admiration for General Douglas MacArthur matched his contempt for Truman. He strongly opposed Truman's firing of MacArthur for insubordination, calling the MacArthur affair "one of the tragedies of our time." Mendel wept openly when the President relieved MacArthur of command in Korea in a humiliating public ceremony in 1951. When MacArthur made the famous "old soldiers never die, they just fade away" speech to a packed House gallery, Mendel had televisions placed in his office and at home to enable visiting constituents and friends to see his hero.

MacArthur was a political "hot potato." Mendel wanted to honor MacArthur (and give a backhanded slap to Truman), but a Democratic controlled Congress was reluctant to criticize a Democratic President. Mendel waited his time.

After several changes in administration, with the support of House Majority Leader John McCormack and Armed Services Committee Chairman Carl Vinson, in 1961 Mendel sponsored a resolution commending MacArthur's "outstanding devotion to the American people, his brilliant leadership during World War II, and the unsurpassed affection held for him by the people of the Republic of the Philippines." It was passed unanimously by both the House and Senate. By then everybody wanted to recognize MacArthur's contributions to the nation. To honor the general officially, Mendel scheduled a luncheon in August 1962.

When the White House learned of the extensive media coverage, President Kennedy invited General MacArthur to visit him just before Mendel's luncheon. Kennedy authorized an Air Force plane to be put at the general's disposal. Our local paper was miffed and captioned an article, "President Likely to Upstage Rivers in Capitol Welcome for MacArthur." It was the first time MacArthur had spoken on Capitol Hill since 1951. The resolution was presented on the Capitol stairs to accommodate the huge media coverage.

General MacArthur receives the Resolution of Appreciation introduced by Mendel. Due to the enormous press coverage, the event was held on the Capitol steps. *Left to right*: Mendel, Vice President Lyndon Johnson, MacArthur. August 16, 1962.

In appreciation MacArthur wrote Mendel the following:

> *The extraordinary loyalty and firmness of your own support ever since our meeting in Tokyo in 1951 has deeply moved me. Without your dynamic leadership this Resolution would never have taken active form.*

In 1952 Waties Waring resigned as federal judge. Mendel wanted the job. He sent discreet inquiries to the President, asking about his chances of being appointed to replace Waring. The President rebuffed his inquiries. Mendel had made at least one powerful enemy, but he was clever. Once it became apparent that Truman had no intention of appointing his outspoken adversary, Mendel publicly withdrew his name from the list of contenders. He turned his embarrassment into a public relations coup by claiming that he felt he could better serve his state by remaining in public office and speaking for the people. This tactic consolidated his position as a segregationist with the white voters in the First District.

In 1952 Mendel gave lip service to the Democratic Presidential candidate, Adlai Stevenson. However, he soon joined other prominent South Carolina Democrats who supported the Republican nominee for President, World War II hero General Dwight Eisenhower. Mendel told me that he had not wanted to support Eisenhower and bolt the Democratic Party for a second time. It had cost him dearly, so Mendel tried to play both sides and professed his loyalty to the Democratic Party of John C. Calhoun, Wade Hampton and, of course, Thomas Jefferson, stating that the national party had been taken over by "outsiders."

It was the voters in the First District who finally pushed Mendel into supporting Eisenhower. The Lowcountry voted 65 percent for Eisenhower, but Mendel was worried about Democratic sanctions and his removal from the Armed Services Committee. Wanting to ingratiate himself with the newly elected Republican administration, he claimed credit for the strong Republican showing in South Carolina even though Stevenson had won the ticket.

Mendel's honeymoon with the national Republicans was short lived. Soon after his election, President Eisenhower issued an executive order desegregating all schools located on military bases. In addition, the Charleston Navy Yard lost jobs due to cutbacks at the end of the Korean War. Mendel became disenchanted with the Republicans whom he had always viewed with distrust.

Brown v. Board of Education may be viewed by some as one of the most wonderful Supreme Court decisions of all time. Southerners called it "Black Monday." And here was Dwight Eisenhower, whom Mendel had trusted to be sensitive to Southern concerns, vocally and dramatically supporting integration. When asked if he would support Eisenhower when he ran again in 1956, Mendel retorted with his most countrified accent, "Hell no! Ain't no education in the second kick of a mule." He was always making homespun comments like that.

Mendel chatting with President Eisenhower.

By then Mendel was very public in his determination to remain in the Democratic Party, but he was still angry at his party for what he viewed as selling out to agitators and race-mixers. Mendel walked out of the 1956 Democratic Convention because of their party's strong civil rights platform. Segregation was the issue overwhelmingly on the minds of the voters of the First District. Mendel eventually endorsed Adlai Stevenson, the Democratic nominee, but neither he nor his constituents cared much for either major candidate. First District voters actually cast most of their votes for an independent protest candidate, conservative Democratic Senator Harry F. Byrd of Virginia. It mattered little. Stevenson carried the state, and Eisenhower was reelected President.

President Eisenhower advocated civil rights legislation. In 1957 he ordered federal troops to Little Rock, Arkansas, to escort Negro students into Central High School, a previously all-white school. Mendel feared federal occupation of our school systems, just as in Reconstruction. He sent letters to Arkansas Governor Orval Faubus, who strongly opposed the presence of federal troops in Little Rock, congratulating him and urging him to keep up the fight.

But as the sixties approached, Mendel tempered his rhetoric. He was rising in seniority. It was not in his best interests to continue to beat the drum for a cause that was losing. As Mendel liked to say, "There are times when a man must rise above principle." He joined Fritz Hollings and others who urged calm and acceptance and thereby sought to avoid many of the problems with violence other Southern states had experienced. He practically ignored the race question in the elections of 1960 and thereafter. Walking a fine line between alienating his constituency and alienating important elements of the federal government caused some to call Mendel a "fence straddler" and a hypocrite. It was posturing, but it worked.

In 1960 the First District voted for Nixon, although Kennedy won South Carolina through the support of the Upstate rural areas. Kennedy was adored by the liberal press. I was a member of the John Birch Society then, and we detested Kennedy. We hated his politics, his womanizing and his relentless glamour. But what we feared the most was a dynasty of Kennedys: John for eight years, followed by Bobby for eight years, followed by Teddy for eight years, followed by 1984, the Doomsday Year.

We did not ask for segregation, but we were forced to endure the upheavals of the civil rights movement. Charlestonians like Septima Clark organized the Highlander Citizenship School on Johns Island, where Negroes were taught about voting rights and were encouraged to engage in civil protests. Many unsubstantiated, unsavory rumors about civil rights activists spread through the community like wildfire.

The struggle over the Voting Rights Act of 1965 was the last time Mendel fought to save segregation. When it passed, he realized that segregation's days were numbered. He also realized that he was better off supporting law and order during those tumultuous days of sit-ins, freedom rides, demonstrations and murders in other Southern states.

Mendel found a political ally in George Wallace, who was likewise struggling to hold back the civil rights tide. Both Mendel and Wallace were Democrats from a different era and a different world. Both were men of power who had very strong beliefs on racial issues. By the mid-1960s, both were men without a party to support their views.

The first week of July 1968, Mendel made headlines by attending a fundraising dinner for George Wallace in Glen Burnie, Maryland. That was a memorable day for me. The previous evening at dinner, Mendel asked me if I wanted to hear Wallace, and when I said, "Yes," I thought it was settled that I would accompany him. The next morning I tried to reach him several times at the office to make arrangements, but Mendel was not available. Finally, that afternoon, I was so tired I wanted to stay home, but I thought he expected me to go. I asked Kathy Worthington to enquire what our final plans were; all she could get out of him when he was rushing out of the office was, "I don't know whether Mrs. Rivers is expected to go or not."

So I dressed and hurried off, telling young Mendel that if his father should call, to tell him to just leave without me if I delayed him. I drove down the George Washington Parkway in a torrential downpour; there was no way to go but forward. The skies burst; cars were stalled along the way. I drove through many freshets and prayed to reach Mendel's office safely.

I was late of course. Mendel was waiting for me, disgustedly, and sat in his chair and told me that he could depend on me to get him late for everything. We had another misunderstanding, for it seems that a group of Alabama Congressmen had a driver, and Mendel had planned to get a ride with them. He had not expected me until he got my message.

After my cheery greeting, Mendel just took his time leaving the office; the traffic was backed up because of the rain, and by then it was the height of the rush hour. Mendel kept changing lanes, and I kept praying. The sunshine finally appeared. Once Mendel squeezed in front of a driver and was furious when she almost hit him. "I never yet saw a damned woman driver with a bit of manners," he said. I bit my tongue and refrained from saying, "I wonder what she thinks about your manners."

We had to consult a map designed for travelers approaching from Baltimore instead of from Washington. It wasn't easy to find the "Barnyard." After two stops for information, we got there a half-hour late. A policeman wouldn't let Mendel park behind the building; Mendel's name meant nothing to that Maryland cop. Finally, we were recognized and were escorted through the kitchen entrance. There we were stopped by another guard who had orders to let no one through.

We entered the dining room just behind the head table and were received with a roaring standing ovation. To my chagrin, I saw that there was only one extra place at the head table—for Mendel, of course. I tried to find a place elsewhere, but the men pushed over, and one left the table so that I could be seated to the right of the master of ceremonies. A dinner was brought in for me.

That crowd, like all of the Wallace crowds, was wildly enthusiastic, giving many hearty rising stands to show their approval. With his usual courtesy, Wallace leaned over to me under the noise of the cheering when he first stood up and said, "I surely appreciate your and Mendel's coming here." He made a good speech and left immediately for another engagement.

We drove back home in a lovely clear evening. Mendel told me, "Wallace is my friend of long standing. I will dine with whom I please. Of any candidate he speaks most closely my sentiments. I don't plan to bolt the Democratic Party now."

Mendel got his picture in the paper with Wallace. There was speculation about his allegiance. Charleston papers made light of it. Republicans were baffled. The *Washington Post* said Wallace must be stopped by a coalition of House Democrats and Republicans voting for a candidate with a plurality. The *Post* had carried mean articles and ugly pictures of Wallace.

The *Columbia Record* had an abusive editorial about Mendel. It made fun of him, calling him "bushy-tailed" and quoted him in the vernacular regarding Wallace. It said, "Mendel is no novice" and implied that he was espousing Wallace so that he could divert votes to help the Republican administration— too complicated a maneuver to understand, and certainly not what Mendel wanted to do. It said that Governor Rockefeller of Arkansas called Wallace a demagogue and implied that Mendel was one, too.

On July 19 Mendel told me of a very interesting compliment that Wallace paid him the day before. I was not allowed to write it down, for Mendel told me that it was not to be repeated. I made this note so that it can be added to my dictations when the issues of 1968 are part of history: Wallace asked Mendel to run as his Vice-Presidential candidate.

The day after Mendel died, George Wallace and his handsome brunette wife flew into Charleston to pay their respects. Four Secret Service men or bodyguards escorted him en masse. They were all dressed in dark suits, and one could feel power emanating from them. Wallace breezed into the house behind the phalanx. His presence commanded attention. He paid his respects and did not stay long; he left with his entourage in exactly the same manner as he had arrived. (George Wallace was later gunned down and nearly killed. He never recovered physically. He later repudiated his strong segregationist stand and publicly apologized to the black people of Alabama and the nation.)

Herringstone Years

Herringstone Farm consumed our time, energy and money for eight years; it deserves to be described. I had read that wonderful book, *The Egg and I*, and aspired to record my misadventures as a city girl turned reluctant part-time farm wife. Ma and Pa Kettle were household names, and I envisioned myself becoming a celebrated author of rustic life in the hinterlands, replete with colorful characters and hilarious anecdotes. I never had time to create my opus, but I did manage to record highlights of the years we owned the farm.

The Shenandoah Valley is one of the world's most beautiful spots, with rolling hills between long mountains that stretch for one hundred miles. Prosperous farms and interesting villages have a quaint old-world flavor. When I first drove through the Shenandoah Valley (or the Valley of Virginia, as the Virginians renamed it) on our wedding trip, I told Mendel that I would love to have a home in that beautiful region. I became smitten by its peaceful pastureland, woodlands, wildflowers and rushing streams. Fascinating old brick farmhouses seemed to express a sense of care given them by generations of owners. I had no idea what the future held.

John Neff was a gentleman farmer who shipped apples and peaches by the boxcar. He and his wife, Dot, lived near Staunton in an old brick house of ample proportions. We had visited them on our wedding trip. Dot's Victorian parlor and the sitting room behind were charming. The old cobbler's bench before the wide fireplace in the den delighted me. The Neffs were the epitome of hospitality, and their home was a welcome retreat from the bustle of the Capitol on many occasions after we moved to

Washington. We'd drive down with Peggy, a toddler, and Lottie, our loveable colored helper from South Carolina. In her black uniform and white apron, Lottie took care of our daughter and gave "Miss Nett" (her name for Dot) a helping hand.

We had been married for nearly five years and Marion was on the way when John called to tell us that the farm next door to them was for sale. By that time Lottie and I had parted. We put Peggy in the car and drove to Staunton.

My first impressions of Herringstone were not happy ones. It was autumn. The somberness of the day and the colorless landscape didn't enhance the large aging wooden house that stood at the top of the steep, narrow, dark driveway of maples that had been planted in horse-and-buggy days. There were unkempt lawns, trees and neglected gardens on either side of the house. Many acres of neglected apple and peach orchards grew behind the dilapidated barn, and there was a large plot that had once been a vegetable garden. We peered through the windows and discovered both low ceilings and some that were loftier. It was evident that the old dwelling had been modified many times by an amateur builder. To Mendel, it had infinite possibilities, with its acres of timber across the road, a spring down in the field and old fruit orchards. For me, it had no charms.

Mendel and the Neffs were enthusiastic about it. After mulling it over, I told Mendel the next morning that it would be all right with me if we offered a fantastically low $5,500 for ninety-eight acres and a house; the asking price was $6,600. The owner was a nurse who had inherited the property from a Mr. Rawlinson. Before his death, she had nursed him, his wife and their daughter through long painful bouts with cancer.

Mr. Rawlinson's father was reputedly the canon of Canterbury Cathedral. The clergyman was an accomplished artist; several dozen of his paintings were in the house, watercolor scenes done in photographic accuracy. The Rawlinsons were a prominent family in Victorian England. One was a famous archaeologist in Asia. Mr. Rawlinson had named the farm Herringstone after his ancestral home.

The farmhouse was begun in 1890. Every time Mr. Rawlinson received a patrimony check from England, the residents of our little area, Stingy Hollow, would see him dashing by in his buggy, kicking up clouds of dust and heading for Staunton to buy new building supplies. He and a helper would make amateurish additions on the place. As a result, there were rooms of many levels with steps between. Outside hardware was on inside doors.

Since he never had to work, he had probably appeared to be quite a catch to the local Miss Cochran, whom he married. Her family home was on the highway to Lexington and boasted a serpentine wall designed by Thomas Jefferson. The Cochran family was part of the Staunton aristocracy.

I felt rather pleased with myself when Mendel and John went into town to present my offer. I had nobly agreed to stay in a place I disliked, Mendel couldn't reproach me for muffing a chance to get that farm and there was no chance the owner would accept the offer.

In no time, it seemed, John called me, and I answered on their hand-cranked, party-line phone. "Well, Marguerite, you are now the mistress of Herringstone."

"*What?*" I was floored. I had been so sure that our offer would be refused. I felt let down, pregnant, uncomfortable and grouchy.

"Well, maybe I will die before we have to live in it," I thought. "Mendel will enjoy it. He can get a pony for Peggy and plant all those apple trees and peach trees and corn he and John keep talking about."

We signed the mortgage papers for Herringstone. I think we borrowed about $4,500. It was put in my name. I made the lawyer very angry. I didn't want to sign any "on demand" note. I insisted on one day's notice, which he had to write into the contract. From that point on in our interview, he addressed me as "Madam." I felt overwhelmed with such a huge debt. I didn't realize that possibly I could have sold a part of our ninety-eight acres to meet an emergency or that if we had lost the place, I would have been much happier.

Mendel loved Herringstone. It became his substitute for the St. Stephen farm the Rivers family had lost. He hung a rope hammock between two pine trees, providing lazy swinging on hot summer days. Sometimes he rode with Peggy on the rusty red tractor as he plowed the fields with an old harrow that was weighted down with stones. The tractor had a hand crank in front that had to be turned vigorously to start the engine. Mendel would often run out of curse words before the motor would turn over. He loved the smell of tractor grease and newly turned earth.

He replanted sixteen acres of apple trees with the finest stock available and replaced eleven acres of peach orchards as well. He put in ten acres of tomatoes, both red and yellow, and was lucky enough to be at the Paris Air Show when the tomatoes ripened.

I hauled bushels of tomatoes into Staunton, but beautiful ripe tomatoes were a glut on the market. They were hard to sell at any price. It was hot. Those were the days before the polio vaccine, and the girls could not be permitted to mingle with the locals or even drink from a water fountain. Sharing a cold Dr. Pepper—the ten, two and four drink—was a real treat.

We spent a few weekends, Christmas holidays and many summers at Herringstone. The Neffs were the only neighbors of consequence, and we had cocktails with them whenever we were at the farm.

Liquor was rationed during the war. Although gas was also rationed, somehow people would find enough to go out and call on friends, ostensibly just to share good cheer. The actual reason for the unexpected visits (which everybody understood) was to see if the hosts just might be hoarding some liquor, somewhere. No visit ever began without the casual "Oh by the way, do you have anything to drink around here?"

On one occasion, two rather notorious Staunton topers appeared at the foot of the driveway, headed in our direction. We knew immediately their ulterior purpose. Mendel saw them from afar and came dashing into the house, shouting, "Here they come! Hide your liquor, quick!" I tried to put it away before they arrived at the door.

Peggy saw it all. Getting into the spirit, she began to skip around the guests, echoing our sentiments, chanting, "Here they come, hide your liquor quick. Here they come, hide your liquor quick. Here they come, hide your liquor quick." She danced around and around, hoping to be noticed. I was terribly embarrassed, certain the visitors would listen to her verses, put two and two together and realize we had hidden our "stash." I shouldn't have worried. The visitors were already "loaded" and far too intent on getting another drink to pay any attention to our noisy little child.

Mendel's drinking had become more and more pronounced during the forties. He did not begin as an alcoholic. Early in life, he promised his mother not to smoke or drink before he turned twenty-one. He kept that promise, but he "made up for lost time" in his twenties. Later he became a heavy drinker who gradually progressed into a textbook binger alcoholic. Bingers don't drink every day. They are sober most days, and they remain sober until some part of them tells them it is time to drink. When they start drinking, they cannot stop.

Mendel was generally sober, but when he drank, he would drink round-the-clock for days at a time. He once drank continuously for almost three weeks. I don't know which was worse, the anxiety of not knowing when another bout would occur, the heartache of watching a wonderful man destroy himself or having to endure his irritable, restless ways when he sobered up. As the illness progressed, he had to be hospitalized at the end of each occurrence.

After Marion was born, he was bitterly disappointed that I had once again "failed" to give him a son. While he was drinking, he once told me I was "too stupid" to have a boy. The damage soon extended to the children. Ultimately, I was forced to tell Peggy that I thought her father was an alcoholic, and that she could never tell anyone because he would lose his job. It was a secret we kept between ourselves for many years.

We continued to try to improve living conditions at Herringstone. Mrs. Lotts, the former owner, sold us some furniture at bargain rates. At first we pushed twin beds together to accommodate the three-plus of us. Gradually, we acquired other bargain furniture at incredible prices, for the war had prevented antique hunters from traveling afar. Six rickety-caned dining room chairs cost seven dollars; old chests of drawers, fifteen and twenty; a walnut sofa, thirty-five; a trundle bed, five.

Mendel bought a piece of furniture, too. I can still remember waiting for him with Peggy. We stood on a windy corner for what seemed an interminable time. My Harris tweed coat did not keep me warm, and I knew that Peggy was freezing in her woolen leggings and coat.

Finally, Mendel drove up. He was in high spirits. He and our guests, the Acey Carraways, had been shopping.

"Well," he told me, as Peggy and I clambered into the car, "we've found a piece of furniture for the house. A wonderful chair!"

"A chair! What is it like?"

"Well, you can lie down in it—it's sort of a barber chair."

They all laughed heartily. They had obviously been enjoying the conviviality of a few cocktails. I was hungry, cold, tired.

"A barber chair? Mendel, how could you be so stupid? A barber chair!"

"It's a bargain. Wait until you see it."

I shed a couple of angry tears before I saw the chair. It was not so bad after all. It was walnut, of slender design, the forerunner of modern reclining chairs. It was actually of Charleston origin, the Judge Holmes chair.

The farmhouse was infested with rats. They even chewed books or shoes left on the floor. Although we hammered flattened tin cans over the holes of entry, without cats or exterminators, the rats kept chewing. Rats scampered up and down the attic at night. Mendel called it the "Rat Hill Downs."

We papered the rooms at Herringstone. The large guestroom eventually became rather attractive. Dot sold me an old bed for ten dollars, the price she had paid. The wallpaper had huge blue-and-white stripes graced by enormous red climbing roses. There was a fireplace and a large, screened porch. I covered a wooden box and a peck basket to create a dressing table and stool. For a while, there was only one bathroom with a huge, turn-of-the-century tub with enameled claw feet. Eventually, we added two other rather crude bathrooms in a couple of cramped unused upstairs rooms.

Herringstone's antiquated coal-burning furnace heated the water for the cast-iron radiators. The outside door leading to the basement stairs had no lock and gave an easy access to the house. When it was cold, Mendel was in charge of the heat department. One cold winter night, Peggy and I waited for him to arrive from Washington. I dreaded having to descend into the dark, cramped underworld to shovel coal.

Three-year-old Peggy obviously sensed my fears, for she said, "Mother, don't go down into the furnace room. I heard two men talking in there. They said, 'Let's kill Mrs. Rivers.'"

"What?" I was horrified, for the room had become chilly.

"Oh yes," she assured me. "They said, 'We're going to kill Mrs. Rivers. Durn it. Dammit. Deemit.'"

That expression was Peggy's recent invention. When I heard it, I knew there were no burglars. Relieved, I went down and shoveled on some coal.

I bucked Mendel about Herringstone all the way and felt much imposed upon. For me it was a lonely, frustrating experience. Having grown up in a city, I did not enjoy the isolation of farm life. The only telephone was a party line with a crank and eavesdropping neighbors; it was antiquated equipment that was probably turn-of-the-century.

There were few diversions for the children, and they usually wanted me to be available for their companionship. Sometimes we played croquet on the grass terrace-garden overlooking the foothills, Betsy Bell, Mary Gray and Little Molly Cottontail. As a surprise, I once created a fairy garden with reflection pool made of a little pink plastic-rimmed mirror surrounded by moss that concealed the edges. It enchanted Peggy, who wanted me to perform the magic again and again. I read to the girls and tried my best to entertain them, but mostly I was forced into farm chores.

Peggy had started school when we were still living on Glendale Avenue, near the Masonic Temple in Alexandria. She ran a low-grade fever most of the fall semester and none of the doctors could figure out why she was so sickly. She stayed in bed while the other neighborhood children attended first grade. When the lease on Glendale Avenue expired, we moved again, this time to Charleston. We put Peggy into a private school, hoping that she could catch up. She didn't. She was still far behind when we enrolled her in at the Staunton elementary school the next fall.

It was bad enough living in the country. It was awful packing the girls into the car every day to take Peggy back and forth to school nine miles away in Staunton. I was terribly concerned about Peggy's repeating the first grade and her inability to learn to read. She could not master the most basic words like "saw" and "was" or the subtler differences between "red" and "read." Dot's daughter would tutor her for hours, to no avail. She was so precocious that I could not understand the problem.

Housing was still scarce after the war but we finally were able to locate another place in the Washington area. The house wasn't much, but considering Washington's housing situation, we knew we were lucky to find it. It was an unappealing, cramped prewar house. The things Mendel and I craved the most were a large kitchen and closets, lots of closets.

Because of Peggy's learning difficulties, we enrolled her in St. Agnes Episcopal Girls School, which was located across the street. By then it was the spring semester and her fourth first grade enrollment. The school insisted upon testing her IQ before they admitted her. To my astonishment she scored exactly the same as the beloved child movie star, Shirley Temple! Peggy had dyslexia. We didn't know about dyslexia back then. Peggy had to memorize every word and never did learn to spell. It took our little genius two years to get into second grade. We should have left her at St. Agnes, but as always, to conserve funds, we sent her to third grade at the public school a few short blocks away.

We commuted back and forth to Staunton a lot in those years. I had no opportunity to make friends. I had no help with the children and spent a lot of time in the big kitchen we created from the old pantry. I enjoyed reconstructing the little garden by the driveway, where paths and borders of perennials surrounded a sundial and a crabapple tree provided fruits for the jellies I made.

Once when driving into town from Herringstone, Mendel recounted a story about a rich "crook." Peggy was listening in the back seat and innocently asked why he couldn't be a crook so that the family could have a lot of money. Mendel slammed on the brakes of the car, pulled over to the side of the road and yelled, "Don't you ever say that again. I am not dishonest." It was true. Years later, a constituent came to Washington. The only sight he wanted to see was where Congressman Rivers lived. After looking at our modest suburban ranch home in McLean, he was quoted as saying, "Now I know that Mendel Rivers is an honest man."

One day a large snake slithered into the house through a rat hole and situated itself under the dining room sideboard. Adjacent to the dining room was a screened porch with a glider beneath the porch window. Marion, a toddler at that time, was wearing little black dancing shoes because nothing else was available due to wartime rationing. Lacking proper ankle support, she stumbled and broke open her chin. The cut bled profusely. Peggy was banished to the glider while the injury was assessed. Suddenly, she noticed the snake and began to yell, pointing out the mysterious dark invader. Always at his best in time of crisis, Mendel calmly got a hoe and went into the dining room. Without fanfare, he chopped off the snake's head, instructed Lee, the part-time colored helper, to remove the reptile's remains from the house and then proceeded to make arrangements to take Marion to a doctor.

Shortly after the war, Mendel gave us a history lesson. He brought home a combination radio and 78-speed phonograph and an album with a "V" and a dot-dot-dot-dash on the cover of the jacket. The album was a five-record recording of Beethoven's Fifth Symphony. Mendel explained how the Allied planes played the first movement on bombing missions over Nazi Germany; the short-short-short-long was the Morse code letter for "V" or victory. Later we supplemented our collection with Mozart, Schubert and Chopin. The children have always felt indebted for this priceless gift of music.

The chickens were another example of the challenges of adapting to life in the country. Mendel asked me if I wanted some lovely milk-fed, double-breasted baby chicks. He had met someone on one of his numerous trips who bred what he claimed were the finest baby chicks in the country. He had offered to send Mendel some.

My response was a horrified "No! I don't want any lovely milk-fed, double-breasted baby chicks or singly-breasted ones either!" I probably said a lot more at that point, as I always felt overburdened at that vacation spot in Stingy Hollow.

Nothing more was said about the chicks. One day the postman drove up the drive to our porte-cochere and blew his horn. I rushed to the door, thinking there was something special awaiting us. "Sign here," he told me. "Your chicks are on the back seat."

"What! There must be some mistake. We are not expecting any chicks!" I glanced at the two cardboard boxes filled with peeping little hungry balls of yellow fluff.

"Oh yes, these are for you, Ma'am. Here is the order slip for them, two hundred chicks."

"But I don't…"

"Here they are, Mrs. Rivers. Your husband must have ordered them."

Mute with annoyance at Mendel and pity for the crowded little chicks, I accepted the two large boxes and stood on the porch watching the postman's car recede down our steep driveway. I wondered where I could put them and how I was going to take care of them. I walked over to Lee's house, a dilapidated place a few hundred yards away. Lena, his wife, was seated on the porch.

"Please get Lee to come over as soon as possible," I asked her. "We have an emergency at the house."

"Very well, Mrs. Rivers," Lena agreed in her prim and proper manner, "I'll send Lee over as soon as he returns from town."

There was no place to put the chicks in the yard. I decided to house them in the old back kitchen that was now in disuse. It was full of rat holes. Fortunately, I had some canned vegetables. I opened the cans and dumped their contents into a large container that I put into the refrigerator for future soups. I nailed the ends of the cans over the rat holes. I put water in low

Marion visits on the porch of our part-time helper, Lena, who lived nearby.

pans on the floor, spread newspapers, closed the door into the passageway and let the chicks out of the boxes. There were adorable. Mendel had known that I'd find some way to house them.

When Lee arrived, he assured me that when nightfall arrived, the chicks would need more warmth than the draughty old kitchen. "You got to get them a brooder."

"A brooder? What is a brooder? Where do you get them?" I didn't want to have to buy one. I was always broke during those years.

"Yes ma'am, a brooder and some chick mash. And then you better get a way to keep them in when you open the door."

Lee found a piece of coarse meshed wire and nailed it across the door opening. It kept the chicks in, and we could easily step over it. I telephoned Dot Neff.

"Guess what now? You don't happen to have a brooder, do you? I am now the mother of two hundred double-breasted, milk-fed baby chicks."

Dot gasped and laughed when she told me that she did in fact have an old brooder. Lee and I got it from her springhouse. We took the brooder back to the old back kitchen. I discovered that a brooder was a heated structure used for raising young fowl. Although it needed a few repairs, it provided our chicks a warm, safe place to snuggle into at night.

Mendel called me that evening. "Any news?" he asked innocently.

"Yes. Those damned baby milk-fed, double-breasted chicks are all over the place. Why didn't you tell me they were coming? Why did you get them? They're adorable."

"I knew you'd love them when you saw them! Now be quite sure to get them plenty of chick feed, and keep the place clean."

I described the arrangements we had made to care for the chicks and asked him how he expected me to keep them in the house in such makeshift quarters.

"Oh, don't worry. When I come down, I'll make a chicken house for them." Mendel seemed quite pleased with himself.

The chicks stayed in the old kitchen for several weeks. They sprouted, dropped their fluffy feathers and got uglier and noisier daily. I liked them less and less. By the time their house had been built in the backyard, I heartily disliked them. They were leghorns. Whenever one of them pecked another too viciously, the blood spots showed vividly and seemed to become a magnet for the rest of the flock. Every one of the other chicks immediately began to peck at the bloody spot. Mercilessly, they all joined in the sport until their victim lay gasping and dying.

One afternoon some months later, I heard a terrible commotion outside. By that time Mendel had also brought some pigs and had housed them in an enclosure next to the chicken yard. I ran to the back to see why all our animals were making so much noise. It was shocking. The chickens were clustered around a hole in the fence, all crowding and squawking and trying to get into the pigpen. The half-grown pigs were running around in circles, squealing and grunting with delight. White feathers were flying all over the place; the pigs had chickens in their mouths. As each chicken would squeeze through the hole, it was grabbed up by a pig and was taken for a fatal ride around the pig yard. I had long lost my respect for the chickens.

We continued to visit Herringstone, but it became more difficult as the family grew. The last three years we hired Latvian displaced persons, Herta and Anton Zvirgdsdins, to work on the farm. The Latvians had fled from the Russians, leaving their family farm with one hour's notice. They had endured the privations of a refugee camp and working in one of Hitler's factories. After the Latvians arrived, I was thankful that I was no longer responsible for the chickens except, of course, taking eggs to the farmers' cooperative, where they were sold for some trifling sum.

Mendel was still enthusiastic, however, and as soon as the chicks grew into pullets, he brought home a huge sack of laying mash for Anton to feed them. Herta, too, was delighted with the chickens. The young hens laid, and everyone but me was extremely pleased.

Farmer Rivers beside the pigpen.

Then a strange thing happened. Herta came to me in great distress. The young hens were dropping dead in the yard, felled by some mysterious ailment. Privately I was delighted. The less I saw of the chickens, the better it suited me. I tried to hide my feelings, however, but when Herta came to me a third time, I called the county agent and asked for a diagnosis of the mysterious killer.

The young man inspected our hens and our chicken coop. He asked questions about the feeding. Herta and Anton were otherwise disposed, and since they spoke practically no English, he did not talk to them. The county agent told me that the hens had been fed the laying mash too soon. Their bodies had been strained too much. They had to be weaned from the laying mash gradually. It was sweeter than regular mash and had to be reduced a little each day until the hens were fed only regular mash. Once the hens matured, they could be gradually fed laying mash again. I thanked him, and he drove off.

I carefully tried to explain the county agent's instructions to Herta and Anton. I pantomimed the chicken feeding routine we needed to adopt. I could tell something was very, very wrong with my explanation. Herta's eyes took on a hard, distrustful expression, and she muttered something to Anton. They exchanged glances and looked at me coldly as I continued to explain and pantomime.

"A little bit today, a little bit less tomorrow," I repeated, pinching imaginary bits of feed in my fingers. "You understand?"

Herta regarded me coldly, her arms folded, hostility emanating from her stance. "Meeses!" she finally said, "We is goot people! We no eat chicken mash!" Poor Herta actually thought I was accusing Anton and her of eating the mash!

I often marvel that we ever established rapport. As they gradually acquired more English and got over their disgust at what they considered my slovenly ways, we developed mutual respect and affection. They told me about Latvian customs.

On Easter Sunday, the men of their community would dress and visit their neighbors enjoying a glass of schnapps. The next day, the women would dress in their finest attire, including white gloves, and visit the neighbors. When the hostess left the room to get refreshments, the women took great delight running their gloved hands on windowsills, under tables and other inconspicuous places trying to locate a little dust. They quietly held up their gloves to point out the offensive dust. This fetish for cleanliness was extremely stressful to the housewives.

Of course, Mendel thought their zeal for cleanliness and order was wonderful. Every scrubbed, rubbed and polished can of spice was arranged in a meticulous geometrical pattern. He thought it was wonderful that everything in our drawers was rearranged after our visits, that all the pins were laid out like spokes on a wheel, that the insides of every piece of furniture were scoured and waxed.

I was pleased to a certain extent, but the Zvirgdsdins' cleanliness was a constant reproach to me. By then young Mendel had arrived. At first Herta would follow me as I held the baby and would carry a pail for anything he discarded. She refused to hold little Mendel or help me with him in any way. I was overwhelmed with my responsibilities and no help with the children. It took us a long time to become friends.

The last year Herta was with us, she volunteered to come up to Alexandria and clean our house for Easter. It was cold. She stood on a ladder outside and shivered as she cleaned our windows in the icy wind. I took care of the children, cleaned inside and fetched her cleaning materials, trying to do my share. After she left, I was exhausted and spent most of Easter resting from our cleaning orgy.

After little Mendel was born, we visited Herringstone less and less. There were other concerns. Peggy's behavior had become worse, and the younger children began to copy her tantrums. She refused to eat and weighed alarmingly little for a nine-year-old child. In desperation I finally took her to a child psychologist, who recommended that she be sent to a home for children with similar problems. Mendel was aghast at first, but he relented and even hired me as a secretary to pay for the added expense. It was a difficult time for all concerned. We hired a colored nurse from Charleston to watch the younger children while I commuted back and forth to Capitol Hill. Peggy seemed to flourish while she was away. When she came home a year later, I am sorry to say that some of her unfortunate habits returned. These were not easy times for any of us. Here is what I composed in 1948 about the farm:

Come to our hill, where a wandering breeze
Scatters pink carpets beneath apple trees,
Where Spring comes softly, and lavishly brings
Myriad magics in petals and wings.
Breathe the warm fragrance of fir tree and pine
And gardens of roses and columbine;
Stroll in our meadow, where wild daisies gleam.
Visit our house, with arms open wide,
Offering welcome to visit inside;
Here city noises and hurrying cease,
Lost in a realm of perpetual peace.
If you'd like peace for perpetual diet,
It's for sale—a bargain! Won't somebody buy it?

When we sold Herringstone, I happily discarded my role as a farmer's wife. I never wrote my masterpiece.

Happy Daze

We used to watch *Happy Days*, a popular television sitcom about a suburban American family in the 1950s. My life in the fifties was a collection of commonplace household routines, unexpected emergencies and official obligations that at times seemed overwhelming. I liked to jest that sometimes I lived in a happy daze.

In 1951 we left our cramped rented house in Alexandria and moved back to South Carolina once again. Mendel would have no part of downtown Charleston. He suggested that we buy land in North Charleston and build there. I absolutely refused. So we compromised and moved to a place neither of us liked, West Ashley. Mendel purchased a lot next door to his friend Leon Patat in a modest, custom-home neighborhood called Wappoo Heights.

I would have much preferred to live downtown and always considered myself an exile. Although we were only five minutes from town, for me it was a million miles away. Today Wappoo Heights is considered "high cotton" by the real estate agents, a term they use for expensive properties. In 1951 it was definitely "middling low," the cotton broker term for "not so hot."

In those days the traffic driving past Wappoo Heights was unbearable much of the time. Folly Road was the only local access route to James Island, Johns Island and Wadmalaw Island. There were a lot of commuters, for island land was still relatively cheap. The road out of town crossed a drawbridge over Wappoo Cut. When the bridge was open, which was often, traffic could back up for miles, and irritable drivers would sometimes make us wait for ages until some kind soul eventually let us onto the road.

Ultimately, Mendel prevailed upon the Highway Department to put a light at the Wappoo Heights entrance. It was not just any light! It was timed to change the instant a car drove over the sensor, a steel plate. Once the mischievous neighborhood children discovered how powerful it made them, they took great delight in stopping traffic as they zoomed over the sensor plate, gleefully driving onto Folly Beach Road over and over again.

In 1950 Ryan's Jail, the colored tenement on Queen Street, had been razed, and wanting to please me, Mendel purchased the desirable old "Charleston bricks" for our home-to-be. He feared that hostilities in Korea would escalate and cause a scarcity of building materials, similar to the one we had just experienced during the war. As usual, he was in a rush, and I was forced to plan my "dream home" while nursing sick children in Alexandria.

Our house was designed by an architect who did the work as a favor. The outside didn't look too bad—brick veneer and Charleston green shutters bolted to the house—but the interior was another matter. The upstairs was primarily wasted space with an inappropriately pitched roof that created elongated, unappealing dormer windows. The downstairs fared slightly better. A friend sold Mendel "cheap" many board feet of grooved cypress paneling, which was put in six rooms plus the entire upstairs hallway. It became the predominant decorating theme of our house—endless cypress paneling. It was a happy day for me when some of it was finally painted white. (Young Mendel used to complain that when the cockroaches started crawling around at night, the cypress knots on the wall would come alive in his bedroom.)

When our house was nearly completed, Mendel casually asked the builder how many feet of setback our house had on the "wild" side of our lot, the side facing the vacant lot between our house and our neighbors.

"Oh, Congressman, you have about two feet."

"What?" Mendel nearly shouted. He was shocked and angry that the builder, a veteran contractor and so-called friend, had situated the house so lopsidedly on our lot. He quickly contacted the owner of the vacant lot, who was glad to sell it to us for the price he had paid because a drainage easement in the middle of the lot had prevented his making a quick profit on his speculative purchase. We paid about $7,000 and built a set-back, two-car garage with a modest rental unit. Mendel later had a handsome wrought-iron fence erected in across the front of both lots.

While the house was under construction, we moved four times that summer. We started off rather elegantly in an old Sullivan's Island beach house. It still had a genuine icebox and a hand pump at the sink. The screens were rusted, and there were lots of mosquitoes. We slept with sheets over our heads, hoping to protect ourselves from the predatory flights of

Wappoo Heights, 1952. *Left to right*: Mendel, Mendel Jr., Marion, Marwee and Peggy.

mosquitoes that buzzed round and round. Then we rented an unappealing motel unit on the Isle of Palms and after that a horrid cinder-block house on the back beach of Sullivan's Island. In the days before air conditioning, people struggled to survive the oppressive, humid heat with fans and scant breezes. It was so unbearable on that windless back beach that we finally relocated to my parents' house in Charleston.

One of the most pleasant recollections of our temporary sojourn at 24 New Street was the shrimp vendor. Shrimpmen, vegetable men and the peanut man were all part of the Charleston scene, but it was the shrimp vendors who were the most colorful. There were many of them, but I remember best the one on New Street. His loud, mellifluous voice could be heard through the open windows as he hawked his wares chanting, "Swimpy, raw, raw, raw."

If a housewife didn't have ready cash, the shrimpman would lament, "Lady come to do-ah, wan-na buy. Have no money, so she go back 'n cry."

Residents would dash to the piazza or an open window and yell down for him to wait so they could purchase those delectable delicacies—fresh-caught local shrimp. The "swimps" were packed in ice and loaded on a weather-beaten, makeshift cart, some paint still clinging to the boards. In my youth the shrimpmen sold shrimp for "fifteen cents a plate or a quarter for two," but by the time we moved back to Charleston, carts had been modernized with scales suspended from wooden contraptions nailed to their crude wooden frames. There were two large wheels at the back of the cart, probably wagon wheels, and the front had a stand to keep the cart from tipping over. The mad dash down the stairs, or chasing the cart if the shrimpman didn't stop, created an air of excitement as housewives and their young charges crowded round.

The shrimpman reminded me of Porgy, an endearing Charleston character made famous by DuBose Heyward in his novel *Porgy*, and later made immortal by George and Ira Gershwin in the folk opera *Porgy and Bess*. Porgy was a cripple who moved around via goat cart. My friend Arden Ball's father was a close friend of Heyward, and Jack Ball showed us the narrow, dark alley next to 49 Broad Street where Porgy parked his cart. Negroes did not have access to nearby public restrooms back then, so Porgy used a foul toilet located there just for him.

We moved into our new home in the fall of 1951 and tried to get acclimated to life in the suburbs. The house was furnished with mismatched Herringstone antiques, a couple of nice pieces I had purchased in Charleston and furniture Mendel got "cheap" from friends who owned tasteless uptown stores. We eventually imported numerous antiques from Scotland and commissioned a Scottish cabinetmaker to create several Charleston reproductions. I carefully researched and selected a Thomas Elfe chest-on-chest and a banquet table made of three attached sections. Never one to do things in a small way, Mendel commissioned two Federal-style sideboards and purchased three antique grandfather clocks.

Our first houseguests were Harry Collins and his charming wife, Irene, who visited us while General Collins was the commanding officer at Fort Jackson in Columbia. General Collins had been the occupying American general in Salzburg, Austria, after World War II. After the harsh Nazi occupation, Harry's democratic style was so welcome that when he died, grateful Salzburgers arranged for him to be buried in one of their ancient churchyards so that he could be near his wife. Irene was an Austrian aristocrat who had been professionally trained as a lawyer; she felt that she could not work after her marriage because the status-conscious Salzburgers would have considered it a disgrace that their cherished General Collins had not provided adequately for his wife. We later learned that Irene knew the von Trapp family of *Sound of Music* fame. She said that the aristocrats resented Maria's marrying the baron and considered her an upstart who had taken advantage of their unfortunate family situation.

The Collinses accompanied us to some function at The Citadel that I cannot even remember. Harry admired Mendel; however, we were unprepared for his farewell "housewarming" gift. The morning after the event, we were awakened by the most amazing racket directly in front of our home. What was causing the commotion? Suddenly, we realized that it was bagpipes. General Collins had arranged a surprise—a serenade from The Citadel bagpipers who had marched almost a mile from a nearby shopping center through our neighborhood in full Scottish regalia, playing their pipes all the while. They stopped in front of our house and played some more. Afterward, we entertained the Collinses and the band with some hastily assembled refreshments. Our neighborhood had never seen anything quite like it.

The fifties passed with reasonable predictability. We sent Peggy to Ashley Hall, hoping that she would become a little lady at last, for over the years her sassy remarks had made quite a poor impression on my circumspect, social family. Marion and young Mendel attended the public grammar school nearby.

Once, a constituent called Mendel at home to complain about the airplanes flying over her house in North Charleston; the flights were noisy and interrupted TV reception.

"I just don't think I should have to put up with all these airplanes," she said, "and I want to know what you intend to do about it."

Mendel asked her, "What kind of planes are they?"

Mendel (right) drives past the reviewing stand at The Citadel.

"I don't know," she replied.

"Are they American planes?"

"Yes."

"You just better thank God they're not Russian planes," he retorted angrily and slammed down the phone.

We were still living in Wappoo Heights in 1958. My father, Charles Francis Middleton, had a long stay in the hospital. I visited him a great deal. It was only then that we finally established a sense of camaraderie. He enjoyed the jokes I culled for him, the slides of our family, which I projected on the walls of his room, and the decorations I taped to the walls.

That year was the last one that I ever made an effort to cultivate a spirit of joy at Christmas. I had tried, but I discovered that I lack the elusive quality that Boo and Nanan so abundantly demonstrated. Perhaps it was because Mendel always chose that time for another binge. Mendel's holiday binges were predictable. He would prowl the house, annoying everyone unlucky enough not to have business elsewhere. We had to hide him from the numerous constituents who came by laden with Christmas gifts "for the Congressman" and expected us to reciprocate with handsome presents. Our family tried and went through the motions, but Christmas was never a joyful season.

However, that year I decided it would be different. From a large basket equipped with jingling bells, I delivered gifts, beautifully wrapped, well in advance, for a change. I decorated Daddy's hospital room. I planned a special Christmas dinner for him and Mother. I asked Boo to share in the preparations. She could be great, but this time, she fell down on the job. Her family had been to the traditional Anderson Christmas breakfast, and she arrived at the hospital late without the card table and cloth I had asked her to bring. I reacted by sounding off with Lucy-like squawks and later decided I'd rather become a realistic, honest, polite version of Scrooge. I have managed to survive Christmas without dramatics each year since that explosion. I wrote this poem that season. It remains my sincerest Christmas card:

> 'Tis the day after Christmas,
> And those in our house
> Exhibit the charms of a hung-over souse.
> And yesterday's presents, so lately displayed,
> Are all put away, or eaten, or frayed.
> And frayed are our nerves, and afraid much am I:
> This day will recur, every year till I die.

My father was a proud man. He had already suffered the loss of his voice due to cancer caused by excessive smoking. He especially disliked this handicap because his greatest joys had been acting with the Footlight Players and singing in St. Michael's choir. He died quietly one afternoon, shortly after his return from the hospital that spring. Mother and I were in the next room. He was in his late sixties and was spared the humiliation of being an invalid. I miss him and have been thankful that we made peace with one another before his death. I learned an important lesson through that experience and tried to pass it on to my children.

Mother, Boo and I were named executrices of his estate. We were completely ignorant of the ways of lawyers, stockbrokers and bankers. We muddled around between their offices for months. Mother was comfortably provided for. She continued to stay at New Street.

Before Daddy's death, Mother had written biographies about two early Charleston artists, Jeremiah Theus and Henrietta Johnston, America's first pastellist. Both biographies have been highly praised by art historians. She also wrote a biography of Martha Laurens Ramsey and a short story about Affra Harleston, one of Charles Towne's prominent early settlers.

Mother visited me in Washington while Mendel was Chairman. I was in the position to take her to diplomatic parties or introduce her to interesting people on the Hill. That impressed her not at all. What she wanted was to discuss the Theus collection with the curators at the National Gallery of Art. I gladly drove her there. When we arrived, did I learn my manners!

The curators rolled out the red carpet for The Important Mrs. Middleton, whom they regarded as the foremost living authority on Jeremiah Theus. They scarcely knew or cared about my husband. They cared deeply about the scholar who rescued Theus from obscurity.

Mother also received several "Women of the Year" recognitions in South Carolina. I am proud of her. She was so unprepossessing, and she accomplished so much after her bout with encephalitis. She even crocheted nine heirloom bedspreads for her grandchildren as well as those for Charlie, Boo and me.

The spring of 1958 was also when Mendel had his worst day ever! Boo and I called it the "L. Mendel Rivers Depreciation Day." The merchants of Charleston organized a two-day promotional "Appreciation Day" sale event that also honored their congressman. Banners and signs festooned the downtown shops. There were radio announcements, engraved invitations, a formal dinner and a parade capped by a speech at Johnson Hagood football stadium. The congressman was scheduled to fly into Charleston for the extravaganza. Sadly, it is still rumored in Charleston that the plane circled the area for a long time before it landed in order to sober Mendel Rivers up before meeting the delegation that eagerly awaited his arrival.

It was impossible to keep him out of sight, since there were numerous activities planned that evening, including a reception at the Hibernian Hall and a banquet at the Air Force Base. The next morning Mendel and I rode in a convertible heading a fifty-five-car parade through Charleston's business district to the football stadium, waving at the crowds as we passed by. Mendel was still "under the weather." Peggy joined us after the parade and courageously offered to chaperone the intoxicated celebrity until speech time. I gratefully went elsewhere.

Under the bleachers, milling about, Mendel's "friends" plied him with liquor, not caring that he was already slurring his words and had a speech to make a few minutes later. One "friend" with the horrible nickname of "Goat" bragged for years thereafter that he kept Mendel drunk that day. Peggy tried to interrupt the flow of drinks directed toward her father, but the "friends" were rude and rowdy, quickly getting drunk themselves. Liquor was spilled, and everyone reeked of alcohol.

It must have taken superhuman effort for Mendel to slowly walk out to a platform situated in the center of the stadium, climb the stairs and address the crowd. We were terrified. Once again, Mendel surprised us.

After he was introduced, he stood up slowly, with great dignity. He may well have been merely trying to steady himself, but from a distance, he looked statesmanlike. He began slowly, as well: "I shall not make a speech today. I am too overcome by this outpouring of your love and appreciation for me." He said a few more words, which I can't remember, and sat down.

I was so relieved, I thought I would cry. He was whisked away immediately afterward while the orchestra played "You'll Never Walk Alone." It was indicative of Mendel's enormous popularity that there was no unfavorable publicity whatsoever, nor any political repercussions.

That same year, 1958, was the year Peggy was a debutante. It was during her college freshman year. I felt like the manager of a Broadway production, for it took the better part of a year to plan her launching party. Peggy went to our state university. It was a pity that we did not make a strenuous effort to send her to a good girls' college, for all she learned at the university was how to loaf and drink beer.

Our family had four debutantes that season. Eunie wanted me to go in with her and Mary Hazlehurst Thurston, our millionaire cousin from Oklahoma. They selected New Year's Eve for a large ball. I saw no sense in entertaining on an evening when the price of everything would be trebled. Peggy and another Hazlehurst cousin, Alicia, from Tennessee, were presented in a modest tea dance, the first of the season. It was a great success; I considered it a personal triumph.

Emmett Robinson suggested our decorations. He said they'd be a cinch to make and to arrange. He drew sketches and a scale for cutting the long swags of white chiffon that were to decorate our Christmas trees. He made us a beautiful stylized tree to decorate a refreshment table. I made simpler ones.

Young Alicia visited us that summer. We spent many exhausting days on our living room floor, measuring, cutting, splicing and ironing the rayon for Emmett's swags. They were rolled on cylinders and carefully stored. We ordered several boxes of green glass Christmas tree balls. A friend took me to her tree farm in the fall to select the right trees in advance.

The invitations were another project. At the suggestion of a veteran mother of two post-debs, I set up an elaborate card file system. We had cards for married couples, single girls, escorts and stags. Trying to find a suitable escort for each single girl was a real chore. It could not be done in the summer. One had to be sure that the individuals concerned were on good terms, and that they were not ill matched physically. No one liked the "put with" system. The young men wanted to choose their dates. If a response were long delayed, we'd have to call to be sure that the invitations had been received.

It was a great moment when both a girl and her escort accepted. We then stapled their cards together. They were triumphantly filed in a special category: DATES. Even with the help of a schoolgirl to run errands and to answer the telephone, pandemonium reigned in our household after the invitations were mailed.

The hotel let us decorate the hall the day before our party. The family rallied to our aid. Greens were hung, the Christmas trees installed, the tables decorated. Then we started on Emmett's swags. The assembled Middleton and Hazlehurst cousins took turns mounting stepladders and trying to arrange those sleazy yards of rayon. Our nerves and the cloth rapidly become the worse for wear. I felt very inadequate, having accepted the help of all those relatives on their one free day before Christmas.

Mary Thurston finally climbed down from a ladder. (She had hired a decorator from New York to arrange her daughter's party.) She looked wary as she called to me, "Marwee, that's the best I can do. How does it look?"

I turned from my ladder and looked. Fatigue made me giggle. Her efforts didn't resemble Emmett's drawings at all. Will I never learn tact? "Mame," I told my volunteer decorator, "it looks like you've thrown a roll of toilet paper at that tree."

Her sister Lois saved the day by devising some bows of white ribbon. We made the bows in feverish haste and hung them above the green balls. They were charming, not as sophisticated as Emmett's swags, but then, none of us were the artist he was.

Although I frequently worried about not having the right thing to wear, this time our family dressed in style. An accomplished dressmaker created a beautiful blue satin gown for me out of material Mendel had brought back from the Orient. He wore a handsome Black Watch tartan jacket with satin lapels and looked quite handsome as he danced with various members of the family. We designed a dress made of peau de soie for Peggy. It had a sleeveless bodice covered with lace and seed pearls and a full skirt that looked almost antebellum with its hoop beneath. The debutantes gave silver charms as favors that year. Our charm had a silver Christmas tree enameled green with the date and the initials of Alicia and Peggy on the back. The tea dance was a great success.

Marion had her first date at age eleven—far sooner than I would have allowed, if she had told me! The urbane, sophisticated matron we know today belies a youth spent doing whatever she could to give her parents gray hair. One "prank" made the local papers, twice. Marion's friends, who were among Charleston's most privileged youth, put her in a car trunk and drove to the Billups service station at the foot of the Cooper River Bridge in Mount Pleasant. The lid of the trunk was deliberately left cracked open, with an arm covered in ketchup hanging out; it just happened to be Marion's arm. They circled slowly through, and someone asked for a shovel. When the attendant said, no, he was sorry, he didn't have a shovel, they drove away, with the bloody hand tantalizingly dangling from the trunk. The attendant panicked. He called the police. The police began a manhunt, which became a dragnet with a seven-mile-radius roadblock. The police put out APBs. They combed the highways. When the naughty miscreants saw a police car heading their way, they wisely drove back to Sullivan's Island. Marion returned home as if nothing had happened. An article entitled "Gory Hoax or Foul Play—Police Search for Answers" appeared in the *Charleston Evening Post* the following day. Another follow-up article had a reenactment of the car with a bloody hand hanging from the trunk. It was no joke to the police. It seems that everybody in town knew about the episode except me, of course. Marion later fessed up, and I inwardly groaned. Those kids had no idea of the repercussions their little prank could have caused.

Shortly thereafter, Mendel decided that we should move back to Washington. He was renting a little apartment in a prewar housing complex known as Shirlington. I was reluctant to make a change. When I saw what he wanted us to buy, however, I was spurred into searching for a better place. Mendel had picked out a bi-level tract house way down the Shirley Highway in Springfield, Virginia. I knew that no amount of strenuous effort could ever make that place appealing.

In the spring of 1959, I scoured the Alexandria area whenever I could leave Charleston. The desirable places in the old section were out of reach financially, or too small for a family of five. I tramped up and down so many stairs and climbed so many ladders it was no surprise when I found that I had a charley horse. I also found a nice brick house on a wooded lot near Episcopal Seminary. It had three stories and traditional architecture; I decided that it would be good for our purposes despite all those stairs and only three bedrooms, for Peggy was away at college.

I returned home, and Mendel started negotiations for buying the house on Trinity Drive. I had to take to bed, for my charley horse had extended into a backache. Our communications system broke down, despite numerous long distance phone calls.

The day after we bought the house my orthopedic surgeon told me the sad news that I'd have to stay on one floor, and that whenever I was up, I'd have to wear prescription shoes and a surgical brace for the rest of my days. That brace was as bad for my morale as it was for my appearance. Suddenly, I looked and felt ten years older. The steel stays poked into my ribs and the harness straps showed through my dresses. My waistline was thickened by three inches. I hated that brace so much that I ignored the prognosis and obtained a book of yoga exercises. For years I faithfully performed "the cat," "the lion," etc., until I was finally able to discard that detested prescribed garment of torture.

The job of packing was lightened by the help of friends and relatives. The children balked all they could, and we put off the move as long as possible.

Finally, one hot June day, we left the Wappoo house, which we had rented, and drove up to our new place, the children in one car, and I in my new brace, swooning on the back seat while Mendel drove our other car. It was not a promising beginning. I had tried to please a group of individualists. I hadn't succeeded too well. Nobody particularly liked that house.

Unpacking took a long time. The novelty of having an invalid mother had worn off; after feeding me and helping me dress, the young people were reluctant to tackle the disorder of boxes and excelsior. Fortunately, my back gradually improved so that I was able to get the place fairly livable after the first few weeks of helplessness.

The girls found few friends to cheer the loneliness of their environment. Only young Mendel and I really liked Trinity Drive. I was lucky in having congenial neighbors and friends. I did more entertaining in that house than in any other place we've ever lived.

Marion was particularly irked at having to leave a special beau. We asked him to visit for a week that summer. It wasn't a success. According to Marion, he had grown up in a home where the maid served demitasses in the living room after dinner and where parents never disagreed or raised their voices. He had, moreover, just visited another family in North Carolina, where he and his friend occupied the guest cottage and enjoyed the use of a Cadillac roadster whenever they went from pool to club to party.

At our house, the guest slept in a rollaway bed, which I'd set up in our tiny library. The young people used my Chevrolet, but Mendel expected the young man to cut our grass if they were to have the privilege of using his membership card at the Bolling Green Air Force Base Club. My economical stews and casseroles were a novelty to him. I was so afraid that they were going to elope that I accompanied them to the railway station on the night our guest departed.

Poor Marion! In Charleston she'd gone with a socially prominent "crowd." Now, she found herself an outsider. After her local friends went off to boarding school, she had little companionship. She learned to study that winter. I was proud of the way she knuckled down to her schoolwork. We were far from accord, however, for as I read of the crimes in the Washington area, I found myself becoming more and more a duenna. She thought me ridiculously alarmed. We had some strained scenes. I hated to see her go out with young people because I already knew her to be fearless.

Milestones

In 1960 I entered another of my awkward phases, my role as crusader. After Marion enrolled in St. Agnes, I met a woman who asked me what my daughter was studying.

"Oh, French, history, English and uh…" I laughed lamely. "I've forgotten the others."

"Have you read any of the texts?"

"Well, no."

"Well, read some and see what you find out. It might prove interesting."

It was indeed interesting. It was also electrifying. I found myself devouring literature I'd never been aware of—books, pamphlets, committee reports, the *Congressional Record*. I was galvanized into action by the first book I found in Marion's room. It was *Doing the Truth* by Bishop James A. Pike and was to be used as her textbook on religion for the second semester. I objected strongly to the book and became an expert on the Bishop, his irreligious pronouncements and his unorthodox behavior.

I felt sorry for Marion. In addition to the ignominy of being a social flop, she was afflicted with a mother who called up the parents of her classmates to complain about a book on religion. All that fall, I wondered how I'd handle the problem of that book. Several mothers shared my disapproval that such a book should be put in the hands of young girls as a textbook on religion, but none of them would face the principal with me.

When I finally confronted the principal with my carefully written analysis of the book, she was prepared, too. She approved of everything in the book, she told me. It was the only suitable text. There were other schools if we

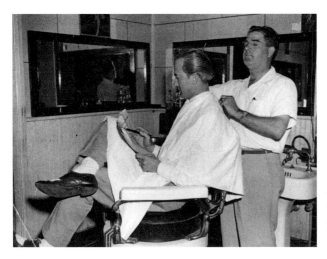

A "trim" for Mendel was an event that could prompt a picture in the local newspaper.

didn't like it, she suggested, with emphasis. I accepted her challenge and sent Marion back to Charleston to complete her final year at Ashley Hall. Mother kindly agreed to allow Marion to live with her.

That summer Peggy attended the University of Colorado summer school. I didn't know that it had a reputation for being a "party school." But Peggy did; that is why she chose it. The last week of summer school, along with thirteen other girls in her dorm, she sneaked out for a "late date," a popular custom at that time. They signed out for an ordinary date, returned and then left the dorm again after hours. The dorm mother did a bed check and discovered that some fourteen of her young charges were very, very missing. She reported their absence, and the hapless girls were required to appear before the disciplinary authorities. All were placed on social probation for one year. Peggy would have been expelled if there had not been such a large group.

Peggy liked the West. After summer school was over, she visited my friend Virginia who lived on a small sheep ranch in Rye, Colorado. Virginia and her husband drove Peggy over several states, looking for a suitable college without the stigma of her being placed on social probation. That is how it happened that Peggy attended New Mexico State University at Las Cruces, New Mexico, the following September. There she met Bob Eastman, her future husband.

Back in Alexandria, I continued my crusading. I had just gotten into stride. I had learned so much about the evils in our churches, I thought that I could do my bit by awakening other people. My efforts to talk to Mendel's colleagues were not highly effective. He insisted that if I asked them over, I should provide drinks and a good dinner. They were tired when they arrived. By the time I started my little enlightening talk, most of them were quite sleepy.

It wasn't long before Mendel decided that I ought to go back to Charleston. I felt that my virtuous efforts were being ignored in a most cruel fashion, but move back I did in the fall of 1961.

Many of my Charleston friends were interested in the activities of left-wing clergymen. However, my inexperienced efforts to persuade groups of strangers at meetings of any size were not received with enthusiasm. I learned that honesty and facts were no match for eloquence and ridicule. I plodded on, accepting every chance to impart my unpleasant truths. The results were so discouraging that I decided to retire in favor of more tactful and forceful speakers. My scrapbooks were more successful. They helped a number of church people lead protests in their churches.

My zeal didn't help me launch Marion into society or prepare for Peggy's wedding. Marion's debut was a pathetic contrast to her sister's. She insisted upon bowing in an off year; there were so few parties, hardly anyone was aware of the season. We had a tea for ladies at our home. After we'd prepared our refreshments on several evenings beforehand, I was so tired I could hardly stand in our receiving line. Of course, Mendel got inebriated just before the tea, and we had to get an office aide to drive him all over Charleston and Folly Beach, while polite Charleston ladies attended the function in our home. I have a dreadful memory of waving goodbye to the last guests at the front door (who moved so slowly—the last group was my mother and several of her elderly friends) as Mendel entered the back door, disheveled and angry because he knew we had deliberately excluded him.

Marion attended the Carolina Assembly Ball that year. It was given by a group of mothers, mostly daughters of St. Cecilia who copied the traditions of the ball in an effort to achieve similar éclat.

My earnest friends and I became mired in our attempts to expose a certain left-wing minister who was scheduled to speak at one of our largest churches. On one occasion, I tried to present my scrapbooks on the deteriorating values in the Episcopal Church, particularly as espoused by the National Council of Churches, to the local diocese at a meeting inside the newly built church across the highway from our home. Mendel and the children attended. Several liberal Episcopal priests attended also, to present the other side. They were trained to speak publicly, and I felt they ganged up on me and overwhelmed me with their erudition and contempt.

I was able to hold my own for a while, but as they continued to pound their points, I became confused and weary. It must have shown, for Mendel rescued me: He left his place in the audience and took over the meeting. He out-talked, out-clevered, out-joked, out-maneuvered and finally just silenced those men. Mendel filled in the breach, my knight at last, fighting for his lady.

Our cause went down in ignominious defeat; the clergyman consolidated his forces in the community and reinforced his prestige, at our expense. It was hard to accept his overwhelming victory. Again, eloquence and cleverness won over facts and honest purpose. The truth may make you free, but it can also make you seem ridiculous. I wrote a poem commemorating that humiliating event that started, "Mr. Clary makes me scary; Mr. W. is a fairy," but regrettably, the rest of that delightful venom has been lost.

After that awful evening, I confined my activities to the John Birch Society. According to the liberal press, members of the John Birch Society saw a Communist under every bed. Boo and I spent much time reading publications and trying to educate our earnest friends, many of whom were as concerned as we were about the encroaching United Nations, the left-leaning National Council of Churches and the liberal trend of our own National Episcopal Church. The Junior League became aware of the growing exposure young people had to pornography, incest, sexual promiscuity, etc. We wrote letters, had meetings and spent hours trying to stop the erosion of our values.

Sadly, the alarm we tried to raise proved futile. The sixties' antiwar protests, freedom marches, college bombings and other unrest had opened the door for civil disobedience.

Bob and Peggy became engaged that fall. He made a hit with the family and friends who attended a party we held for them. He stayed with us at Christmas and enjoyed the parties and hunts; he adapted himself to the chaos of our household with ease.

I'd like to forget most of my recollections of Peggy's wedding. I tried to get organized, as I had for her debut, but my efforts all seemed too gangly. The months of preparation were confused ones as we plugged along. The card files that had been so helpful for the debut party were ineffective for the wedding. I found myself playing dreary rounds of solitaire with those cards. I'd make piles of the names of those who must be invited, then eliminate friends in favor of political acquaintances whose presence was distinctly not desired. Mendel gave me no help but was busy with more important matters in Washington. He never wanted to undertake tedious decisions. I was trying to save money, as usual. We progressed from plans for a home wedding to a church wedding. Our reception at home had to be transferred to the country club. That meant having extra cards engraved and mailed to all the invitees.

Peggy was a wonder. She made several cotton dresses for their honeymoon trip to the Bahamas. She addressed all the invitations and kept her head during a host of minor crises. I would never have survived without her and Mrs. Struhs. Mrs. Struhs had come to my rescue before, when at the last minute, we begged her to serve our thawed refreshments for Marion's debut tea. Nothing upset Mrs. Struhs. As the acceptances dribbled in, I'd give her guesstimates of the number of guests we might have.

"There may be four hundred and fifty, Mrs. Struhs," I'd say.

"Perfectly fine, Mrs. Rivers," Mrs. Struhs would declare. "I'll get some more shrimps and another big turkey and another ham."

A day or so later, I'd call her again. "I think we'll probably have no more than three hundred now, Mrs. Struhs," I'd say apologetically.

"Perfectly all right, Mrs. Rivers," that amazing woman would reply.

There were further hurdles and much exhaustion. Our maid, Louise, had a death in the family; so all during the final, most hectic week, we had no help.

Even the March weather was against us—dismally rainy, windy and cold. But weddings are usually hard on the bride's mother. Why should I have expected to produce a masterpiece? We ended up having a formal evening wedding. It was wonderful to see how our friends and relatives shared in celebrating another milestone in our lives.

The reception was pretty, in spite of the delay. The bridegroom's mother kept us waiting while she went back to the hotel for a corsage. I delayed the receiving line, while our guests waited outside in the rain until the groom's mother eventually appeared. Looking back, I would never do that again!

Peggy and Bob looked very happy in pictures of the event. They left the next day for the Bahamas, where Peggy got the rest she needed so badly. I packed and stored some of her gifts and packed some for her to take to Wilmington, Delaware, where Bob worked. They had lived in Wilmington for only two weeks when Bob was transferred to Detroit. They worked very hard to make their apartment in Grosse Pointe attractive, and later they moved to a little house that looked like it came right out of Hansel and Gretel. Two years after she was married, Peggy received her bachelor of arts degree from Wayne State University, and a month after that, young Robert was born. Yes, I am very proud of my eldest daughter.

I'm proud of Marion, too. She attended Converse College, which was one that Peggy had scorned. She put her nose to the grindstone and was graduated in three and a half years, always getting on the Dean's List.

Young Mendel was extremely bright and attended Princeton for a year before transferring to Georgetown University. He lived with us for a while and then rented a house in Georgetown.

Once as a special treat, Mendel took his son to a baseball game. The ballpark was located in one of the most dangerous areas of downtown Washington. (It was after a great section of the city had been burned by riots in 1968 and the city had, for a short period, been under martial law.) Although the vehicle had the number-one license plate, it was a South Carolina license, and Southerners were anything but popular with some of

Washington's inner-city elements. Mendel drove around. Suddenly, he said, "Son, that's what I'm looking for, the police station. Get out of the car and go in there and tell them Congressman Rivers wants a place to park."

At the time young Mendel was twenty-one. He was almost paralyzed with sudden fear and could barely move, much less give an authoritative directive to a cop (who would likely be about young Mendel's age, anyway). According to young Mendel,

> Cops didn't help guys my age. They arrested us. I edged, or rather slunk, inside the police station. I saw a nice young policeman and tried to speak coherently. I kept talking so fast that he could not understand what I was trying to say. The more rapidly I said, "Congressman Rivers says he needs a place to park," the more startled the policeman looked. I think he thought I was crazy. Eventually, I was able to communicate sufficiently for him to understand, and surprisingly, he did find a place behind the building where the car could be parked.

It was a long time before young Mendel realized that his father honestly believed it was a favor, forcing him to confront an unfamiliar, scary situation.

So time passed. Mendel continued to move about rapidly and constantly. I joined him whenever it was possible. In his position, Mendel stayed in only the best accommodations when he went on military inspection trips. But he was a child of the Depression and loved to feel thrifty. Often he had his aides purchase bottled water on the local economies instead of paying the inflated hotel prices. He never traveled without numerous pieces of baggage, which he insisted upon counting himself to ensure that they were all present. He tried to instill this habit in his children. He was generous, always coming back from abroad laden with gifts. Most of the array was the usual postwar souvenirs, but Mendel also had an eye for valuable prewar Japanese wood-block prints, fine perfume, oriental carpets, petit point evening bags and leather gloves.

Mendel had wonderful sayings: "You gotta think big" and "Never be afraid to ask questions or you will never know the answer." Sometimes he would refuse to share his opinions with us. Once, while we were in the middle of Sunday dinner, just to be conversational, Peggy asked her father what he thought about an issue. His reply was sharp, "What the hell do you care what I think? Think for yourself. I don't want you going around quoting *me*." It was years before Peggy realized that being forced to form her own opinions about politics had been a gift, not a reprimand.

Before he became Chairman, Mendel purchased a bi-level tract house in Springfield, Virginia, in the same development that I had tried to avoid years before. The house was comfortable, but discouraging aesthetically; my visits to Washington were brief and not too interesting. I usually went there for some official affair that didn't mean much to me.

I wasn't happy or particularly unhappy. When Mendel visited Charleston in the winter, he had me pick camellias and carefully pack them in Spanish moss to prevent their turning brown; he delighted in giving boxes filled with those lovely delicate blossoms to his friends, colleagues and staff in Washington.

Shirley Temple Black visits Chairman Rivers in Washington.

The excitement and commotion of Mendel's visits were sandwiched between periods of relative quiet. I stayed at home a great deal. Housekeeping and the children absorbed most of my energies, which have never been abundant. I puttered around the house and garden; I indulged in my favorite respite from boredom, that which Logan Pearsall calls the polite, unpunished vice of reading. I put on weight.

Occasionally I felt like a disembodied spirit, floating between two environments. Neighbors, friends, relatives and a few outings lessened the monotony of life at Wappoo Heights. I still longed for a house in town, where, in one short block, I could meet a dozen people I enjoyed seeing. And of course, being associated with Mendel—restless, dynamic, inimitable Mendel—there was always the fillip of the unexpected to enliven my days.

Before I knew it, I found myself approaching the half-century mark. It was at about that time, I remember, that Mendel used one of his distinctive crooked similes and likened me to a mollusk. I wrote another verse:

> *I know I am growing old—alack!*
> *When I see Shirley Temple Black,*
> *Now matronly, with double chin,*
> *I realize the state I'm in.*

The sign reads:

U.S. CONSTITUTION — Art. 1 - Sec. 8

The Congress shall have Power ...
To raise and support Armies ...
provide and maintain a Navy ...
make Rules for the Government and
Regulation of the land and naval Forces.

Chairman Rivers with his strategically placed sign quoting the U.S. Constitution. It confronted all who testified before the Armed Services Committee, 1965.

Mr. Chairman

After twenty-four years of service in the U.S. House of Representatives, Mendel finally rose to the powerful position of Chairman of the Armed Services Committee. He had mellowed from the impetuous young congressman who defied President Truman and the Democratic Party years before. He had served his apprenticeship and had matured in judgment as he aged. His still slim, tall stature and flowing white hair were reminiscent of John C. Calhoun. Like other South Carolina politicians, Mendel greatly admired Calhoun and frequently compared himself to that august statesman. For decades he had delighted in defiantly rejecting conventional contemporary crew cut tastes in haircuts. He enjoyed this nonconformity but dressed impeccably in custom-tailored suits and colorful Italian silk ties.

He had stopped fighting for lost causes like segregation and was impatient for Carl Vinson (his predecessor as Chairman who served in Congress for over fifty years) to retire. Mendel became the ranking member of the committee in 1961 when Representative Paul Kilday of Texas resigned to serve as a judge of the Court of Military Appeals. The new position had given Mendel far greater influence in Congress.

At last, after years of waiting, Vinson stepped down and, in December 1964, Mendel was in line to become Chairman of the House Armed Services Committee when the new Congress organized in January.

And then the unthinkable happened. For reasons known only to him, Mendel decided to start drinking just before Christmas. Worse, he disappeared, and there were lots of rumors as to his whereabouts. The prolonged absence nearly cost Mendel the chairmanship. The Speaker of the House John McCormack reportedly tracked him down by telephone, somehow, and told him that if he wanted to be Chairman, he was to return to Washington that moment, to organize his committee. Or else. Mendel returned, and the rest is history. People said that Mendel had a personality transformation after he became Chairman. Whatever the cause, the drinking tapered off, and for more than two years before his death, he never touched another drop of alcohol.

Mendel had often lamented that he thought Carl Vinson would *never* retire so he had had plenty of time to plan how he would run the committee. When he finally got his chance, Mendel became Chairman very much in his own right.

The chairmanship delegated to him the responsibility for the nation's defense and the well-being of the officers and men who made up its army, navy and air force. He saw that responsibility as somehow flowing down through the years personally to him. As a man of power, Mendel Rivers would permit no mere Secretary of Defense—and no mere President of the United States—to reduce the Congress to junior partner in the struggle to preserve his country. He took it personally because men of power take everything personally. And he was right: a rubber-stamp, bipartisan Congress fails to represent the people and fails to challenge the President to do his job better.

Feeling that national defense transcended partisan haggling, one of the first things Mendel did was to close the caucus cloakrooms on either side of the Armed Services Committee room in the new Rayburn Building. As he and Russ Blandford were discussing the layout of the committee suite, Mendel asked him about the purpose of two smallish rooms on either side of the main chamber. When Russ told him that they were intended for the majority and minority members to strategize policy, Mendel looked at him with "fire in his eyes."

He snapped back, "We have no majority or minority. All members of this committee are Americans, interested in national security." This response impressed Russ, a no-nonsense, former Marine officer, because it had been a private conversation, not a public relations gimmick.

In addition to the committee offices, Mendel was assigned a handsome four-room suite nearby. It was vastly different from the two-room office in the Longworth Building where I had once worked as a stenographer.

There was an outer reception room staffed by one woman and a charming, warm entrance to Mendel's inner offices with their spectacular view of the Capitol dome. Behind the reception area was a room for his administrative assistant and office manager; adjacent to the receptionist was

Mendel in his Washington office. A Chinese Communist 7.62-millimeter carbine, captured in the Mekong Delta by units of the River Patrol Force and presented by Vice Admiral Hyman Rickover, hangs in the background.

another huge room for the rest of the staff. In the old Longworth Building, the outer office had been strictly functional, crowded with numerous desks, typewriters, files and lots of mail. The cacophony of the typing, telephones and constant interruptions is with me still.

Like all congressmen, Mendel had the franking privilege (the right to simply sign his name for official postage, instead of having to use stamps), and the staff was told in no uncertain terms that it was illegal to use franked mail for personal correspondence. Mendel's signature was in beautiful, legible penmanship. He always used green ink, a lawyer's trademark.

There was an unveiling ceremony for Mendel's committee room portrait in May 1968. Only three other portraits were there—those of the former chairmen, Dewey Short, Bill Bates and Carl Vinson. This was a special occasion, and numerous colleagues, military brass and friends crowded into the committee room to wish him well, and to be seen, of course. Peggy flew in from California and brought our four-year-old grandson Robert to the party. As was usual at such occasions, we were the pampered, proud satellites of our illustrious patriarch. We listened to the customary commentary by important dignitaries; lots of pictures were taken. Chairman Rivers was in his element.

Mendel's Scottish ancestry served him well in the political arena. He had the reputation of being able to put a chill into any witness just by looking at him. The Highlanders were a fierce, proud, independent lot, and like the

Chairman Rivers in the Carl Vinson Committee Room, 1965.

Robert Eastman copies his grandfather's stance.

fighting Scots before him, Mendel used his weapons well. His rapier was his tongue, his shield was his audacity and his battleground was the war of wits so enjoyed by men of power, as the Secretary of Defense soon learned.

Robert McNamara, a Kennedy appointee, had started off well as Secretary of Defense in 1961. He had captivated Chairman Vinson and other committee members with his facile recollection of backup information about the numbers of tanks and planes, etc., each branch of the service had available. McNamara had little use for politicians, military leaders or any who did not share his enthusiasm for statistics. McNamara was egotistical and used to having his own way.

But some younger committee members began to suspect that McNamara's reports to the committee were inaccurate. As the conflict in Vietnam escalated, committee members felt that McNamara was not qualified to select bombing targets from a map located in Washington. The field commanders in Vietnam found McNamara arbitrary and difficult. Some committee members believed McNamara was constantly scheming to thwart their efforts to fly on military planes. His micromanagement style was legendary, down to requiring clerical workers to account for such minutiae as pencils and erasers.

Mendel was determined to put the Secretary of Defense in his place. After he became Chairman, among his first official acts (perhaps his very first) was to direct the creation of a wooden sign, which he caused to be installed at the very front of the Chairman's podium, directly facing all witnesses. The wooden sign read:

> *The Congress shall have the power…to raise and support armies…to provide and maintain a navy…and to make rules for the government and regulations of the land and naval forces…The Constitution, Article 1, Section 8.*

That simple sign faced Secretary McNamara squarely when he testified before Mendel's committee for the first time and every time thereafter. In fact the paint was not completely dry for their first encounter. It was testy.

McNamara kept referring to former Chairman Vinson and how he and the former Chairman had always had an understanding. Finally, Mendel had had enough. He looked at McNamara and told him quietly and carefully, "But Mr. Secretary, Chairman Vinson's gone. He's g-o-n-e." He drew out the last syllable. Then he proceeded to inform the Secretary of Defense that the Congress was now prepared to assert its proper role in national defense.

And the Secretary never referred to "understandings" again.

Mendel's run-ins with McNamara were frequent. Year after year Mendel fought for, and McNamara opposed, raising military pay to the civilian equivalent. Mendel believed the entire U.S. Navy should be nuclear-powered, so it could go anywhere, any time. McNamara argued for diesel-powered ships because they were cheaper.

Mendel delighted in pronouncing the Secretary's middle name, Strange, in the most derisive of tones, dragging the name out until it seemed to have four or five syllables. To me his appearance was equally "strange." Instead of the conventional crew cut, McNamara had slicked-back hair parted on the side, which, coupled with his rimless glasses and thin, humorless lips, reminded me of an arrogant Nazi. To my knowledge, nobody from the top to the bottom of the military could stand the man. (Today McNamara is viewed by many as the chief architect for the failed policies in Vietnam. Since that war caused so much heartache and hardship, perhaps it is fitting that he lived to see how history will remember him.)

Once Mendel was talking to a friend when his secretary interrupted to tell him that Secretary McNamara wished to see him the following morning at ten o'clock at the Pentagon. Without looking in her direction or changing the tone of his voice, he said, "The time is all right, but the place is wrong." McNamara took the hint, keeping the appointment in Rivers's office.

Headstrong as he was, and short as the fuse of his temper might be, Mendel preferred to maneuver rather than to launch frontal assaults on McNamara's defense policies. McNamara was aware that he himself lacked the ability or the clout to have his way. Instead, he would ask President Johnson to intercede.

On these occasions, Mendel would neither argue nor threaten. Instead, he would say mildly, "Fine Mr. President, if that's what Bob McNamara wants, just have him get it through my committee."

When the military pay bill came before the Congress in 1965, Mendel proposed a 10 percent increase, while McNamara argued for no more than 4.5 percent. The Joint Chiefs, fearful of a floor fight over the pay increase, thought it would be great if Mendel would just call the President or Mr. McNamara and settle it at about 6.5 or 7. This was duly reported to Mendel. His reaction was typical, and typically astute.

Lyndon Johnson is a pretty smart operator, and he operated here on the Hill for a long time. If we were to do that, then I'd owe him something. Now if he were to call me and say "Mendel, I'll settle for six-and-a-half," we'd just have it done. But if he doesn't call, I ain't calling him to use up any favors or obligate myself. To hell with him. We'll just ram through the ten percent.

As it worked out, the bill was passed by a vote of 435 to 0 at 10 percent. It was the first pay increase for enlisted personnel since 1952.

McNamara succeeded in having the *John F. Kennedy* aircraft carrier diesel powered, and Mendel was furious. As Chairman, he fought the executive branch for a nuclear propulsion program, and eventually the Congress authorized nuclear submarines in spite of McNamara's opposition. The final run-in with McNamara was over nuclear-powered frigates. In the end Mendel authored a provision that required the President of the United States to order them built unless he wrote the Congress that it was not in the national interest. McNamara went to Lyndon Johnson and asked him to write a letter saying it was not in the national interest, but the President had sense enough not to do it. Out of that confrontation came a new Secretary of Defense.

After Clark Clifford replaced McNamara, Mendel told a group of visitors, "The President has repealed me; he now has a Secretary of Defense I can't criticize!"

Like all master politicians, Mendel was a dynamo, putting in incredible hours of work. Yet he knew how to conserve his energies. A superbly disciplined man, he had trained himself to put his head back and plunge into sleep within eight seconds, waking up a quarter of an hour later, fully refreshed and ready to go. He dutifully kept up his work as Chairman, making unannounced visits to military installations, inspecting defense plants and talking to those who could add to the store of knowledge, which made him the best-informed man in Congress on weapons systems, military hardware, planes, tanks and missiles.

Mendel had witnessed the French debacle in Indochina. The Korean conflict had already demonstrated how futile it was to fight a ground war against what seemed

Cartoon depicting the Rivers-McNamara feud.

like an infinite supply of Oriental troops. So Mendel was skeptical of President Lyndon Johnson's plans to send American combat troops to Vietnam. He publicly questioned what they were there to do and whether they would be allowed to do their job and win a military victory.

As the war dragged on, he pounded away at one theme: There is no substitute for victory! Whatever the soldiers who are there say we must do to win, is what we must do. Period! If we are not willing to do that, then bring the boys home.

He was relentless. Win the war, damnit, or bring the boys home, was his constant refrain. "Tell world opinion to go fly a kite," he enjoyed saying. "If we need to invade North Vietnam to win, then let's invade. If the Russians don't like it and want to join this war, let 'em join. I don't fear the Russians. I fear Americans who don't want their own country to win a war."

Among his valued possessions was a "peace sign" (the upside-down Y inside a circle) on a chain. On closer inspection, the "peace sign" was actually a stylized B-52 bomber, with the words underneath: "Bomb Hanoi." He spoke at pro-war rallies and even ventured onto a few college campuses to spread his message. His feelings were hurt when he was ridiculed by antiwar students at a college in Los Angeles. He felt misled; the school administration had assured him that the college was conservative and pro-war.

On the floor of the House, when he was piloting a defense bill to enactment, he tried always to accomplish what he felt was necessary without confrontations or any show of muscle. On some occasions, he called on his encyclopedic knowledge of congressional procedures. On others, he drew on his understanding of his colleagues. He was ushering a military authorization bill through the House, when a congressman representing a strongly Jewish district rose to his feet. "I move to amend this bill to require that no American troops will ever again serve in Southeast Asia."

Mendel knew that he could oppose the amendment and, after a battle, defeat it. No such broad prohibition had a chance of passage. It would have meant an hour or two of the House's time and some abrasive debate. Instead, he responded: "I accept the amendment. But I amend the amendment to read 'and/or Israel.'"

The Jewish congressman stood up quickly: "I withdraw the amendment."

As Mendel later remarked to a close friend, chuckling as they walked through the Capitol, "I just handled a situation with great statesmanship. Calhoun would have been proud of me. The whole thing took forty seconds."

He was not always so fortunate. Young Mendel attended Georgetown University and occasionally journeyed to Capitol Hill to sit in the House Visitors' Gallery and watch his father on the floor below. He told me this tale: His father was presenting a major defense authorization bill, and there came a strong challenge from a liberal colleague over certain provisions of that bill. The exchange became quite heated. Mendel lost his temper and concluded some retort with the words, "since the gentleman doesn't care about his country." It was a foolish comment, made in the heat of disagreement.

But the other man was hurt. He didn't respond to the insult. Instead, he had an ally, another congressman, rise on a point of personal privilege and then state acidly, "Mr. Speaker, I note that my distinguished colleague, unlike the Chairman who challenged his patriotism, at least had the courage to put on a uniform and fight for his country."

Neither side looked very patriotic. They both looked and sounded like children. Fortunately, Congress has a mechanism to "clean up the record." It's known as "revising and extending remarks." Any member of Congress may ask for unanimous consent to revise and extend his remarks before they are printed in the *Congressional Record*. No other member ever objects, because someone might object when he needs to correct a gaff. The congressman then tells the Clerk of the House what to put in the *Congressional Record* as his exact verbatim words, and it so appears, nicely cleaned up for public consumption, in the next day's record.

Mendel and his antagonist both raced to the podium. They just stood there, glaring at each other. Then each in turn asked for unanimous consent to revise and extend his remarks, no one objected, permission was granted and the incident was over.

There were times when Mendel seemed stubborn to the point of foolishness, but there was method to what seemed like madness. Usually, Mendel endeavored to learn what made people tick.

Friends and colleagues were shocked, for example, at his reaction to President Charles de Gaulle's ouster of all NATO forces from France. Congress was up in arms over this blow to free world unity and bitterly resentful of this display of French hostility to the United Sates, but there seemed to be little that could be done. One of his best friends in later life, Frank Jameson, recalled,

> *Mendel came out very strongly one day with the statement that we were going to remove all our war dead from France. Unilaterally, de Gaulle had thrown us out of France, and it had cost us over one billion dollars just to move the communications system from Paris to Brussels. It was a very*

*serious thing, much more serious than many people realized. Mendel said,
"The hell with it. We'll pull the war dead out. I'll put a provision in this
year's authorization bill that we're just going to dig up every American body
in France and bring it home. That ought to get his attention."*

I replied, "Mendel, that's going to be a very expensive process."

"Sixty-two million dollars. We can afford it." He knew the figure exactly.

*We argued about this for a period of five or six weeks, and Russ
Blandford, Chief Counsel of the Committee, would call and say, "Frank,
you've got to convince the Chairman that this is a terrible thing."*

*All the arguments against the moving of American war dead were laid
before Mendel, the religious implications, the fact that some of those in
American cemeteries in France had been killed during the First World War,
that if the dead were returned, there would be a need for new religious
services, that it would open old wounds in the families of the dead.*

*To all of this Mendel would say, "Well, you don't understand. You just
don't understand."*

*That was his answer to every objection raised by me and others.
Knowing how fond Mendel was of my mother, I pointed out that she had
lost a brother in World War I and would be very upset.*

*He just told me to shut up, he didn't want to hear about it. "You don't
understand the problem, but I'll tell you this. I ain't gonna do it."*

*Surprised, I answered, "This is really great. I'm delighted you changed
your mind."*

*"Frank, I don't even want to talk about it. It's decided, and I ain't
gonna do it."*

Many months later, Jameson told that story to Ridgeway Knight, then
the American ambassador to Portugal. Jameson commented, "You see,
sometimes he got off on problems that were ridiculous."

Knight looked at Jameson strangely and replied,

*I never heard that story. But I was in the Embassy in Paris at the time.
That was the only strategy that got Mr. de Gaulle's attention, and as
you'll notice, de Gaulle softened up immediately, and that's why Mr. Rivers
changed his mind. Any nation that would dig up its war dead and bring
them home, de Gaulle couldn't take that. And that was above the State
Department, above the President. Rivers was playing a very lonely game,
and he accomplished what he wanted.*

Mendel had no patience with sycophants. If someone agreed with him
about everything, he would concoct something outrageous and then turn on

the person who had agreed with it. From that time forth, he would regard the yes-man with suspicion. Conversely, he respected those who would stand up to him. As one of his colleagues reflected:

> *He could rage and roar or be sweet as pie, but he never let us forget that he was Chairman of the committee and that his way had to be our way. But if you fought him and you were right, he liked you for it and went along with you. He could be arrogant or humble, headstrong or accommodating, charming or boorish. But he knew the Congress and he knew how to get things done. He was the most astute operator I've ever seen.*

To achieve what he thought important, Mendel might put himself in a ridiculous light. But there was one principle he never compromised: his loyalty to friends. Long after Carl Vinson had turned over the Armed Services Committee and retired to Georgia, Mendel could call him to discuss committee business. "Uncle Carl," he would say, "you're the master." The calls to Vinson were made out of a long-standing affection and the recognition of what "the master" had done for him. Rivers had enemies in Congress, and his crotchets would sometimes drive his best friends up a wall. But those who received his loyalty returned it.

Eddie Hébert, a former newspaper editor who brought to the Congress all of his journalistic irreverence for the mighty of the world, reflected:

> *Mendel and I grew up in Congress together. When Mendel became Chairman, I was his hatchet man, you might say. We shared the same political philosophy. We were both Jeffersonian Democrats, and he idolized Calhoun. We both believed in states' rights democracy. We got along so well together that I did the My Lai job for him. Everything was leaking out of the big committee room, and he asked me to take it over. I told him that I would take it on the condition that Mendel would keep his mouth shut.*
>
> *Mendel couldn't understand reporters; that was his big failing. There were some conflicting leaks out of the big committee. Russ Blandford and I told him to keep his mouth shut. We told him to say "No comment," no matter what reporters asked him. Russ and I walked down the hall with him, and there was old Mendel saying to the reporters, "No comment, no*

---

* The My Lai incident occurred in 1968 when a group of American soldiers whose unit had suffered heavy casualties in the area entered the village of My Lai and killed over three hundred unarmed old men, women and children. Photographs were taken secretly, and a Vietnam veteran talked about the massacre to a reporter some time later. The scandal caused shockwaves both in the nation and in the military.

comment." And he gets to the elevator and just before the doors close, he says, "It's a goddam lie!"

We would have liked to have fainted. And he couldn't understand he'd given them the story. That's all they wanted, a denial or an affirmation.

We were holding closed hearings, and we had everything locked up tight, and Mendel and Blandford were out in Oklahoma somewhere. Mendel was speaking before some high school kids, and he told them, "We saved the Green Berets, and I'm going to save Lieutenant Calley."

Mendel would get mad when reporters asked questions. I'd tell him, "Mendel, that's their job. They're supposed to ask questions." He'd answer them and then he'd want to write the headlines for them, and then he'd want to write the story.

He could come up with the damnedest expressions. You remember the DC-3? Mendel would call McNamara the DC-McNamara, you know, where you had to push out the bombs. He was a character who won't be forgotten.

It was wonderful to serve with him and under him when he was Chairman.

During the height of the Vietnam conflict, Mendel's integrity was put to the test. He was in a position where he could influence where military personnel were stationed. One day in Washington, a colleague called Mendel's office to set up a meeting with a woman who wanted some help. The colleague's request was vague, and Mendel suspected that something was amiss. He asked Russ Blandford to come across the hall to his office. By the time the woman arrived, there were two people present. She was attractive and well dressed and requested that Mendel ensure that her son would not be sent to Vietnam. To sweeten the arrangement, she opened a briefcase that was packed with large-denomination bills still wrapped in crisp bank bindings. Mendel asked Mrs. Bull, his office manager, to come in and witness his asking the woman to leave the office, money in hand. Immediately afterward, Mrs. Bull prepared a memorandum describing the incident; this was filed in his personal safe until his death.

Mendel became very security conscious after he became Chairman. He told me that he never flew commercially because he could not run the risk of being taken to Cuba on a hijacked plane. Syndicated columnist Drew Pearson harped on this frequently, claiming that Mendel had demanded and received unrestricted use of military planes to fly back and forth to his district, a perk denied other congressmen. According to Russ Blandford, one reason that Mendel flew on military planes was to get firsthand information about their capabilities. The flights did not cost the taxpayers anything, for they were training missions that would have flown regardless. And Mendel often drove his automobile to and from the district.

About the same time he started carrying a loaded revolver. He warned me never to open the front door without a "gun in one hand and a dog in the other." These precautionary measures were probably because of the Kennedy and King assassinations and the Wallace shooting. Had there been actual threats, Capitol security would have provided protection.

Mendel never lost his fondness for rising early, about 4:30 a.m. If he found someone to converse with, his voice would carry throughout the entire house. He would go to the office early and was well known on Capitol Hill for his unusual hours. He became great friends with any who would join him for an early breakfast, many of which he cooked himself in the kitchen he had installed in the Armed Services Committee's suite.

As Chairman, Mendel was able to create and maintain a coalition of votes that guaranteed passage of the legislation he sponsored. Once, when his leadership was attacked, Mendel modestly replied, "Whatever anyone thinks of us and our committee, one can't criticize success because we've never gotten 150 votes against us, and Caesar, in all his glory, could not make that statement." (After Mendel died, F. Edward Hébert succeeded him as Chairman. He did not fare as well, for the Democratic Party, which had been known for its solid Southern, conservative block, was becoming a party of splinter interest-groups, many of which were extremely radical. The Democrats still retained a majority in the House, and their caucus refused to support Hébert. Russ Blandford often remarked that it had been remarkable how Mendel had been able to hold together a coalition.)

In the late 1960s, Mendel used his considerable influence to help make the College of Charleston a state institution. The College had been founded as America's first municipally supported institution of higher learning in 1770. For many years it required four years of Latin or Greek as a standard graduation requirement, making it this country's only college whose graduates could transfer to Oxford University in England without an entrance examination. The College survived the American Revolution and British occupation as well as the Civil War and Yankee occupation, two World Wars and the Great Depression. It went private in the mid-twentieth century in an attempt to avoid having to accept Negro students.

During the civil rights movement, the College lost its federal funding due to its anti-integration position. Its segregation policy also jeopardized its tax status as an educational institution, which discouraged charitable giving. The College kept raising tuition fees, while it shrank in size. As enrollment declined to only a few hundred students, entire departments were closed. Its accreditation was in danger.

Its President, George Grice, was a Charleston native. Mendel couldn't stand Grice. He saw him as one of the sore losers of the civil rights movement. George inspired some of my husband's best Mendelisms: "George Grice is proof positive that stupidity is the occupational disease of educators" and "If there were two men in this world I have no respect for, they would both be named George Grice."

In 1969 the state of South Carolina began considering the creation of a university consortium in Charleston. Coincidentally, George Grice resigned as President. At Mendel's intervention, the Board of Trustees offered the presidency to a dynamic retired naval captain named Theodore S. Stern. Mendel had known Stern through his various testimonies before the Armed Services Committee and later as the Commander of the Charleston Naval Supply Center, the third largest Navy Supply Center in the world. Stern had impressive credentials.

Mendel lobbied legislators and the Governor to have the College become part of the state system. He cleverly played Solomon Blatt of Barnwell County, longtime Speaker of the House and avid fan of the University of South Carolina, against Edgar Brown of Barnwell County, longtime President Pro-Tem of the Senate and avid fan of Clemson University, by reminding each of them privately about the important roles their beloved institutions would play in the new state system. And besides Blatt and Brown, there were other state politicians who feared competition with their personal favorite alma maters.

Conservative Charlestonians wanted to retain the College's private status and opposed having the institution become part of the state system. But Mendel persisted. He had a strong sense of history and knew what an invigorated College of Charleston could do for his city and its economic base.

Mendel spent months lobbying. Gradually, he brought all the players together. By the time the matter came up for a vote, Mendel had smoothed away all opposition. Having once been a member of the South Carolina Legislature, he attended the voting session and sat on the dais with his arms folded across his chest, watching as the votes were cast. The measure passed unanimously. The College has gone on to become one of South Carolina's great educational institutions. Enrollment has increased more than tenfold in the years since Mendel's efforts. Standards are high; it offers an impressive array of programs and degrees.

Ted Stern has written admiringly about Mendel and the other Charlestonians who preserved the College's legacy. They were successful in keeping the hub of the College at its original site on George Street and in expanding the downtown campus.

Mendel in a pensive mood.

Edward and Robert Eastman
in the "trophy room."

Many organizations gave unusually elaborate tributes and plaques to Mendel, which he proudly displayed in his Washington office. These were later relocated to the "trophy room" in our Wappoo Heights home. In South Carolina, Mendel received recognition continually, for he did much to help the state regain some economic prosperity, something it had lacked since the Civil War. Although many of the military facilities in his district had been there since the nineteenth century, Mendel was accused of putting so many military installations in his district that it would sink.

After he became Chairman, Mendel disposed of the little bi-level in Springfield and purchased a modest ranch house much nearer to Washington in McLean, Virginia. It took only ten minutes to pass through one traffic light, turn right onto the George Washington Parkway and drive into Washington. I moved back to Washington again and lived there until Mendel's death in 1970.

Those last years were pleasant for both of us. Mendel had quit his drinking. The children were finally grown. Marion was working on the West Coast. Young Mendel was in law school, and Peggy moved from California to Delaware. It was nice to see them on their own and yet near enough for occasional visits. When it was necessary, we would go back to Wappoo Heights, but for the most part we enjoyed our middle-class existence in McLean, an existence frequently touched by the wonderful honors that continually came Mendel's way. I had finally learned to be more accepting, and he had become less demanding, perhaps because somewhere deep within he realized that his days were numbered.

Visiting Our Oriental Allies

One of Mendel's first orders of business the year he became Chairman was to visit our Oriental allies and make an official inspection tour of the Vietnam military situation. Luckily, wives were invited on the trip, and off we went to exotic lands that had evoked a sense of mystery and adventure (minus the shooting war, of course) since the time of Marco Polo.

This chapter is taken from my diary.

We were hurtled into a brilliant sunset that evening in September 1965. Bound for the Pacific, our first destination was Korea and its Armed Services Week. Our special plane, Air Force Number Two, housed a cheery complement—General Mark Clark, who been UN Supreme Commander when he was stationed in Korea in 1952; four Senators whose names I forget; and four Representatives, Mendel, Porter Hardy of Virginia, Craig Hosmer of California and Speedy Long of Louisiana—all accompanied by wives, escort officers and clerks. We were a jolly party and enjoyed our flight, being frequently amused by Renie Clark's quips.

The rosy sky seemed magical, for it went on and on. Many hours later we discovered that even a gorgeous sky could become monotonous when it lasted interminably. Its disappearance after a refueling stop in Alaska was actually welcome.

When we finally landed, the Koreans welcomed us with tremendous fanfare. Although as Chairman, Mendel was the most influential person in the party, the Senators outranked him. We were lined up according to protocol with the Senators first, husbands preceding their wives. We

Mendel, Generalissimo Chiang Kai-shek, President of Taiwan, and General Mark Clark, 1965.

descended from the plane to a handsome red carpet and were greeted by the longest receiving line I have ever encountered. The receiving line was headed by the Minister of Defense, Kim Sung Eun, along with all the important men in his department or in the armed services. Each man was accompanied by his wife, dressed in the lovely silk gowns of Korea, with a small child standing beside her. The children enchanted us with their smiling, doll-like faces as they presented a bouquet to each woman in our party. A military band played for a parade of troops who were reviewed by our officials. After the close of the ceremonies, we were whisked off to our hotel in Seoul, accompanied by the shrieks of police sirens as our drivers threaded their way through a tangle of automobiles, trucks, small three-wheeled cars, bicycles and daring pedestrians.

Our spacious suite at the Hotel Bando abounded in fresh flowers. It even had a large dining room. As Mendel showered, I prepared to unpack. After shedding my rumpled traveling dress, I had put on an old robe of Marion's that had taken up less space in the suitcase than mine. When there was a knock at the door, I opened it to a smiling Korean man, who bowed low and declared he was the manager of the hotel.

"Good day, Madam. I hope that you and the Congressman are comfortable and that everything is satisfactory."

"Very lovely and satisfactory. We are happy to see all the beautiful flowers in our rooms," I replied with all the grace I could muster, feeling decidedly uncomfortable being trapped there wearing that shabby borrowed robe and suffering from a case of jetlag. After brief exchanges of polite phrases, the manager bowed and made his departure.

I hadn't had time to draw a breath before there was another knock. It was an escort officer bringing messages to Mendel. On his heels came a man from the American Embassy with greetings and invitations from the ambassador. He was followed by porters bringing in the rest of our luggage. (I bought myself a lovely robe at my first opportunity.)

The defense minister gave a formal state dinner party that evening. We were served fried chicken and a dessert of canned peaches instead of Korean cuisine, doubtless a hospitable gesture to American visitors. Mendel sat by the Minister's wife, and they conversed through an interpreter. The Minister and I spoke English. He was interested to learn that Mendel would soon have his sixtieth birthday and later presented Mendel a handsome embroidered screen. I made a faux pas at dinner. I followed the Minister's use of knives and found myself trying to cut the meat with a dull knife. A serving man politely picked up my steak knife and handed it to me, saying gently, "This is

Korea, 1965.

for the meat." The American Ambassador, Winthrop G. Brown, seeing our travel-weary faces, tactfully suggested that the floorshow be omitted.

On the following days the men were taken on inspection tours of various military posts. One day the women joined them at the DMZ, the demilitarized zone between North and South Korea. We rode there in a bus. Shoulder-high cosmos in lovely clusters of pink and rose grew along the bumpy, dusty roads. Only the heads of pedestrians were visible as they bobbed up and down beyond the cosmos blossoms. Signs warning of land mines were also plentiful along the way.

The DMZ gave one an eerie feeling, knowing that the enemy was watching us through telescopes. A clowning Communist guard stood in a sentry box that had lace curtains at its small windows. He provided comic relief. We laughed heartily as he held a curtain as if it were a face veil, wriggling his hips like an Egyptian dancer. He obligingly posed for snapshots.

We were extensively entertained by both the Korean and American officials at luncheons and dinners. While the men were entertained at a stag party one evening, the minister's wife gave a dinner party for the women. There were about twenty people seated on cushions around a large low table. All of the Koreans wore traditional gowns except one solitary wife who was dressed in Western style and smoked cigarettes. She was a contrast to the others, who were disposed to giggle behind their hands like a group of old-fashioned schoolgirls. The Korean gowns were perfect for their style of entertaining. The gowns flowed voluminously to the ground, and a woman can sit down at a low cushion gracefully and without endangering her modesty.

We Americans were another story. We were clad in our American stylish short skirts and dresses, for hemlines were well above the knees. We couldn't sit at a cushion or move in any direction without showing off our legs and feeling and looking awkward. A great many Korean delicacies were served. I felt that I should try them all and tackled everything that was offered. The Minister's wife, by whom I was seated, poured my tea into small cups and my wine into thimble-sized glasses. It was uncomfortable sitting Oriental style, and I continually shifted my knees from one side to the other, modesty be damned.

After our departure from Korea, when I read a Korean etiquette book that was given to me as a farewell gift, I discovered that I had blundered. I should have poured the wine and tea for my hostess to reciprocate. I should not have sat with my feet curled toward her. I was not expected to taste every dish of food offered. How unfortunate it was that our State Department did not provide us with such vital information prior to the trip.

Marwee at far right of Korean pagoda, 1965.

The last day, we enjoyed a luncheon at the home of the Korean President. Previously, in a ceremony in his drawing room, husbands were paid tributes through an interpreter and were presented medals and gifts. We conversed with the President and his lady through interpreters who stood behind our chairs throughout the meal.

A splendid parade climaxed Armed Services Week. It was truly moving to see the young soldiers who rode by in tanks and trucks that were decorated with flowers, especially when I was told that after the parade, they would be heading for the jungles of Vietnam. We cheered and waved Korean flags from the President's box, and marveled as the daring pilots of the Korean Air Force put on a spectacular show. It was a memorable day.

On our departure from Korea the same impressive formal ceremonies were reversed. We watched the review of the troops, the music and the long receiving line with children and flowers for the ladies. As we made our farewells to our hospitable, courteous allies, the band played "Aloha Oe." My eyes were brimming with happy tears by the time I entered Air Force Two.

After Korea, our party made a few brief stops in the Orient. Japan was wonderful, but entirely different, cleaner, modern and yet enough of old Nippon to be picturesque. The American ambassador was not available due to the change in our schedule, so we were never guests at the embassy. Most of our time was spent shopping. Mendel gave me pearl earrings. We saw a Shinto procession at the shrine by the Hilton hotel. One priest looked like a medieval character in his robes.

An amusing incident occurred when the automatic lock on our hotel room door failed to work properly. Mendel fumed and had me call for a maintenance man. He tried to fix it, but it still wouldn't bolt from the inside.

Watching his efforts, Mendel commented, "You see? Anyone with a pass key could get into this room."

"Oh, no, sir," said the clerk in his Japanese accent. "Nobody can get in. You see, you hang this sign on the door. It say, 'Do Not Disturve.'"

Renie Clark had her birthday in Japan. We celebrated with a lobster salad and champagne luncheon. Mendel drank coke. General Clark looked terrible after we ate. He turned bright red. We feared a stroke. Later he was fine.

We arrived in Taiwan on October 5. The highlight of our trip was the visit to the home of President Chiang Kai-shek. When we arrived at the hillside mansion, several interpreters ushered the group into a spacious reception room and requested that we form a line according to protocol precedence. Shortly thereafter, our host entered and proceeded down our line, welcoming us through the interpreters. Afterward, we sat in two rows of chairs, the men and women facing each other, again in prescribed order. After the men had chatted with the generalissimo, it was their wives' turn to speak to him. He was exceedingly dignified and courteous in his efforts to make us feel welcome. As the afternoon was warm, we gladly used the fans that had been given us as mementos of the occasion.

The generalissimo invited Mendel and Mark Clark to breakfast at 8:30 the next morning. Typically, Mendel said that was too late for him, so they rearranged the time. Later, while we were flying in Air Force Two, Mendel told me what they had talked about. Mark Clark had told the generalissimo that he could march two thousand Citadel cadets to the polls to vote for Mendel, but that his help was not needed. Mendel told him about the Charleston gardens and the Formosa azaleas and gave a brief account of the early rice culture in the Charleston area. Mendel urged the generalissimo to visit the United States, where many held him in great esteem; he added that U.S. foreign policy was playing into our enemies' hands.

President Chiang's son and daughter-in-law also entertained us at dinner during our brief visit. We were entertained by Chinese and American officials and liked the friendliness and optimism that were evident everywhere we went. We admired the Taiwanese people. After having fled from the Communists on the mainland, they were industriously building a prosperous country. We had a lovely send-off by people who seemed like old friends after just two days' acquaintance.

(Madame Chiang was away at the time of our visit to Taiwan. I met her in Washington when Mendel gave a luncheon in her honor after he became Chairman. It was in the Speaker's dining room. I have corresponded with her and her nephew, Dr. Kuhn, during the ensuing years. She is a gifted lady who has used her talents to help her country and to assail Communism.)

On October 11, 1965, we flew to Hong Kong. Mendel had previously requested that the commanding general of the United States Army in Vietnam, General William "Westy" Westmoreland, fly from Saigon to meet with the congressmen in Taiwan for a briefing. (Years later General Westmoreland mentioned to me that he still appreciated Mendel's thoughtfulness in giving him a brief respite from the war front.)

Mendel was very cross and had a lovely time cussing me out for something trivial—my slowness in ordering breakfast, I think. I suspected that he was nervous about the trip. He gave me minute details on packing our gear, for we had purchased loads of junk in Hong Kong.

Jack Wiegland took us to the airport, where the men took off in two small jets. Mendel, General Clark, Speedy Long, Porter Hardy, two generals and Colonel Naler made up the party. I don't know if the Senators went. "Westy" told me that we would meet in Bangkok tonight or tomorrow. (Jack was head of counterintelligence and entertained British and Chinese often, as well as people like us. He pleased many friendly children with Chinese greetings. His wife said he got the highest grades in any language from the army school. He almost killed himself learning, and now he doesn't need it. Most of his classmates divorced, due to the strain of mastering Chinese.)

Recollections of Hong Kong are already hazy. The whole trip was spent in our accustomed rush. We shopped mostly. I bought five sweaters at Mohans,

Representative Gerald Ford greets Madame Chiang Kai-shek as their luncheon host (Mendel) looks on, 1968.

two for each of the girls. I planned to go to church and made Lynn Hardy very late waiting for me after my hair appointment. We commuted by ferry, and it was fun to watch the children and people in a holiday mood.

The Chinese are very friendly, gregarious and jolly. I still marvel at the bareness and tiny size of the sampans. Some had wooden headrests instead of a bed, but apparently, many had no sleeping quarters at all. The sampans usually had enamel chamber pots and cloth curtains for wind or rain protection. Cooking is done on a hole in the floor using what looks like charcoal sticks. A few sampans sported aluminum armchairs wrapped with pink or blue plastic strips. There was absolutely no privacy. On the dock were several pans of water. A girl washed off her hands and face and rinsed her mouth in one of the less filthy ones. We saw young boys in gray trousers and white shirts marching in some sort of school procession. They all looked happy and well fed.

Min Ho, the daughter of our good friend General Ho, who was attached to the Chinese Embassy in Washington, invited us to dinner at their home. I would have liked to have seen it when her grandfather was in his heyday.

Their apartment was spacious and beautifully furnished. They rent out five apartments, yet there is ample space for the Hos' family of four. The moon was full, and the view over Repulse Bay was exceptional.

We went to a furniture store, and Mendel got some beautiful things that were shipped back to the United States. I was so grateful to him. My favorite purchase was a handsome trunk made of dark rosewood with burled wood panels. It has two large brass straps with charming Oriental locks and is an imposing piece. We planned to use our treasures in our McLean home where they would blend nicely with our other Oriental furnishings.

I wish I could describe the scene in our room. It was like a stage comedy. Mendel got very cross, insisting that I had to help with the packing. He then called Mohans and had some of their boys pack for him. It was so confusing that the waiter almost giggled when Mendel tripped on the handles of my hatbox. Of course it was nerves. They were all excited about the reporters. I don't know what had transpired, for Mendel sent me to visit Renie when Westy arrived.

Bangkok was impressive. I enjoyed the boat trips on the canals. Graceful Thai girls in small boats of produce headed to market while others walked by on the embankments carrying baskets of fruit that were hung on both ends of poles balanced on their shoulders. Their clothes were colorful. As our boat glided beneath the bridges, many Thais waved in friendly greetings.

I had been nervous about Mendel's trip to Vietnam. It was an enormous relief to return to the hotel and see the remnants of his hasty visit strewn around the room, shoes scattered across the floor and a shirt flung across the bed. Mendel never discussed his trip to Vietnam, and I wish now that I had asked him about it when we did our dictations a few years later. Sometimes I wonder why I have not been more curious in my life.

As soon as we landed in Guam, the ladies went on a hilarious trip in a helicopter while the men were taken on an inspection tour. It was so noisy that Renie Clark, Marian Hosmer, Lynn Hardy and I passed notes, and the three Senate wives sat up very straight and remote. I don't know why the others did not participate in our fun. I later learned that one of our girls, Roberta Young, was scared stiff by her placement near the open door. Renie kept looking for the head and clowned around saying that she wanted a parachute so that she could jump for a ladies room. She moved in her seat so much that her seat belt broke, and she fell into some piled-up stuff. I laughed helplessly. Our military escort finally helped her up. We flew endlessly over Guam and decided it must be Australia. We kept passing notes, all the while getting more hilarious. Our mirth helped break

Marwee reflects after the whirlwind trip to the Orient.

the tedium of the long, loud, reverberating helicopter flight that had been planned for our enjoyment as a special treat.

I write on October 17 as we fly over the Pacific heading back home. It will be quite a blow to step on anything but red carpets and not to have flowers presented at every turn. It has been grand to have Marian Hosmer along. She loves to laugh and thinks Mendel is a riot. She asked me to jot down some of his Riversisms:

"No matter how thin the pancake, there are always two sides."

"A thought in his head would sound like thunder busting in a gourd."

"She could sour milk by long distance telephone."

"She looks like a bale of cotton with the middle band busted."

Hawaii was lovely. The people were hospitable and the air sparkling. We ended our trip on a gay and pleasant note. It was a happy contrast to Manila, the only place I was pleased to leave as quickly as possible. Last night we wore jessamine leis at the party given by Admiral Sharp's command. General Winters was host in his absence. That dear Kitsy Westmoreland, dressed in a muumuu of orange and pink, was there looking lovely. She brought Renie and me Japanese aprons as our "getting back to reality" gifts. Everyone has been wonderful.

We went to bed early. Service wives kept phoning last night to thank Mendel for all he has done. I finally had to request no more calls about midnight. Mendel awakened me at 4:30 a.m. telephoning the Washington office. All was well there. We have been back in Drew Pearson's columns recently, but no one knows what he said.

What a trip! By Wednesday, it will all seem like a pleasant dream.

We go down to Charleston for the unveiling of Mendel's bust Wednesday. Hope Evelyn, our cleaning woman, can dust the house before I get there. We just flew over San Francisco and had a grand geography lesson from the pilots, seeing the Donner Pass, Reno, the snow-capped mountains, Lake Tahoe. We are going about five hundred miles an hour. Mount Hood looks impressive two hundred miles away. We will soon see Salt Lake. Mendel says he'll call Peggy, who is living in Detroit, as we fly over Chicago.

We saw the Korean Defense Minister and his family again the following summer when they paid an official visit to Washington. Before they arrived, the Korean Embassy kept calling Mendel's office to find out what we planned to do for them during their visit. Of course they expected us to reciprocate for their lavish hospitality during the Armed Services Week. I've always felt

Mendel Jr. and Koko Kim at a reception for the Korean Defense Minister (Koko's father Kim Sung Eun) when he visited Washington, 1966.

that entertaining foreign dignitaries is a function of the State Department, and I wondered why State never offered to do anything for them.

Mendel found two men at the House restaurant who would serve, and we had a little supper party on our pleasant sun porch in McLean. We managed to express our appreciation for the lavish hospitality that we enjoyed in Korea and sent welcoming gifts to their Washington hotel.

We also tried to make Koko, the Kims' eighteen-year-old son, feel at home in the United States. He lived with a Korean diplomat's family and had few opportunities to speak English. Koko learned one helpful sentence, however. To almost any remark, he gravely replied, "A very sound idea." The summer before young Mendel entered Georgetown University, we urged him to befriend Koko and teach him some American expressions.

One day, we asked young Mendel how his efforts to teach Koko were progressing.

"Oh very well," young Mendel replied. "He teaches me Korean expressions, and I teach him English ones."

"What expressions have you taught him?" his father asked.

"Oh, you know, the usual: 'Jeet jet?'"

"That's great, son. You have learned a nice Korean accent."

"Dad, that's not Korean. That's English. Don't you know 'Did you eat yet'?"

The Serviceman's Best Friend

Vietnam was fought not only in the jungles of Southeast Asia but also at home. Time-honored values were questioned more and more as the conflict dragged on and on. Inflamed emotions, demonstrations, drugs and bombings on college campuses dominated the news as much as the battlefields half a world away. The makeup of the Congress reflected the unrest. Liberals against conservatives. Antiwar factions against anti-Communists.

I am proud to say that Mendel Rivers became the military's strongest ally although he never served a day in any branch of the armed forces. (He was too young for the First World War and was serving in Congress during the Second.) He was called the "Serviceman's Best Friend," and no one has ever replaced him as the armed forces' strongest Congressional advocate. One colleague stated, "He lived and breathed the American Serviceman, more than that, he lived this nation. 'The Star Spangled Banner' and 'America the Beautiful' still brought tears to his eyes."

Mendel was also a realist. He accepted the fact that neither the President nor the Congress were willing to support their own military and let them win the war in Vietnam. What he minded, I believe, was the dishonesty of the politicians, a dishonesty that was killing thousands of American soldiers. Mendel even invited the Chairman of the Joint Chiefs of Staff to testify about the strategy for winning the war. When the invitation was ignored, Mendel took to the press.

Mendel was an ardent disciple of General Douglas MacArthur, who believed that there was no substitute for victory. Early in the Korean War,

"The Big Boss" admiral's cap presented on Pearl Harbor Day by 198 grateful Vietnam servicemen from the first planeload who were able to purchase Christmas-leave, round-trip tickets home for $376. This was one of Rivers's last functions before leaving for Birmingham, Alabama. This happy photo appeared on the front page of the *Washington Post*, a newspaper usually critical of Rivers, 1970.

Mendel had urged President Harry S. Truman to use the atomic bomb if the Communists did not pull back. He had urged an invasion of Cuba during President John F. Kennedy's administration. After North Korean forces captured the American spy ship USS *Pueblo* off the coast of Korea in 1969 and imprisoned her crew, Mendel was outraged. He ranted and fumed at home and publicly urged, "Retaliate! Retaliate! Retaliate!"

He fervently advocated military superiority and supported expensive weapons systems without hesitation. When the air force needed a new long-distance cargo plane to replace the aging C-141, it decided that the times required something new and different, something that could fly fast or slow, could land within one hundred yards on bad runways and could carry twice the payload. That new vision of airpower was the C-5A Galaxy, the pride of the air force. Mendel decided a new cargo hauler was not just a good idea, but essential to winning the Vietnam War and the larger cold war. He championed the C-5A.

It was an excellent airplane, but it was typical of the new breed of high-tech military wonders being produced by the American military-industrial complex: It took far longer than projected to bring on line, and it cost far more. Its cost overruns were huge, and they occurred over and over. There were the inevitable suggestions of possible corruption, somewhere. The overruns became a front-page news embarrassment to the air force and more fuel for the growing antiwar movement.

Mendel was a rock. "Of course it costs more!" he would bellow. "A plane like this has never existed before. We're having to invent new technology every day. How much are you willing to spend to keep your freedom? You know, we can just cancel this airplane and let the Communists take over, and that will save all kinds of money. Maybe then you'll be happy."

The C-5A did get built, and it has served the country well for decades. Its maiden flight was a ceremonial flight to Charleston Air Force Base in 1969. The date had been chosen because it was the anniversary of the D-Day invasion of Normandy in 1944. There at the C-5A rollout—along with hundreds of military brass, families and the curious—was L. Mendel Rivers, Chairman of the House Armed Services Committee and local hero. The crowd watched the huge craft descend slowly out of the sky. It approached the runway. It landed. It taxied. It lost a wheel. The wheel rolled along side the airplane, just next to it, for hundreds of yards. The rolling of the wheel next to the plane seemed to last forever. It seemed a flaw in the airplane. It was an embarrassment.

Mendel was the guest of honor, of course. He rose to speak. Everyone wondered how he would deal with the errant wheel. Would he be angry? Would he gloss over it? Would he blame someone?

He never missed a beat. He made the usual introductions and then went straight to what everybody wanted to hear: "I guess you all saw that wheel come off that airplane. What the hell do you think we put twenty-eight of 'em on there for? They'll never miss one." Then, just in case anybody hadn't been listening: "There are some [such as U.S. Representative Proxmire, who was noted for his "Golden Fleece Awards, et al] who would rather have seen a wing drop off. All I can say is to hell with them."*

He was passionate about the "nuclear navy." He was a close friend and supporter of Vice Admiral Hyman Rickover, who was head of the U.S. Navy Nuclear Propulsion Program. Mendel believed that every major U.S. navy ship should eventually be nuclear powered. He complained loudly when the USS *John F. Kennedy*, an aircraft carrier, was designed and built with a conventional diesel power plant. "What the hell good is that ship going to be, if we can't get her fuel?" he asked. There was no answer. But Mendel won the war. Over time, the great majority of U.S. navy warships were built nuclear powered.

During his first meeting with Admiral Elmo R. Zumwalt Jr., the newly appointed Chief of Naval Operations, Mendel began holding forth over the breakfast he had cooked in the kitchen he had installed in the Armed Services Suite of the Rayburn Building.

"Admiral," he said, "I don't want you to be like some of those other sons of bitches who were CNOs. I want you to be like Tom Moorer. That's my idea about how I want you to be."

Zumwalt looked at Mendel from beneath his dark, hooded eyebrows and answered, "Mr. Chairman, I hope I have the attributes of all my predecessors, and if any of them had some faults, I hope I can avoid some of those. But whatever the case is, it's going to be a Zumwalt navy."

"You know, I think I like you, Admiral," Mendel replied.

Mendel was vitally concerned about the morale of enlisted men and the servicemen on the front lines. He was known to keep generals waiting in his reception area while he patiently listened to the needs of an enlisted man.

---

* History has vindicated Mendel's support of the C-5A. On September 20, 2005, thirty-six years after the giant airplane landed at Charleston Air Force Base and lost a wheel, the National Geographic Channel broadcast a documentary entitled *Megaplane* and described the C-5A thus: "The C5 Galaxy revolutionized military airlift and changed the art of war. It is the champion of the air. Its massive size and long range enable it to perform operations no other Air Force plane can do." With its incredible 36,000-cubic-foot capacity it can haul any piece of ordnance in the U.S. Army's arsenal: two Abrams tanks or fourteen Humvees or seven Hueys or two platoons and their gear or various combinations of the above (or anything else asked of it) and still fly at less than one hundred miles per hour or greater than five hundred miles per hour. It can be refueled in flight and can fly indefinitely.

He was scandalized when he learned in 1962 that a petty officer on active duty could qualify for welfare in New York. He vowed that would never happen again.

In 1963 he established, through the vehicle of the House-Senate Conference Committee reconciling the military pay raise bill, the principle linking military retired pay to increases in the Consumer Price Index, the same as federal retired pay for civil servants. In 1964 he championed the cause of "hospital rights," guaranteeing medical care in military hospitals for military retirees and their dependents. In 1965 he fought both the Secretary of Defense and the President himself to get the first pay raise since 1952, and the largest single pay raise ever for enlisted personnel. The CHAMPUS Program (Civilian Health and Medical Plan for the Uniformed Services), finally enacted in September 1966, owes much of its existence to the efforts of L. Mendel Rivers. He was instrumental in getting an additional pay grade, E-7, established to help retain senior enlisted men. He championed mobile home allowances and cheap airplane fares for soldiers.

As Chairman, Mendel was one of the most active correspondents on the Hill. Much of the mail came from outside his district. He aided whom he could, especially the innumerable servicemen who had problems of all descriptions. Their regard was made manifest whenever possible.

He went to great lengths to get information because he found that sometimes top military personnel were disingenuous. A close friend observed,

> *People used to think Mendel went to PXs to shop for Marwee. He didn't need a damned thing there. He would go through that place comparing prices and was a genius at knowing whether the troops were getting a good deal. Part of his brilliance was that he could talk to troops from the war zone and find out first hand what was going on and then talk to four-star generals or admirals knowing what he was talking about and not have to listen to a bunch of excuses.*

Interestingly, it was a long time before Mendel had the opportunity to meet a Vietnam veteran from his district. He met with our cousin, George Palmer, after his return from combat in 1966. Although it was a social call, it was also a debriefing. Palmer told him about how worthless the M-14 was in jungle warfare where constant shooting loosened a screw and caused the front site assembly to fall off. Infantry marines in the field had to purchase their own uniforms and boots on the black market, although the rear echelon had all the uniforms they wanted. Palmer still regrets that he did not take this opportunity to tell him that it was obvious overseas that the

Johnson-McNamara system of running the war from Washington, ignoring the wisdom of the men on the ground, ensured ultimate defeat.

Although he had serious health problems and desired to retire, Mendel felt that his leadership was needed in the Congress during the troubled times of Vietnam. "I am the granddaddy of the Hawks, and I think we should get it over with as fast as possible."

As the Vietnam conflict grew more and more out of control, the personal hardships of the career military, the draftees and their families got worse and worse. If they needed help, and Mendel could help, he would delight in saying, "I am *your* Congressman now."

He meant it. He had a simple philosophy: "Those who give their lives for their country should enjoy a standard of living equal to that which they are defending for others."

When cursing and spitting upon returning soldiers seemed so fashionable, Mendel rose to their defense over and over. He suffered personal abuse from some of the news media. Yet he never wavered.

"What have you soldiers, sailors and airmen done for me?" he would ask rhetorically. "Why, you've only saved my life and my country through two world wars and two regional ones. I love you all."

Mendel greets the students at the newly named L. Mendel Rivers Elementary School in Altus, Oklahoma, April 1970.

Vietnam.

Writing in the August 1966 issue of *Naval Affairs* magazine, Bob Nolan said it all:

> *Ask the average American of voting age who his United States Representative is and chances are he will be unable to tell you. Ask the average American serviceman the same question, and he will quickly reply, "Representative L. Mendel Rivers"…Today's GI, no matter which of the fifty states he is from, considers Chairman Rivers his Congressman…We recently received a letter from one of our shipmates in Vietnam stating, "If a presidential nomination and election were held now, with only the military voting, Chairman L. Mendel Rivers would be elected hands down…L. Mendel Rivers is the serviceman's congressman."*

Mendel's passion for the military extended to our home. I proudly wore a bracelet with the name of one of our brave MIAs. Mendel always wore an American flag in his lapel, and he gave the children countless patriotic trinkets. We were a flag-waving family. We may not have been trained to salute smartly, but we tried to stand tall; we felt it was our duty.

Over the years the military gave Mendel many honors. A navy housing development near Hanahan, South Carolina, was named "Men-Riv Park" and Charleston Air Force Base had a "Rivers Gate." Falcon Elementary School, near an air force base in Altus, Oklahoma, was renamed L. Mendel Rivers Elementary School in April 1970, because of the town's appreciation for Mendel's allowing an air force training school to located there instead of Charleston. (The base had recently been downsized and the community was suffering financially.) Far away in Vietnam, Cam Rahn Bay had its own Mendel Rivers Parkway.

California Governor Ronald Reagan visits Mendel in Washington.

Out and About with VIPs

VIP is an acronym for "Very Important Person." Over the years we have met many influential, rich and famous people, the kind of celebrity who makes the news. I used to make a silly joke about my being a VUP, a Very Unimportant Person. Celebrity and power attract each other and sometimes the tagalongs seem to have a little difficulty with the role they are asked to play.

Mendel had become friends with Jack Kennedy when he was a member of Congress. Jack earned the reputation for being a "three-day congressman," for he was usually in Washington only Tuesday through Thursday. His office was located three doors down from the old House Armed Services Committee suite in the Cannon Office Building. The suite had at one time been occupied by James Knox Polk. We were invited to Jack's wedding to Jackie O, but we had a conflicting schedule—a trip to Europe.

In 1960 we happened to meet President-elect Kennedy on a Palm Beach dock while we were visiting the Charles Johnsons. Charles and Edith Johnson were delightful hosts. They loved to throw parties and to have guests visit them. Our entire family once stayed, very pleasantly, in the servant quarters of their huge house in Biltmore Forest. Charles made a fortune in car dealerships. His yacht was moored next to the Kennedys'.

Frank Boykin and his wife were also in our group. Frank was a colorful member of Congress from Alabama. His motto was, "Everything is made for love." Coming from a humble background, he was extraordinarily successful in business. He seemed to have the Midas touch. What Frank Boykin invested in, even when he didn't intend to, made money. For example, he purchased land in Alabama strictly as a hunting preserve. Soon thereafter, he learned it contained one of the largest subterranean salt domes in the world, and the mineral rights alone were worth millions. He gave his wife, Ocello (pronounced Oss-la), many handsome jewels, which she wore proudly. Her nickname was "Diamond Lil."

Frank admired Mendel and wrote him many flattering letters, all of which expressed in an entire page what anyone else would have said in a sentence. Frank was the most voluble man I ever knew. His letters were run-on, and so were his thoughts. Mendel said he was regarded in Congress as a "clown." But he was kind to Mendel, and Mendel loved him. Frank was less clever in politics than in business. His state, Alabama, lost population in the 1960 census, and the state lost one seat in the House of Representatives, so its congressmen were forced to run against each other, with the bottom vote getter losing his seat. Frank trailed the ticket.

Back to Palm Beach and the Kennedys: When I left to greet our hostess, Mendel and the Boykins chatted with JFK. I wasn't even aware of Kennedy's invitation to come to lunch the next day. Mrs. Boykin and the men were delighted, naturally, and planned to go, but Edith, our hostess, and I felt that the invitation was much too casual for ladies to accept without a more formal invitation from one of the Kennedy ladies, as that was considered good manners in those days. We decided to wait until Jackie or his mother seconded the invitation.

Nobody called that evening or the next morning. Edith and I went bargain shopping while Mrs. Boykin remained on the yacht, waiting for the phone to ring. When Edith and I returned to her apartment to deposit our treasures later that morning, the telephone was shrilling as we opened the door. It was Frank Boykin asking why we had not come to the Kennedys.

"We weren't sure the women were invited," Edith told him.

"Well, they expect you all right. You get Ocello and come on."

So the three of us proceeded to the Kennedy home where we were admitted by Secret Service men. We had to go through a covered passageway before we reached a courtyard, where we were greeted by a fat Irish maid in a white uniform. "You'll find Mr. Kennedy at the pool," she said, indicating the direction with a wave of her arm.

We made our way over the lawn to where Jack Kennedy was floating in a swimming pool. I will never forget the way he casually reached up a wet hand, which we were forced to shake as we awkwardly bent over the edge of the pool.

"Just sit down," he told us. "I haven't finished my swim."

We seated ourselves in comfortable poolside chairs. After a while we were joined by Joe Kennedy and our husbands. Part of our conversation remains vivid even after all this time. Ocello Boykin admired Edith's sweater.

"I got one like it in Hong Kong for twenty-five dollars, and they cost eighty here. What did you pay for yours?"

"I think about that, maybe seventy-five."

"Where did you get it?"

"Saks."

At this point Mendel tried to bring me into the conversation, asking, "Where did you get your dress?"

Although I never shopped for clothes at Sears, Roebuck, it just happened that I liked a dress on a model that I had seen in Sears while shopping for some house paint. "Sears, Roebuck," I said, expecting everyone to laugh. There was deadly silence.

No, it wasn't the clever, funny one-liner I had hoped to impress the Kennedys with. I shouldn't have done that to Mendel. But the Sears dress was pretty, and I liked it! It looked good on me. I guess Mendel was embarrassed by my comment, along with everybody else. Later that day, he handed me a fifty-dollar bill and told me to get myself something pretty.

Rose Kennedy joined our group at poolside. She was a tactful lady who started out in a lovely picture hat, but who hurriedly went back into the house to deposit it when she saw that none of us wore hats. Jackie, who was expecting with John-John, never did appear. I sat at the table by old Joe, who entertained Lyndon Johnson, who arrived late, and me with reminiscences of his life in Boston and as an ambassador in London.

In 1960, when we lived on Trinity Drive near Episcopal High School in Alexandria, we had an unexpected and delightful houseguest, the Honorable Oscar Herrero. He had been the Cuban Consul in Charleston under the Batista regime. We had gotten to be friends with him and his wife while they were living in our fair city.

After Castro took over, Mr. Herrero was dedicated to the liberation of Cuba. He had come to Washington for an interview with Admiral Arleigh Burke, Chief of Naval Operations. We invited him for lunch, and, to our delight, his visit was eventually extended for a month. (Due to visa problems, his wife had been detained in Mexico for a month while she was visiting their daughter.)

Mr. Herrero had escaped from Cuba on the last boat. He talked about what was really happening on the island, commenting that the *New York Times* was portraying Castro as an agrarian reformer, a sort of modern-day Robin Hood. He told us that Castro was actually a Communist.

Mendel had already spoken against Castro in 1959. He asked Mr. Herrero for further details, thinking that he would schedule a speech in the House. Mr. Herrero produced reams of beautiful, flowery prose describing the conditions in Cuba. As it would have been impossible to make a speech from such material, I offered to help convert it into something more in Mendel's style. For several days Mr. Herrero and I worked long hours on the material. Mendel scheduled the speech.

By the time we finished rewriting Mr. Herrero's comments, there were only a few hours left for Mendel to prepare his talk. I rushed Mr. Herrero into Washington. As luck would have it, Frances Palmer, the sister of my brother's widow, had planned a luncheon in my honor that day. It was too late for me to back out, so I dashed to her home in Alexandria. Unfortunately, by the time I arrived, the luncheon was over. Some of the guests graciously stayed on while I ate in the living room from a tray perched on my lap.

As quickly as was courteous, I drove back to Washington to accompany Mr. Herrero to the House Gallery. Sadly, we watched Mendel deliver his address to an almost empty House. Congress was not in full session due to an upcoming recess. There was no press coverage at all in the evening papers.

Mendel was deeply disappointed that his speech concerning vital national security interests had been ignored. The office mailed out thousands of copies of the speech to friends, but it received virtually no national publicity from a liberal press that disdained the politics of conservative Southerners. History has proven Mendel, not the *New York Times*, was right about Castro. Most of the time Mendel had good political instincts, and he never hesitated to speak the truth, even when it was unpopular.

Over the years Mendel became known for his "Bird Luncheons." The name sounds innocuous, but they were far more than mere excuses to get a bite to eat. Mendel would contact favored constituents, usually well-to-do supporters in the rural counties of the First Congressional District, and they would arrange to have watermelons, tomatoes, flowers and freshly killed game flown up from the District to Washington. The constituents were proud to contribute. Mendel would brag about them by name, who sent what and how much. The Bird Luncheons became an annual event, and Mendel would use the occasion to honor a friend (General Douglas MacArthur) or colleague (Vice President Hubert Humphrey) or sometimes a group (the Chairmen of the Joint Chiefs of Staff). The constituents who provided the refreshments were always invited, and they were frequently quite happy to travel the 525 miles to Washington, to be recognized by Mendel in the presence of the nation's powerful. Mendel boasted that "anyone who's anyone in the Military-Industrial Complex is here today."

Before Admiral McCain* took over the Pacific Command, Mendel had a luncheon in his honor on July 19, 1968. It was wonderful to see the ease with which Mendel entertained. He looked very handsome in his light silk suit. He wore a brown tie with tiny, wiggly, distorted letters in what appeared to be a monogram but which, stretched out and magnified, spelled the words of a dirty phrase schoolboys scribble on walls. Mendel was still a schoolboy at heart.

The luncheon was in the Speaker's Dining Room. Speaker McCormack, a close friend of Mendel's, let us use his china, glassware and silver. Mendel's invaluable office manager, Mrs. Bull, had ordered beautiful flower arrangements with a price limit of only twenty-five dollars. There were three bowls of roses in yellow, pink and talisman shade. They were especially lovely.

I got there quite early for once. After having my hair done, I raced home, changed my dress and arrived before anyone else. There were fifty men and four women (Ocello Boykin, Anna Chennault, Roberta McCain and me). I chatted with the Boykins in the dining room while a large crowd gathered outside in the hall.

I went out and greeted Anna Chennault, who had come with a congressman from Ohio who left after escorting her there. Anna Chennault has been well received in Washington because she was the pretty, petite, savvy widow of the famed World War II commander of the Flying Tigers, General Claire Chennault. She possessed that aura of dainty femininity so characteristic of Oriental women.

After a while, we went into the dining room. I was seated between Paul Nitze, Secretary of the Navy, and Admiral McCain. Secretary Ignatious was the other guest at the head table. Mendel had placed Admiral McCain on his right and Mrs. McCain on his left. The Boykins were seated at the table around the corner. Only the head table had place cards for the guests.

---

* McCain's son John was a navy pilot who was shot down over North Vietnam. He gained national respect for the way he conducted himself as a prisoner of war when the Communists tried to make him a political pawn due to his father's position. John McCain replaced Barry Goldwater in the U.S. Senate and ran for President in 2000. When he beat the Republican front-runner Governor George W. Bush in the New Hampshire primary, he dashed to South Carolina to campaign. This was the primary where George W. Bush performed his infamous pandering to Christian conservatives at Bob Jones University in Greenville, a successful ploy that won him the South Carolina primary and arguably the Republican nomination. McCain was the first political candidate to successfully use e-mail for fundraising, raising $500,000 in a single day.

Left to right: Marwee, Admiral McCain, Mendel, Roberta McCain and Secretary Ignatious at one of Mendel's celebrated Bird Luncheons in the Capitol Speaker's Dining Room, 1968. Only rarely were ladies included.

Mendel tapped the water glass with a knife for attention. "Since I did not invite the Chaplain, I will officiate." He then proceeded to make a very lovely prayer and blessing, much better than many professional prayers. We sat down, and then Mendel offered a warm welcome and promised there would be no more speeches.

When we started eating, Nitze asked me, "Did Mendel start making speeches as soon as he could talk?" I told him of Mendel's being so shy in law school that he could not stand up and answer questions he had studied and knew. Nitze told me that he had never spoken to more than five people at once until a few years ago when he came to Washington and had to address a large group at a hotel as a fill-in for his superior (the Secretary of the Navy, I think). On the way over, he said he thought of running away or dying. Fortunately, he was met at the hotel by a delightful man who also sat by him at the luncheon and put him at ease enough that he was up to the challenge when he was called upon to address the crowd. Nitze was an attractive man. (Mendel said he thought he was the one who was always gutting him over at the Pentagon.)

Halfway through the meal, Speaker McCormack appeared. Mendel told him that when he declined, he had invited me in his place. Mendel got up and moved to a seat beside Mrs. Boykin so that McCormack could sit in his usual spot at the head of the table. The Speaker ignored the meal that was brought for him and chatted for a while. As a courtesy Mendel asked him to say a few words.

McCormack stood up and spoke a few words, and a few more, and more, and more, and more. When he started, the group thoroughly enjoyed his remarks about his friendship with McCain's father and the account of how they had helped a young officer named Tom Collins who was continually getting into scrapes. McCormack might have stopped then, but he was "The Speaker," so he spoke further.

The group slowly lost interest. People slouched down and became restless. When McCormack turned and called Admiral McCain "Colonel," it was unfortunate. He was oblivious to everything but the intoxication of addressing an audience. Even when the Majority Leader, Carl Albert, came in to give him a message, he ignored him. Carl stood behind Mendel, looking noncommittal, while the sweet old man, who was so kind to come to Mendel's party in the midst of his crowded days, droned on and on. When he eventually finished and Albert did speak to him, he left in a hurry to attend a luncheon honoring members who had served fifty years, an engagement that he had obviously forgotten.

Mendel then introduced each guest. Everyone remained huddled close together—Frank Jameson, Admiral Rickover, Jake Smart (the head of Euro, who had flown over for the party), Jerry Ford, lots of other members of Congress and top officers—fifty in all. He rattled off those names with great ease, making a brief remark about each person. He only faltered once, and yet McCain had selected all the guests. I find it wonderful that Mendel, with his dreary days at North Charleston as a background, could hold his own so beautifully with men who started off with good schools and social props, and that he could actually outshine most of them.

We first met syndicated columnist Drew Pearson at his daughter's wedding during Mendel's first term in Congress. The groom's father was Homer Comings, a Justice Department friend of Mendel's. Many prominent Washingtonians attended the wedding reception at the Carlton Hotel; all the guests were checked three times before they were admitted. We were introduced to Pearson as we went down the receiving line. For a long time Mendel and I read his column, Washington Merry-Go-Round, and listened to his radio program.

After Mendel became influential in military appropriations, Pearson sniped at him whenever he had the least opportunity, often calling him a "security risk" because of his drinking. There was a kernel of truth in his columns: Mendel had a problem, as did many other congressmen, including some never criticized by Pearson. But Mendel loved his country. He was a congressman, not a general or a spy. He rarely had access to his country's most sensitive secrets.

We felt Pearson's articles were misrepresentations, partial truths and sometimes outright lies designed to wound politically and humiliate personally. Some of Pearson's "scoops" came from dead people. They were hurtful, and Mendel despised the man. He passed out numerous copies of the Kluckhorn and Franklin book that exposed Pearson's journalistic tactics. Pearson once wrote an especially outrageous column that claimed that Chairman Rivers had passed out near an open safe and that its classified contents were strewn all over the floor. It was common knowledge on the Hill that sensitive information was never stored where Pearson alleged the incident occurred.

In June 1966, Pearson wrote a nasty article about Mendel's drying up at Bethesda Naval Hospital that appeared the day Mendel was scheduled to sponsor a major military appropriations bill. Outraged, Mendel's colleagues retaliated. When he stood to present the legislation, Speaker McCormack, who was a strong anti-Communist and a good friend, introduced Mendel as "one of the greatest Americans I have ever met." Mendel received extensive Floor praises and finally a standing ovation. Such praises just don't happen on the Floor of the House. The drinking was never mentioned. Mendel was deeply gratified for this unprecedented act of support. Everyone else was relieved that his position on national defense had not been compromised by Pearson's article. Known for his quick, pithy retorts, Mendel was later quoted as saying that he had to quit going to the hospital: "It's bad publicity."

In 1968 Pearson and Jack Anderson published their blockbuster, *The Case Against Congress*. About eight pages were devoted to Mendel. It contained lots of distortions, but I could not help but enjoy some of their funny cracks. For instance, it said that in Mendel's district, the military installations broke out like brown spots on an old man's hand. They wrote that one of Mendel's aides (not named Dillard) had testified before a federal grand jury called by Bobby Kennedy and that $30,000 had passed under the table from a contractor named Kelly. Kelly didn't give Mendel or Dillard any $30,000, only a case of Scotch in gratitude for Mendel's getting him an appointment with Admiral Wills. The authors made great sport of the honors Mendel received, of the military brass that bowed and scraped to him and of his solicitation for Carl Vinson.

There was a lot of speculation about how Drew Pearson managed to punctuate Mendel's every trip to Bethesda Naval Hospital with an ugly column. For a fee, any number of people could have provided Pearson with unfavorable information. One rumor was that a senior Rivers staff member was the informant. Mendel never confronted the man, preferring to unceremoniously transfer him back to the Charleston office; the man resigned shortly thereafter. Another speculation was that the ex-wife of a former staffer was the culprit. I personally witnessed the thinly veiled contempt of a military attaché who was assigned to escort Mendel in Europe during one of his drinking episodes. In addition, the drinking was publicized by Mendel himself, who, as one friend recalled, "would get on the phone and call the President and other people and ramble on."

When he was "on the wagon," Mendel could serve liquor and never drink a drop. But, knowing it could happen again at any time, everyone tried to protect him from himself. His staff once put ginger ale in a champagne glass when he was obliged to make a toast to the Chancellor of Germany. Russ Blandford witnessed a military attaché, who was known to have a drinking problem, hand Mendel a full glass of liquor at a Washington reception. It was supposed to be a soft drink. Mendel took a sip, realized it was alcohol and made a funny face. He then proceeded to quickly polish off the rest of the beverage although he had not consciously intended to start another binge.

His office staff, friends and family protected Mendel, and no one witnessed the full spectrum of the havoc his drinking caused. More remarkable was the respect and support he had from his colleagues. With extraordinary drive and determination Mendel was able to return to Congress again and again after his binges and fight for our military at a time when conflicting ideologies were ripping our nation apart.

Eddie Hébert, Mendel's successor as Chairman, commented on how Drew Pearson would get on Mendel's back and how Mendel wanted to strike back at Pearson. "I'd say, Mendel, don't you understand that Pearson's column does not appear in every paper in the country? The Associated Press and the UPI appear in every paper in the country. If you get on the Floor and denounce Pearson, the wire services will have to tell why you denounce Pearson, and they're going to have to say what he said about you that you deny, so you let everybody know it. Keep your mouth shut."

It was no secret that there was a lot of bad blood between Mendel and Drew Pearson. One night we were at the White House attending a dinner party given in honor of Speaker McCormack. We were circulating around the East Room before the receiving line was set up. Receiving lines were set up by aides according to rank, with husbands preceding wives.

Mendel spied Pearson across the room. He commented, "Isn't that Drew Pearson? I am going over there and *fix* him." I trotted along beside his determined strides, delivering an anxious plea, "Oh, no, Mendel, don't do anything here! You can't make a boor of yourself. Just leave him alone!" I had horrible visions of Mendel carrying out his oft-repeated threat to knock Pearson down the next time he saw him.

Mendel ordered me to leave him alone, and we walked up to the group that included Pearson. Mendel stood about a foot away from him, thrust out his chin and glared at the columnist. Although Pearson noticed his presence, he continued to talk with utmost aplomb. He was a rather distinguished looking old man, and I have no doubt he was probably used to enraged congressmen. We were like a tableau.

So, when I saw that I couldn't deter Mendel, I slunk off and stood by Betty and Gerry Ford. We watched from afar. Mendel continued to stand right beside Pearson, who nonchalantly ignored him. After several minutes, much to everyone's relief, Mendel finally strode back and joined us. (Gerald Ford asked Mendel to switch parties and become a Republican. This switch would have cost him his seniority.)

Why did Drew Pearson despise Mendel so? I don't think it had much to do with Mendel or with the alcohol. In my opinion, Drew Pearson decided that certain members of Congress represented all that he saw as the backward part of America. Mendel Rivers was one of the most flamboyant of those members of Congress, and Drew was in a position to try to discredit those congressmen. It wasn't personal. It never is in Washington. Washington is far too vicious to be personal.

There was a humorous side to Drew Pearson's unwanted publicity. When one has been associated with Congress for a while, the expression "Floor of the House" becomes so familiar it needs no explanation. But to outsiders it had other meanings than the main chamber of Congress.

Once an irate man telephoned our home and demanded to speak to the Congressman. "I'm sorry," I told him, "he is not here now."

"Well, I know he is there. You just tell him Oscar Snertz wants to talk to him. He'll talk to me."

"I'm sorry, Mr. Snertz, I can't. He's on the Floor of the House."

"Oh, I see. Drunk again, eh?" Mr. Snertz hung up the receiver.

Proud Grandpa escorts Edward (left), Robert (right) and Peggy on a VIP tour of the Capitol, 1969.

Mendel's association with Lyndon Johnson went back a long way. According to Russ Blandford, LBJ had been on the Armed Services Committee when he was a congressman, and the committee members disliked him. Johnson was known as an "if he couldn't win 'em, he'd buy them" type of guy. He was a chain smoker. Mendel told Russ about a disagreement the two of them had while crossing on the street between the Cannon and Longworth Buildings. The interchange become so heated that the two exchanged physical blows. Johnson was the larger man.

In 1964, Lyndon Johnson was the incumbent President and the Democratic nominee for President to succeed himself. He was JFK's surviving Vice-President, and he was the odds-on favorite to win reelection. The Democrats were headed toward a resounding victory in November.

But not in the South, and especially not in South Carolina. There, the Republicans, under the flag of Barry Goldwater and the "new" conservatives, were gaining converts among white voters. In the South, times were changing. Lyndon Johnson understood that well. He wanted to win, but he also wanted to win in the South. He sent his wife, First Lady "Lady Bird" Johnson, on an old-fashioned "whistle stop" train tour of the South. It was called the Lady Bird Special, and wherever it stopped, Lady Bird held a rally for her husband. It stopped in Charleston in the fall of 1964.

Lady Bird and the local Democrats held a rally at Pinehaven Shopping Center, and Mendel attended. He probably felt he had no choice if he wanted to become Chairman, and he dragged me along. It was not a pretty event. There we sat, on a high wooden platform in the cold evening breeze in a North Charleston shopping center—Lady Bird, Mendel, the other local Democratic officials and me. The crowd was not friendly. It was mostly youthful, white, enthusiastic Republicans, clean-scrubbed children of privilege, caught up in their new political cause, cheering for Goldwater. They heckled poor Lady Bird, and they tried to heckle Mendel, who was embarrassed. After all, this was his district. He was the local congressman. Lady Bird was his guest, in his town, and he couldn't control his own people.

But Mendel wouldn't be intimidated. He stared at the hecklers and spoke directly to them: "In 1952, I supported the Republican candidate for President of the United States, and what did it get me? I got a Republican President who tried to close down half of our military installations here in the First Congressional District, and believe me, I got a belly full of Dwight Eisenhower!"

It was fine rhetoric that might have drawn applause ten years earlier, but it didn't impress the hecklers. They continued their noise, and so did Mendel Rivers. He blasted the Republicans, and the young Republicans heckled. The louder he spoke, the more they heckled. Mendel was angry.

I watched the hecklers carefully. Gradually, I realized I knew those young people. They were the sons and daughters of my friends from church, my friends who lived below Broad Street and my friends from the John Birch Society. The hecklers were from "my people," and they were opposing my husband.

Mendel was a conservative Southern Democrat in a party increasingly dominated by Northern and West Coast liberals. Southern conservative Democrats were fleeing to the Republican Party. Mendel couldn't go there. His chairmanship, indeed all of his political power, depended upon his continued good favor with the national Democratic Party. So he yelled at the young Republicans, the faces of the future, and they yelled back at Mendel, the face of the past, and I kept my mouth shut.

It was a long night. Lady Bird was happy to leave Charleston. But she and Lyndon never forgot Mendel's performance. He stood up to his own constituents for a woman from Texas. In order to protect her, he made his own voters angry. In politics, that is the ultimate self-sacrifice. After that awful night, Mendel scheduled an extended trip to Europe and did not return until things calmed down back home.

Some time later, we attended an afternoon affair at the White House, a reception for the brass hats of the uniformed services. We went to the East Gate and were told to go to the Pennsylvania Avenue entrance, which annoyed Mendel. He had to inch the car through the parked cars in the lot along that street. I waited for him on the front porch and watched cabinet members and their wives arriving.

When Mendel returned, we went upstairs to the Oval Drawing Room. Guests included the Secretary of Defense, the Joint Chiefs of Staff, four Congressional Medal of Honor recipients, Bill Bates and us—quite an exclusive group!

Lady Bird received us graciously. She was particularly nice to me, coming to speak to me about four times. LBJ came in late, and we had lots of pictures taken with him. He left the room, briefly, and brought back a tie he had brought Mendel from Europe. It was gratifying to see the expression of friendship.

Mendel invited Lady Bird to visit us in Charleston next spring, and she promised to come. (Later, I mentioned that it would be to his political ruination if she took him up on the invitation next year. I reminded him of the cold reception Charleston had given Lady Bird when she visited in 1964. Mendel said he would handle it.)

When we went downstairs, we realized that the Armed Services' top brass and their wives had been crushed together in the East Room waiting for only heavens knows how long. A lot of people came up to speak to us and asked where we had been all that time. Everyone proceeded to go through another receiving line. (During LBJ's administration, liquor was always served to the guests waiting in the receiving lines.)

After the reception, we returned to our car at the curb. En route, a guard said, "Sir, the Secret Service found a gun in your car. It has been removed."

Mendel spewed out, "You go get it and tell them to keep their goddamned hands off my gun!"

I would have been aflutter after I had been caught carrying a gun at the White House. Mendel was offended because his car was searched.

On another visit to the White House, LBJ was very cordial. Mendel told him, "Come on and get some pictures with me. Some day they will be a happy memory for you."

Mendel with President Lyndon Johnson.

Mendel was probably one of the few persons extant who didn't get excited when someone told him, "The White House is calling you." His standard reply was, "The White House? Find out who it is. If it is not the President, I'm not coming. I told them I wouldn't talk to those children."

Years later when Mendel lay dying in the hospital in Birmingham, Lyndon or Lady Bird called me from Texas every day to enquire of his health. This thoughtfulness was much appreciated.

Mendel really liked Senator Hubert Humphrey, just like he liked the Kennedys. He even honored Humphrey at a Bird Luncheon. On July 31, 1968, we were invited to a dinner for Humphrey. I was not elated at that prospect. Mendel thought it would be a good gesture to attend. After all, he was Chairman only by the vote of his colleagues.

Someone sent Mendel two tickets to the Humphrey affair. They cost $500 each. I went with Jan and Gene Norris from up the street and Mr. and Mrs. Bass, friends who were in the aviation business. (They were very naive.)

I sat by Mendel and Senator Russell Long, the Kingfishes' son. He was very friendly and kept saying he was in agreement with Wallace. At our table were Governor Smith of West Virginia and his man, a mulatto, Dr. Matthew and Mr. Olsen on Humphrey's staff.

Mrs. Vance Hartke came up and draped herself on Long's shoulder. She was rather pretty. She hoped to persuade Long to attend a party she was organizing. The Senator told her that he would attend if the party were a small one. Mrs. Hartke said, "About thirty or thirty-five then?" He replied, "No, about five or seven or nine." Mrs. Hartke kept all those men at our table standing during our meal while she ignored them and tried to cajole Senator Long.

I kept being spoken to by table hoppers. There was loud applause for Humphrey even as we were retreating after his speech. This is the sort of trivia I wish I recorded for years, sidelights on the Washington scene. I am not sorry when I go out in those mobs of Washington pseudo-society that we haven't gone in for any level of Washington society.

After the election, that horrid Representative Richard Bolling of Missouri tried to remove Mendel from his committee chairmanship, claiming he did not support the Democratic nominee and betrayed the party. Although Bolling and his liberal friends in Congress were unsuccessful, it proved that Mendel was going to continue to have troubles with left-wing Democrats.

On June 4, 1999, Peggy and I met with Russ Blandford, who had been Chief Counsel for the House Armed Services Committee. Blandford commented that in light of history, Mendel died at the right time. Russ had witnessed the shifting power structure in the Democratic Party during the early seventies when the conservative Southern Democrats were eased out by an increasing number of liberal Democrats from other parts of the country. Mendel had gotten into trouble for sticking his neck out and supporting Eisenhower back in 1952. The Democratic caucus had subsequently declared that anyone who supported non-Democrats could be stripped of seniority. This was a very difficult time for Mendel. He was walking a political tightrope. In retrospect, I realized that he was under enormous pressure, and wish I had been more supportive of the role he was forced to play. His successor, Eddie Hébert, was "deposed" when he was not able to retain Democratic support for his chairmanship.

I never understood the bond Mendel had with certain people. My Charleston heritage got in the way. We were Episcopalians, descendants of Anglicans, Scotch Presbyterians and French Huguenots. We seldom associated socially with anybody else. It is not that we disliked them; they just were not "one of us." Baptists were a particular source of amazement because they did not drink, they did not smoke, they did not dance nor did they play cards; they went to church all the time and sponsored "Blue Laws" that forbade conducting business on the Sabbath.

Mendel had no such prejudices. In the North Area, there were limited outlets for boys. When new churches came, Mendel tried them all and at one time or another had been an officer in the BYPU, the Epworth League, Christian Endeavor and the Episcopal Young People's Service League; he even won the boys' "Best Camper" cup at the Kanuga Episcopal retreat. Mendel later formed strong friendships with John Hamrick, founder of the Baptist College at Charleston, and Bob Jones, founder of the university that bears his name in Greenville.

Mendel became friends with the Evangelist Billy Graham in the late forties after he heard Graham speak at one of his rallies in Washington. One summer the girls went to camp with his daughters; we visited their North Carolina retreat numerous times. Billy Graham had spent the night in our Charleston home on several occasions. Before one of the celebrated Bird Luncheons, Billy Graham stopped by Mendel's office to change his clothes after playing golf with the President. Of course the evangelist was a teetotaler, so when he popped by unexpectedly, the staff had to scramble to hide the bar in Mendel's inner sanctum that had been set up to entertain the arriving dignitaries. Predictably, Mendel could not understand why they had failed to get Dr. Graham to sign the guest book that day.

Mendel taught me to be punctual the hard way. I was getting off to a poor start the morning we were going to a special Citadel function. I forget now whether the speaker was President Eisenhower or Billy Graham. Mendel was determined to be ahead of time, something inconceivable to Charlestonians who generally regarded being on time as a half an hour after the party starts.

When I wasn't ready, Mendel suddenly shouted, "The hell with you! You get there the best way you can. I'm going!"

I was horrified as I watched him back down the driveway and leave. Frantically, I started calling neighbors and relatives trying to get a ride into town, for one of the children had my car.

The Reverend Billy Graham spoke before The Citadel Corps of Cadets. *Left to right*: Mendel, Rennie Clark, Billy Graham and Mark Clark, President of The Citadel.

I was greatly relieved when the doorbell rang and I opened it to greet the mother of one of the girls' friends. I asked her for a ride, and she obligingly started off. It was drizzling. The lady drove with extreme caution. In fact she was so cautious that I wondered if we would ever reach The Citadel. She was not renowned for sobriety or brilliance, and it did not take me long to realize that she had probably whiffed a few "hairs of the dog" before she appeared at my house. I agonized as she stayed in the slowest traffic lanes. At one point she drove carefully behind a parked car and waited there for minutes before she realized her mistake and was able to get back into traffic.

My discomfiture did not end when we reached The Citadel chapel. The ceremony had started. The entrance was deserted except for two people standing in the rain waiting for me: a resplendent cadet officer and valiant Rennie Clark, who had no intention of letting me face the embarrassment of a late entrance alone.

Once he became "The Chairman," Mendel attracted celebrity. When he visited Hollywood, he visited actor Charlton Heston, here dressed in his Moses costume. This picture made the papers.

We couldn't just sneak into a back seat in the chapel. Being VIPs, we had to be escorted by the gold-braided, red-sashed, somewhat snooty young officer. He took us into the vestry room so that we entered in the most conspicuous manner imaginable, facing the congregation. We were led to the front pew where we had to step over the legs of assorted worshipers until we finally sat down by our frowning and dignified spouses.

Rennie was a great gal. When The Citadel awarded Mendel an honorary doctorate, Rennie and I were seated side by side at the graduation; Mendel took part in the procession, wearing a gown, mortarboard and tassel. What happened next, I don't quite understand. Mendel was usually well groomed and dignified. He had poise and flair, or at least I thought so. But on that day, he somehow managed to get the tassel of his mortarboard parted on one of the points just in front of the middle of his forehead. There it dangled, neatly split in two equal little clumps. Back and forth, back and forth it swayed. It was all I could see! He looked ridiculous, and for some unfathomable reason, he didn't seem to be aware of his appearance. He just walked along, solemn and filled with pomp and circumstance—with a tassel neatly split in half and dangling in front of each of his eyes! Rennie saw it. She clutched my hand. Soon we were rippling in suppressed mirth, two schoolgirl gigglers on the very front row, the wife of the President of The Citadel and the wife of the distinguished, solemn, bi-tasseled congressman.

Farewell L. Mendel

Mendel Rivers gave his life for his country as surely as any soldier on any battlefield. At the time of his death, I was told that Mendel was considered one of the most powerful men in America, about number ten if my memory serves me correctly.

At the end of his thirty-year career in Congress, there was a saying in our hometown: "Charleston has three Rivers: the Ashley, the Cooper and the Mendel." He was an institution. People rich and poor depended upon him. In some ways his powerful position helped create the backbone of our economy. And certainly, losing him was unimaginable to the military he so fearlessly championed and to the family who loved him dearly.

Mendel had confided to me after the November 1970 election that he would not run for office again. I asked him what he would do when he left Congress. "I'll be the best damn trial lawyer Charleston ever saw," he said. "I'll turn that jury every which way but loose."

But before he left the Congress, he wanted to personally ensure that his pet projects were sponsored through properly. Nobody realized that behind a bold façade was a man dying before their very eyes. Not wanting to expose his weakness, Mendel had played his hand close to his chest; only a few doctors knew how serious his heart condition had become. They had told him early in 1970 that he had only an 80 percent chance if he were operated on immediately. He chose to wait.

Things were not going well. By 1970 My Lai had shocked the nation, the bloody Tet offensive was history and the inhumane treatment of our POWs had become widely publicized. The strident antiwar faction was gaining

Marwee and Mendel, August 1970.

momentum; the Paris peace negotiations were bogged down. Our nation was war weary, and Mendel was reluctant to undergo heart surgery before the Congressional session ended. In addition, three milestone events had been planned toward the end of 1970, and Mendel wasn't about to miss any of them.

Mendel received the D.C. Chapter of the Air Force Association Distinguished American Award in August. This was a major recognition, if not the premier recognition of his career. The head table guests were the Military Who's Who: Deputy Secretary of Defense, Secretary of the Army, Chairman of the Joint Chiefs of Staff, Chief of Naval Operations, U.S. Air Force Chief of Staff, Commandant of the Marine Corps, Under Secretary of the Air Force, U.S. Army Vice Chief of Staff, U.S. Air Force Chief of Chaplains, President of the Air Force Association, President of the Navy League, President of the National Defense Transportation Association, President of the D.C. Navy League, President of the D.C. National Defense Transportation Association, Chief Counsel of the House Armed Services Committee and Senator Strom Thurmond. The room was crowded with admirers.

The most popular conservative speaker in the nation, Vice President Spiro Agnew, was asked to make the Tribute. Having the much-acclaimed Agnew honor Mendel was a coup for the Air Force Association sponsors and the highest compliment Mendel could have been paid. At the time, we thought this was as good as it gets, for the Vice-President was well known for his pithy, often witty remarks about the liberals. (It was a huge blow to conservatives when Agnew was later discredited.)

Speaker John W. McCormack must have declined an invitation, as his name was not on the program. He came in late when everyone was eating. He refused to make any fuss and stood unobtrusively in the back corner of the room leaning up against the wall while the speeches were being made. It was obvious that he had attended to pay homage to his colleague solely out of friendship.

Peggy and my grandson Robert attended that auspicious occasion. We were all proud of Mendel sitting at the head table chatting with the Vice President. They were joking and kidding around like two schoolboys. At our table a Congressional Medal of Honor recipient had an interesting story to tell. He was a pilot. His buddy was shot down over North Vietnam while they were on a mission, and he was ordered back to base. Knowing they could both be captured, he disobeyed orders, landed his plane just long enough for his buddy to jump in and then flew back. He was disarmingly candid about the medal, saying that they needed heroes; in other circumstances, he would have been court-martialed. Nearby was a handsome young soldier in a wheelchair. His friends were touchingly attentive, and then I looked down. He had no legs, only stubs. One could tell by the height of the torso that he had been a strapping, tall young man. That soldier in the wheelchair underscored the heavy price we were paying for Vietnam. I felt great humility looking at that fine young man whose life had been so abruptly altered. I never forgot him.

The second major function was the October 27, 1970 dedication of the L. Mendel Rivers Library at the Baptist College at Charleston. John Hamrick, President of the college, and Mendel had been friends for many years. Both were forward-thinking men who realized how important it was to inculcate sound principles into our youth so that our heritage could be understood and preserved. Both sensed that the greatness of America was based on a strong belief in Biblical principles, which they considered the foundation of our country's legal system. Mendel felt that one of the most satisfying experiences of his years in Congress had been having a small share in the building of the Baptist College.

Dr. Hamrick loved to tell this story about Mendel: the college had had difficulty in getting the building loan for the library approved. Before a speaking engagement, Mendel asked Dr. Hamrick about the loan's status because he wanted to announce the loan in his talk. When he was told that it had not yet been approved, Mendel was disgusted. He picked up the phone and called the responsible party who gave him the usual, predictable bureaucratic double-talk. Mendel's reaction was classic, "While I hold on to this line, you get your committee together on your other line, and I'll hang on until I get your answer." As Dr. Hamrick told it, "He hung on. He got the answer. He made the announcement that morning."

At the library groundbreaking ceremony on November 27, 1968, Dan Houghton, Chairman of the Board of Lockheed Aircraft Corporation, flew in to make the principal address. Mendel spoke for over half an hour. At one point, a sudden breeze caught the flag beside the speakers' stand and whipped it across Mendel's cheek. His reply was truly Mendelian: "It could be a lot worse. But for the grace of God and the courage of our people, it could be the Hammer and Sickle." The audience, consisting of several hundred pastors, denominational leaders and friends of the college, loved it. It was a fine occasion.

At the library dedication two years later, the rains threatened all day. They finally blew in, just as the ceremonies began. It was a day of great honor for Mendel. House Armed Services Committee Ranking Member Eddie Hébert made the introductory remarks; "The Star Spangled Banner" was played by the renowned trumpeter Al Hirt. Mendel's speech was to be followed by evangelist Billy Graham. Toward the end of his remarks,

Mendel commented that the rains were subsiding just in time for Billy Graham to speak. Unfortunately, when Dr. Graham took the podium, the rains started again, this time with intensity. Shielding his face from the downpour, Billy Graham laughed and announced, "Mendel Rivers! You may be a great congressman, but you are no prophet!"

After his death, the school hung a portrait of Mendel at the library entrance showing him speaking at the podium with a huge unfurled American flag in the background.

The third event was the keel laying of the USS *South Carolina DLGN 37* on December 1 at Newport News, Virginia.

Mendel had fought hard to get nuclear vessels through the Congress. The *South Carolina* was a nuclear-powered guided missile frigate. It was a big victory for the Armed Services Committee and for Mendel. The Soviet navy had been rapidly ramping up, and Mendel was determined not to let our navy "melt away" under his watch. He relied heavily on the intelligence information provided by Vice Admiral Hyman Rickover, known as "the Father of the Nuclear Navy."

Rickover had an autocratic, sour disposition and was detested by many for his unorthodox recruiting methods for the nuclear propulsion services. Mendel was one of the most avid supporters of a nuclear navy and had saved Rickover's job. Rickover had "superannuated," meaning that he had become too old to serve on active duty in the United States Navy. But Mendel and others faithfully caused Congress to enact, and then to reenact, special laws permitting Rickover to remain on active duty, years and years after he would otherwise have had to retire. (Admiral Rickover was extremely loyal to Mendel. After his death, Rickover used his influence to have a nuclear-powered attack submarine named *L. Mendel Rivers*; he corresponded with me for over twenty years thereafter.)

The keel laying ceremony was unusually elaborate. Republican South Carolina Senator Strom Thurmond was on the Senate Armed Services Committee and, according to protocol, he outranked Mendel. Thurmond was asked to make the keynote address. I was told privately that this was a strictly political choice. (Is anything not political in the world of the military-industrial complex?)

But the primus inter pares invitation to Thurmond offended Rickover. He did not want Mendel to be slighted in any way. Mendel was asked to make the closing remarks, and the ceremonial plate attached to the keel quoted him. It stated simply: "The American people stand to lose everything if we fail to discharge our awesome responsibilities in respect to our national defense."

Just in case there was any mistake about Mendel's importance in the occasion, I authenticated the keel by hammering a small die into the metal plate with Mendel's quotation. For good measure, Rickover asked Mendel to hammer a die beside mine. Peggy, as my "Matron of Honor," sat on the podium with all the VIPs.

The ceremonies were predictably boring. The numerous, droning speeches read endlessly from typed pages had lulled the crowd; they were restless and ready to break and eat. After Thurmond's speech, Rickover finally had the opportunity to personally make up for what he considered an enormous slight. He praised Mendel effusively. In fact, his eloquence was almost embarrassing. It was a long talk for a man who had a reputation for being rigid, serious and quiet:

> *He is one of the great men of our Congress. He is dedicated to peace, but aware of the awesome responsibility our Nation bears in defense of our freedom. Where our national security is involved he is brave, resolute, stubborn. His legislative acts are heroic....No man possesses in so high degree as he the peculiar awareness of military realities. His efforts on behalf of American security are tireless. He has a marvelous gift for stepping beyond the appearance of things, going beyond it, and penetrating to the very essence of the matter...*
>
> *He is one of the most un-intimidable men in the United States. He knows that a good leader is doing his job when half the people are following him and half are chasing him...*
>
> *The day will come when this man, one of our great legislators and a prophetic thinker, will be recognized at his true value.*

In spite of Rickover's astonishing remarks, the crowd had become lethargic. Then Chairman Rivers rose to speak. And Mendel was a seasoned speaker. He stood up, looked around and smiled broadly. Slowly, he made the customary recognitions of the VIPs on the podium, ending with, "I don't know what I can say. I think the best thing to say is, Let's eat." He laughed at his own joke.

Mendel understood timing. Like the legendary Johnny Carson, whose funniest "joke" was to suddenly glance directly into a strategically placed camera that just "happened" to catch his eye, Mendel used the magic of silence and the comedic/dramatic pause. He knew that a hungry audience would enjoy a two-line speech inviting them to eat heartily. He held their attention as he slowly glanced around and then carefully delivered his punch line. Carson would have appreciated it.

And then Mendel began his magic. Within minutes, he had the attention of everyone, picking out a dignitary here and a friend there for some personal, warm, humorous comment. It was a thing of beauty to watch. Suddenly,

Mendel became once again the "silver-tongued orator from South Carolina," December 1, 1970.

everyone present wished he would "pick me next." I watched Mendel's golfing partner, Admiral Red Rayburn, Project Manager of the *Polaris* submarine. He had flaming red hair streaked with white and loads of freckles, and he had been nearly put to asleep like the rest of us. Now he sat laughing heartily, just because Mendel had recognized him. And so did many others.

Revitalized, the crowd eagerly listened to twenty minutes of comments about a strong national defense and upcoming legislation Mendel planned to introduce to modernize the U.S. fleet. Unlike the previous speakers,

Mendel did not read a prepared speech. He was once again "the silver-tongued orator from South Carolina." He concluded: "I am determined, as is your great Committee on Armed Services, that in your lifetime your Navy will not melt away...Lord God, be with us—lest we forget this commitment with our destiny which I plan to keep, so help me God."

With Mendel's oratory still ringing in our ears, we went to lunch. Little did we realize that this was one of Mendel's last public appearances. After the meal and a lot of the usual stilted small talk, the guests began to drift away. We eventually boarded the plane of dignitaries returning to Washington. Mendel was the very last person to enter. He climbed the steps at the rear of the plane and sat in the vacant seat beside Peggy. He was pale faced and panting from the effort and simply could not catch his breath. He looked exhausted. Frightened, Peggy asked him what was wrong. He told her that his heart hurt and he was going in for open-heart surgery soon. She was shocked, for this was the first she had heard. Mendel didn't talk on the flight back and dozed off in his seat. It had been a long day. When we returned home, Mendel, who always went to bed early, uncharacteristically stayed up to visit with Peggy and Bob. She did not realize at the time that he was saying farewell in his own inimitable way.

Before he entered the hospital, however, Mendel had one last major task to perform. He had been deeply concerned about the plight of our POWs and the inhumane treatment they suffered at the hands of their captors. Torture of our POWs was an established fact of that war; some were known to have been cruelly crammed into suspended bamboo cages designed for captured jungle animals. Mendel decided to do what he could to get our men released.

At the end of November 1970, a group of army commandos staged a daring raid on the Son Tay POW compound near Hanoi. Although they arrived at the compound successfully and were prepared to complete the mission, the commandos discovered that the POWs had been hastily evacuated just before their arrival. Hanoi immediately promised to retaliate and punish the Americans still in captivity. In spite of ninety-three failed sessions prior to the raid, the growing antiwar faction condemned the action, claiming that it was damaging to the Paris peace negotiations.

Mendel was outraged by the complaints of the antiwar faction. He decided to make the commandos heroes, if he could. Secretly, he hoped they would try again and again.

Mendel liked to plan events on nationally significant dates. December 7 was the anniversary of Pearl Harbor, and he scheduled his last public appearance—a major statement in support of the commandos—for that day. On December 7, 1970, he forcefully urged his colleagues to support what became known as the "Tiger Cage Resolution" to commend the heroic commando raid. He stated in part,

> *I would want the world to know that I would tell that crowd in Hanoi, you will either treat them with human dignity or some of you will not be here tomorrow…So far as I am concerned, Mr. Speaker, if I were the President of the United States, I would deliver an ultimatum to this crowd and let them guess where the next blow was coming from.*

The resolution was adopted over the objection of the antiwar members of Congress.

Mendel's passion for a strong national defense overshadowed every other aspect of life. In that last speech, he hammered his theme one last time.

> *The future of this nation hangs by a thread. Our priceless heritage of freedom is in terrible jeopardy…*
>
> *The greatest Soviet Naval strength is in its submarine force—the largest ever created in the history of the world…The surface Naval vessels of the United States are, as compared to the Soviet Union, in worse condition than those of the undersea fleet…The Soviets now have an air superiority capability which we will be hard pressed to match.*
>
> *To some, it is a crime for the United States to be ahead of the Soviets in any area. The leaders in the Kremlin are now evidently unimpressed by both our military capability and our national determination to survive. The dissident voices in our nation who would destroy the very fabric of our society are being interpreted by the Kremlin as the voices of the American people.*
>
> *While we debate the question of maintaining our military capability, the Soviet Union forges ahead. We seem hell-bent on national suicide.*

Hearing him, no one suspected that this would be his final day in the United States Congress.

Mendel had been instrumental in obtaining $376 round-trip flights home for our servicemen in Vietnam. The first planeload of 198 servicemen landed in California on December 5. They sent a delegation to Washington to thank Mendel personally. They scheduled their ceremony to coincide with Mendel's speech and presented him with gifts and an admiral's field cap embroidered with six gold stars and "The Big Boss." Mendel proudly donned that hat and was photographed in a picture that appeared in the *Washington Post* and in numerous publications after his death.

On a personal note, it was only after I reviewed the notes from my 1968 interviews with Mendel that I realized that I had denied the obvious for years. As far back as 1954 his physician told us that although Mendel had the constitution of a bull, his rheumatic heart could not take any more alcohol abuse; another binge could kill him. He knew every drink could be his last, but he seemed powerless to quit for the next fourteen years. After Mendel had finally quit the drinking, he began to lose weight and have shortness of breath. This continued throughout 1968, 1969 and 1970. We kept hoping that his condition would improve. But by the latter part of 1970, my husband was a severely weakened man. He had lost weight for no apparent reason and became winded from climbing stairs, but so did a lot of people. He had terrible shortness of breath whenever he did the mildest exertion and his ankles swelled to an alarming size. We knew Mendel's heart was the problem.

It took a lot of courage for Mendel to undergo that open-heart surgery. It was a new procedure. The Capitol physician, Dr. Pearson, recommended Dr. John Kirkland of the University of Alabama Hospital in Birmingham, telling us that his reputation was even better than that of the pioneer open-heart surgeon from Texas, Michael De Bakey. He agreed to an operation only when he knew he could postpone it no longer. Mendel knew that his chances for recovery were uncertain at best. That last night before he left for Birmingham, Mendel hugged his son in the garage at Pinetree Road, and he started to cry. Young Mendel didn't understand. He thought his father was being silly, for he considered him invincible.

Mendel had always maintained a good relationship with the local press and made certain that the hometown papers were fully apprised of newsworthy events. He had an especially warm relationship with Barbara Williams. When announcement of his upcoming surgery hit the AP wire, Williams did not expect a personal call. Mendel told her, "They think I may go out with my feet first, but I will try to fix them," and then implied that he expected Mayor Palmer Gaillard to take his seat if anything happened. (Certainly Gaillard expected to win, for in the special election to fill Mendel's seat, it was an open secret that his wife went to Washington to look for housing while he was campaigning in the district.)

On December 8, we flew to Birmingham. The operation went smoothly, and everyone was greatly relieved. Eddie Hébert came down to confer with Mendel, and as he said later, "[The] Mendel Rivers I talked to in that hospital bed was the same Mendel Rivers that you knew…passionately dedicated to that in which he believed and barking instructions to me on what to do."

Retired President Lyndon Johnson or Lady Bird called the hospital every day to inquire about Mendel's health. President Nixon called me once expressing the same interest.

Unexpectedly, there were complications! The family flew in from all over the country. In his final hours, Mendel was hooked up to monitors and was given a tracheotomy that prevented his being able to communicate except with a pencil and pad. He, who had been such a master of words, was rendered speechless.

His last words to his son were prophetic. He could not speak, and he was frustrated, as he lay abed. He looked at his son and tried to form words. Young Mendel had no idea what he was saying. He flailed about for a pad, which young Mendel gave him, and wrote these words: Where am I?

I have often wondered, where indeed?

He was feisty up to the very end, brushing off the tender touches of those who sought to say goodnight on that last evening. We left his bedside and huddled together in the hotel, talking about nothing in particular until exhaustion overtook us. A few hours later the phone rang with the grim news.

It seems amazing that absolutely no plans had been made in the event that Mendel did not return. The family tried to carry on by getting up long before the sun rose to call friends and admirers whom they felt should not hear of Chairman Rivers's death on the six o'clock morning news. Later that awful morning the family and staff flew back to Charleston to make arrangements for the funeral.

When we arrived home, we were greeted by the minister of Grace Church. He was so impressed with his role that he had dashed over to the house when he heard we were en route. He kept trying to force me to make protocol decisions for seating the large number of VIPs who had come down from Washington and was so insensitive and self-important that he followed me into my bedroom. I could not even change my clothes to receive visitors. The children were eventually forced to usher him out, for the house had already started to fill with friends and dignitaries.

Sadly, the minister also demonstrated a less-than-Christian concern for the welfare of the magnificent honor guard that stood vigil over Mendel's casket. Mendel was laid out in state for a day before the funeral. In the lapel of his navy blue suit was a diamond-studded, solid gold American flag. (On his wrist was a platinum watch, and I have often wondered why we were so stupid as to lay such lovely jewelry in the earth. Such is the emotion of the moment.) Surrounding the casket was an honor guard that represented the five services. One of the servicemen had been in the hospital and left without authorization to participate. He knew he risked being court-martialed. They stood guard stoically hour after hour. We went to great trouble to make certain that seats were roped off exclusively for their use. Later, we learned that the church staff never bothered to inform these proud men of their reserved seating. Their seats stayed unoccupied, in a crowded church.

The military had responded quickly to the sad news. Top brass flew to Charleston from all over the world. Russ Blandford remembers recuperating from an operation in a hospital in Oberammergau, Bavaria, when a sergeant whispered to him, "The Chairman is dead. What can I do?" Blandford suggested lowering the flag to half-mast. This requires a Presidential order, and as he left the hospital, Blandford saw the flag flying in the mourning position. Flags flew at half-mast on U.S. military bases around the world.

On the cold and rainy morning of the funeral, Peggy received a touching call from a serviceman who was weeping in his hospital bed as he said, "It is raining, and I think God is crying for us all." So many servicemen looked upon Mendel as their protector, almost their father figure in the government. That young man expressed eloquently what we were all feeling. Mendel was their hero. He stood for what was fine in America, and they knew he stood for them.

The funeral for Chairman L. Mendel Rivers was extraordinary. Prior to the service, long lines of people slowly, somberly filed by the casket. Everybody followed the English tradition of a stiff upper lip. During the service not a tear was shed. The servants who attended were scandalized that no one cried. The two young grandsons were left at home, much to their dismay, so that nothing would distract from the pomp and circumstance. To this day they feel slighted for this exclusion.

President Nixon did not come, but he sent a special handwritten letter expressing his sympathy. Secretary of Defense Melvin Laird delivered the note and attended the funeral services. (Somehow I later lost that wonderful letter and it is preserved only in photographic copy in Marion's book, *Rivers Delivers*.)

After a packed, formal service at Grace Church that was piped to three other locations in Charleston, people lined the streets out of the city to pay their last respects as the funeral limousines filled with family and dignitaries passed on their way to Mendel's final resting place in St. Stephen. On Interstate 26, drivers on the opposite side of the highway, who were not required to stop, did so anyway, respectfully standing beside their parked cars, right hands laid across their hearts. It was an awesome send-off by the people of his district, for it seemed that the whole area mourned the passing of their friend as they watched the hearse drive slowly by. Watching the enormous outpouring of affection took away a little of the sorrow we all were feeling as we drove to St. Stephen.

The little St. Stephen Episcopal Church graveyard was crowded. Flowers surrounded the casket. We were seated according to protocol. Everyone was somber. Young Mendel gave a touching eulogy. It said in part:

Today, L. Mendel Rivers is laid to rest. It is fitting that he be laid here in St. Stephen, among the people with whom he grew up, for in a very real sense L. Mendel Rivers was one of the people. Everything he was came from you, and it can fairly be said he was the product of you, his people. I hope you never forget this, because he never did.

L. Mendel Rivers was the quintessence of three very human, very wonderful qualities. First, he was dynamism, movement, ceaseless activity, that drew people to him like a magnet. Secondly, he was love, so that once he had drawn people to him, they always stayed there. He had a large heart that was full of love for his people. And thirdly, he was courage. He chose his positions, his ideas, with great care. But once he had taken a stand, he never wavered, he never deviated, he never detoured. He simply didn't know how.

He quoted a poem that his father loved by John G. Neihardt

Let me live out my years in heat of blood!
Let me die drunken with the dreamer's wine.
Let me not see this soul house built of mud
Go toppling to the dust—
A vacant shrine.
Let me go quickly.
Like a candle light
Snuffed out just at the heyday of its glow.
Give me high noon,
And let it then be night.
Thus I would go.
And grant that when I face the grisly Thing,
My song may triumph down the gray Perhaps.
Let me be as a tune-swept fiddle string
That feels the Master Melody—and snaps!

He concluded, "L. Mendel Rivers died mourned by millions of people and surrounded by his family. No man could ask for more."

An interesting side note about the funeral preparations was that sentimental Peggy suggested asking the Charleston Air Force Base to fly a lone C-5A fly overhead during the interment. She discussed this with Mendel Davis, who assisted with many funeral arrangements. Davis told us later that he contacted the Wing Commander of the 437th Military Airlift Wing at the Charleston Air Force Base, and the Pentagon approved a formation of fighter planes to fly the "missing comrade" formation but refused to authorize a sentimental flight of a C-5A, not even for L. Mendel Rivers. So General Kennedy contacted Shaw Air Force Base in Sumter, South Carolina, and arranged for a C-5A training flight to fly directly over St. Stephen at precisely the time the casket was being lowered into the grave.

The only concern was how long the eulogies would last. An air force representative at the funeral coordinated by radio with the oncoming plane and notified them when Mendel Jr. finished making his closing remarks. The C-5A flight was timed to be after the fighter jets flew over the casket in the missing comrade formation. To those on the ground, the C-5A's salute when it dipped its wing over the casket seemed a part of the ceremony. (Years later we were told that this farewell gesture and deception, if it had been known at the time, could have had serious repercussions.)

A bugler played taps and the flag that had draped Mendel's coffin was removed and folded according to military tradition. All was quiet as the casket was slowly lowered into the ground. We sprinkled the coffin with dirt in the centuries-old ceremony, and Secretary Laird presented me with the folded flag. The crowd of dignitaries, friends and family silently turned, got into their cars and drove away. It was late December; it was damp and the long afternoon shadows underscored the chilly gloom of death. All knew they were witnessing the end of an era. We left empty, each nursing private sorrows, holding back the grief so close to the surface.

How precious and how transitory is the gift of life and how little we value what we have. It can be snatched away so abruptly. There is such a short, exquisite space between the last breath of life and the afterlife. It is never easy to say goodbye.

Afterword

Mendel had not been in the ground twenty-four hours when his namesake and godson, Mendel Davis, approached me and told me he was running for Mendel's seat. He asked for my support.

It was an emotional time. I remembered my husband telling me that he had groomed Mendel Davis for politics and that Davis showed great promise. Palmer Gaillard was Mayor of the City of Charleston and also wanted to run for the seat. My natural inclination would have been to see Mayor Palmer replace my husband. After all, Palmer was my age, lived downtown and had supported my husband for Congress in 1940 when it really mattered. To me, Mendel Davis was merely a nice young man whom Mendel had taken under his wing.

Looking back on it, there were many reasons why I agreed to support Mendel Davis: He had worked faithfully for Mendel for years and had become a friend of the family. He was at our side throughout the terribly sad events of Mendel's passing. At that time, he almost seemed like a member of the family. And, of course, he was Mendel's namesake and the son of Mendel's dearest friend. I can only say now that I thought I was doing what my husband would have wanted.

Young Mendel toyed briefly with running for his father's seat. He was twenty-three when his father died, and the U.S. Constitution requires that a person be twenty-five years of age to serve in Congress. Young Mendel could have probably won the election based solely on the emotion of the moment. However, he could not have taken his oath of office until close to the expiration of his first term. Fortunately, he did not yield to the temptation of running.

The crew saluted smartly as the *L. Mendel Rivers* slid off the dry dock to the strains of "Anchors Away."

There were three elections to fill Mendel's vacant seat: a Democratic primary, a Republican primary and the general election. Everybody I knew expected Palmer Gaillard to sweep the Democratic primary and then face Dr. James B. Edwards, winner of the Republican primary, in a close contest that might go either way. It turned out very differently.

I cut a TV commercial for Mendel Davis, in which I stated, "No man can fill Mendel Rivers's shoes, but Mendel Davis is the man who can walk in his footsteps." Davis aimed his campaign at reminding voters that he was the man preferred by L. Mendel Rivers and his family. My support was decisive.

The voters wanted Mendel Rivers, and when I supported Mendel Davis, they also wanted him. In all honesty, I have always wondered if many voters actually believed they were voting for Mendel Rivers during that primary.

A Jim Edwards story confirms this. After he secured the Republican nomination, Jim Edwards campaigned vigorously. Again and again he encountered this response: "I'd like to vote for you, Jim, but I'm voting for Mendel." (Which Mendel? Did the voters actually believe that Mendel Davis was the resurrected Mendel Rivers?)

In any event, Davis trounced Gaillard and two other highly prominent local politicians in the Democratic primary. He won eight of nine counties, including Charleston. In two other counties, Mendel Davis garnered, as a political unknown, six times as many votes as his nearest opponent. In the general election, he went on to easily defeat the Republican nominee, Jim Edwards, winning eight of nine counties.

I believe that I made Davis Congressman!

I was shocked! I never expected Davis to win. And then I knew: It wasn't Davis's victory at all. It was Mendel Rivers's. It was his greatest political coup! From the grave, Mendel Rivers had elected Mendel Davis to Congress. More impressive even than his defeat of the Charleston political machine in 1940, Mendel had managed to elect an unknown, a novice—just a kid, really—to Congress, on the magic of a name.

And the magic continued. In 1972 my son ran for a seat in the legislature. (In those days, state House members were elected in a group, with voters voting for the top twelve candidates.) Young Mendel led the ticket, receiving more votes than any of a dozen political veterans. And all on the strength of that peculiar name that Mendel turned into pure gold.

I attended Davis's primary victory celebration and expected to be recognized as the one who got him elected. The ingratitude was a terrible disappointment. One of his family members approached me to tell me how grateful his family was for what I had done. At that moment another family member grabbed the first one and pulled her away, ignoring me and saying gruffly, "Come on. We are not supposed to be talking to Mrs. Rivers any more."

From then on, neither Davis nor any member of his family paid me any further attention. I felt shunned! This conduct was deeply hurtful, and I have had a difficult time dealing with it. I felt that Mendel Davis had forsaken the First Rule of Politics: Always remember the people who made you what you are.

Mendel Rivers lived by that rule, and people loved him for it. Obituaries were full of wonderful tributes; condolences came in from friends, constituents and enlisted men and their officers from all over the world. The outpouring of grief continued for weeks in the form of warm personal letters and beautiful cards, hundreds of them.

To be fair, certainly many did not love Mendel; in fact, some hated him. *Pravda* wrote an unkind article about his death. But how his enemies dealt with his passing I don't know, nor do I care. In time I expressed my personal loss in a poem I entitled "Homing":

> *Though restless as a creature caged,*
> *He'd seized each chance to roam—*
> *At first it did not seem so strange*
> *When he ceased coming home.*
> *All through the years, I'd loved to hear*
> *His whistle at our door,*
> *And running downstairs, find him there,*
> *Still whistling an impromptu air,*
> *Gift-laden, coming home.*
> *Sometimes I think I almost hear*
> *That homing signal thin and clear,*
> *I knew so well before—*
> *Before his piping, heard afar*
> *Beyond this troubled, noisy star,*
> *Had set another door ajar;*
> *A welcoming, wide door.*

People mourned Mendel's death in countless ways. There were editorials all over the state expressing loss. His magnificent strength was sorely missed both by the family and the military he so fearlessly championed. Mendel's instincts were correct. We should never have gotten involved in Vietnam. After we did, we owed it to our soldiers to plan for victory.

Although Mendel was sent off in a style that befitted his position, something seemed missing. Mendel had championed the U.S. Navy boldly, and nobody had mentioned naming a vessel in his memory at any of the funeral functions. He died December 28, and into the New Year no announcements were forthcoming. Mendel had instilled in Peggy the importance of timing, so knowing that loyalties fade rapidly, she persuaded young Mendel to join her in petitioning prominent people they thought could influence getting a ship named after their father. As usual, the children never told me about their letters.

Marwee was proud of how well young Mendel held his own with the "big brass," 1971.

I was surprised some weeks later when Admiral Rickover phoned to tell me that the navy had authorized a nuclear-powered attack submarine to be named the *L. Mendel Rivers*. He said he had wanted to announce this honor at the funeral. Rickover indicated that it had been difficult to obtain the authorization and that the letters the children wrote made a huge difference.

There were wonderful ceremonies connected with the *L. Mendel Rivers*. First a keel-laying and later a christening were held in Newport News where the sub was built. At the keel laying I was proud of the way young Mendel held his own with the handsome Chief of Naval Operations, the articulate Secretary of the Navy and Eddie Hébert, the new Chairman of the House Armed Services Committee.

> *Marcus Antonius remarked, "The evil that men do lives after them; the good is oft interred with their bones."*
>
> *Not, we trust necessarily. A man struggled thirty years to keep his country strong. During his lifetime he received his measure of praise and glory. But he found himself time and again cursed and attacked by the*

shortsighted, vilified by the foolish and he was forced, like all men who strive for greatness, to make that choice of agony between a family he helped create and the career he had chosen. And when it was all over, he must have wondered, as all men wonder, was it in the end worth the struggle…

It is his spirit, his resolution, his passion to his cause, that lives on. It is the spirit of a man who believes: I will not excuse, I will not equivocate, I will not retreat a single inch and I will be heard. Indeed, I believe he was…

As always happens when a leader falls, we have seen many supposed friends virtually disappear and we have learned that in the very best grains there is chaff. But we have seen another variety of friendship. We have seen friendship which thrives not on its own gain, but on its love for a man.

We have seen a man's dream come true. We have seen a man who groaned, and I heard him, believe me, when he learned they were going to make the John F. Kennedy *conventionally powered. And that groan reverberated all through the Navy. And a man who couldn't wait to retire the last, bulky, conventional battlewagon…*

That same man's name now stands on the Navy's newest vessel in her newest concept of naval warfare…She will bear in her hold the tools of war and destruction but she will bear in her heart that serenity of peace, that serenity of strength of L. Mendel Rivers, which alone brings peace on earth, unquenchable, unconquerable, indomitable, 'til war itself shall be no more.

Peggy and Marion were asked to co-sponsor the ship, and performed their duties well. I was as proud of them as I was of young Mendel.

After the keel-laying, there was a christening to launch the ship. This is a time-honored tradition in the navy with deep spiritual significance. As the ship leaves the land and receives her name, she begins to form her personality. It was an exhilarating experience to see the crew saluting smartly on the fair weather planes which stick out on each side of the sail, as the boat slid into the water with a powerful swish. I was told that Admiral Rickover personally selected every member of the crew. They set the tone for the future, and the *L. Mendel Rivers* performed admirably for almost thirty years. It was the next to last submarine of its class to be decommissioned.

The third ceremony connected with the boat was the commissioning, wherein the District Commandant accepts the ship on behalf of the navy. Those ceremonies were at the Charleston Naval Base. Navy brass, family members and the predictable politicians attended.

The sub was home ported in Charleston, and the *Rivers*'s wonderful captains invited us to attend each change of command ceremony and just

Peggy and Marion christen the USS *L. Mendel Rivers*, a nuclear-powered attack submarine, 1973.

about every other occasion. Our family was proud to be associated with that wonderful boat.

In 2000 the *Rivers* made its final visit to Charleston en route to the West Coast where she was slated for demolition. (Hull fatigue sets in at approximately thirty years, and submarines are routinely scrapped before attaining that ripe old age.)

On Father's Day I entertained the last captain, his wife and six of their children in my condo, and afterward Captain Portner personally escorted Peggy and me on a farewell VIP tour of the sub. At age eighty-seven, I was the oldest person except Admiral Rickover ever to enter the vessel. My grandson, Edward Eastman, had done some reconnaissance training with the Navy Seals while he was in the Marine Corps. Edward was extremely disappointed to have missed underwater maneuvers from the *Rivers* by a two-week training cycle and went on the *Finback*, a sister ship, instead. We asked the captain to show us the cramped, dark forward area where the Seals bunked.

Peggy waves goodbye to the *L. Mendel Rivers* as it departs its home port at the Charleston Naval Base, March 29, 1995. *Courtesy of the* Post and Courier.

I did my best to preserve Mendel's memory. A close friend offered to publish a book about Mendel's extraordinary life. It was a dear and wonderful gesture. We were enthusiastic. We hired a writer and received some of his first efforts. They were such a disappointment! The project floundered, and I realized that someone else would have to write that biography. Mendel had been doubtful that I would ever produce a quality volume, but I tried. I transcribed our 1968–69 morning dictations. I wrote memoirs. There was so much to record that eventually I just bogged down. Fortunately, Marion joined in the project. In the end I turned my writings over to her, and she faithfully completed what Mendel and I had started so many years before.

I was invited to be the honored guest at countless other functions given in Mendel's memory. Tributes from the military and friends continued on and on and on.

The South Carolina Legislature had Mendel's portrait painted posthumously and hung it in their chambers, although I hear disturbing rumors that the portrait has since been removed to make room for ambitious living legislators.

In Charleston a mounted bronze bust was placed in a small courtyard between the County Office Building and the Old Courthouse on

Meeting Street, directly across from the entrance to Washington Park. General Mark Clark, World War II hero and former Chief of Allied Forces in Korea, was the organizer, and this is how he described Mendel: "[Rivers] was my idea of a statesman, a man who staunchly advocated those things that were good for his country regardless of their impact upon his own future."

In Sumter the Shaw Air Force Base VIP Visitor's Suite and Tactical Command Building was named after Mendel, as was the plaza at the new Charleston Naval Hospital. In 1986 the new recruit processing Reception Center at Fort Jackson in Columbia was named for Mendel. There were still other occasions, and we loved them all.

Honestly, I had no idea how important Mendel was to the military so long after his death and that I was still considered a VIP by the military. I had particularly wanted the whole family to attend what I thought would be the last honor given Mendel, naming the Fort Jackson Reception Center after him. My enlisted grandsons Edward and Robert Eastman were attending a Marine Special Operations school in a secure area under the naval chain of command in Virginia. It was a very hush-hush operation called Amphibious Reconnaissance School, or ARS. I went to a lot of trouble to get their phone number from the commanding general and happily called the boys to give them an invitation. I was told later that they were taken from class and ordered to do elevated pushups while being asked, "Who is your grandmother?" They were given special leave to attend the ceremony and ordered to return immediately. They were amazed that I would dare to do such a thing.

Another time when my grandson Robert was stationed at Camp Pendleton, I contacted Mendel's friend Major General Raymond Murray, a Marine Corps legend, famous, among other things, for fighting with Chesty Puller and for commanding the historic breakout from the Chosin Reservoir during the Korean Conflict. I asked General Murray to look up Robert. Lance Corporal Eastman was called before his company commander and told to report to the company colonel, who enquired why he had not told his superiors that his grandmother was a VIP. To further Robert's embarrassment, when the general visited Camp Pendleton, he was invited to sit with General Murray and his wife while many staff officers paid their respects and asked for autographs in the cafeteria; a full colonel asked Lance Corporal Eastman if he wanted a powdered donut. Robert asked me to never again request visits from our friends in the Corps.

In December 1999, L. Mendel Rivers was named as one of the "Magnificent Ten Charlestonians Who Shaped the 20th Century" by

Here we are at the South Carolina Legislature portrait ceremony. *Left to right*: Margaret Middleton, Mendel Rivers Jr., Robert Eastman, Marwee, Peggy and Edward Eastman.

Charleston magazine. He was credited for having kept the Lowcountry economy afloat during the post–World War II era.

Progress has been erasing many of the visible monuments to Mendel's efforts. He did not create the Charleston Naval Base or the Charleston Naval Shipyard, but he took them to heights of prominence they had never before known and would never know again. I remembered back to when Peggy and I had walked along High Battery, the seawall that protects some of Charleston's most glorious mansions from an angry sea, and beheld a lone ship coming slowly down the Cooper River. It was the USS *Nicholson*, and the date was September 29, 1995. The *Nicholson*, a destroyer, was the last vessel to leave the once-powerful base that had finally been shut down almost exactly twenty-five years after Mendel's last birthday (September 28, 1970). We watched that solitary voyage and thought lovingly of Mendel.

We may have had our differences, but there was affection and appreciation as well. Mendel spoiled and indulged me and gave me many privileges and opportunities over the years, the loving protection that every woman should have. He showered me with things from all over the world. It was exceptional when he came home without some sort of gift or token of his thoughtfulness—anything from a newspaper clipping to a bag of groceries. He opened doors that millions of women never see, much less get a chance to walk through.

While putting together my final words, it came clearly into focus that the yardstick of success has many notches. My successes were less flamboyant than Mendel's, but I too delivered, albeit in a manner more befitting a Southern lady. I quit drinking and tried to nurture three children who never fully recovered from the corrosive effects of growing up in an alcoholic, political home. I accomplished many things that would have pleased Mendel. We shared the same love of honor and country. We both tried, each in our own way, to preserve a heritage we saw eroding through the intrigues of a tiny minority "hell bent," to quote Mendel, on tearing down every institution in our land.

Mendel Rivers knew that the politician lives for today's expediency, but the statesman looks to the well-being of tomorrow's nation. I believe this is why people loved him. He stood for something, and he stood for them. Mendel instinctively knew that God loves a warrior, and he did what he could to sing the clarion call of victory in a war-torn nation. His like has not been seen in the halls of Congress since.

When you read these words, I will no longer be here. So, I pass the baton on to future generations. I gaze into your eyes and see steadfast resolution, courage, strength. I salute you. Do not forget that liberty cannot flourish in

Farewell L. Mendel.

the chaos of war. Do not be misled by the delusions of the intellectually elite who are more interested in tearing down our institutions than in preserving an honorable, practical reality tempered by the sweat of painful experience. It is only through a strong national defense that we will survive in a world threatened by the evil and the jealous who are dedicated to our national destruction.

On my last journey, I look to the immortal verses of a brave young American pilot who wrote one of Mendel's favorite poems.

> *Oh, I have slipped the surly bonds of earth…*
> *Up, up, the long, delirious, burning blue,*
> *I've topped the windswept heights and with easy grace*
> *Where never lark, or even eagle flew.*
> *And while with silent, lifting mind I've trod*
> *The high untrespassed sanctity of space,*
> *Put out my hand, and touched the face of God.**

* John Gillespie Magee Jr., High Flight, September 3, 1941.

Reflections of a Son

By L. Mendel Rivers Jr.

Mendel Rivers was a man of power. That is not an idle statement. He was elected to Congress and became Chairman of the House Armed Services Committee. That office delegated to him the responsibility for the nation's defense and the well-being of the officers and men who made up its army, navy and air force. The high office itself bestows upon its occupant a measure of power. For many men, in fact most men, that is all the power they will ever acquire.

But other men acquire power by virtue of their personalities. They want power. Combine such a personality with a powerful office, and you get a Mendel Rivers. As a congressman, he was given the opportunity to do many favors for many people. He understood the importance of those favors—a job at the Charleston Naval Shipyard for someone's favored nephew; helping someone's son get into, or stay out of, the army; locating missing social security checks—always that one "five-minute call by the right man" that seemed to turn lives around for the little people. All congressmen do it; Mendel Rivers just did it better than most. Each favor is an obligation that tied the recipient to Mendel Rivers and polished the legend that a phone call to Mendel meant a phone call by Mendel that solved vexing problems. "Rivers Delivers," he liked to say. "I bring home the bacon."

With each succeeding election cycle, Mendel Rivers's power grew. Over time, he could do more and more favors. And he learned how to reach out to many constituents at one time, by bringing back to his district large-scale federal projects and ever larger defense-related contractors, who hired locals for good-paying jobs that had never existed before in the First Congressional

District. Whole fortunes could be made, just on the projects Mendel Rivers brought to the First Congressional District. He took full credit for them all, including the ones that would have come to the First Congressional District without him. In time, he became a living institution, and it became more and more difficult to tell what was his and what wasn't. He enjoyed the blurring of the lines.

Mendel Rivers was a fascinating mixture of contradictions: simple and complex, arrogant and humble, patient and explosive, tough and tender, brilliant and foolish. One could both adore and despise him at the same instant. He could be a bully; he was an alcoholic. He was driven by internal insecurities and would have been even more irascible if he had been a teetotaler. The alcohol helped him to release much of his negative energy and anger. He was also hardworking, generous and honest. If he thought he had godlike qualities, he also remembered his roots. If he made fun of you one day, he also exalted you the next. Had Mendel Rivers never entered or even heard of politics, he would have been the same, a man seeking, with considerable success, to control. He could live no other way. For Mendel Rivers, the use of power was obvious. He liked to ask rhetorically and out loud: "What good is power if you don't use it?"

He never said how he wanted to be remembered, but I think it would have been as a flawed man who rose above adversity, tried to love those who loved him and actually cared about his country in a dangerous era.

My parents lived in a time of rapid social change. My parents, for example, despised rock 'n' roll music and called it "jungle music." They hoped it would go away and that society could return to "normal." Like many of the changes they had witnessed, they found this new music beyond distasteful. It was a moral issue. Rock 'n' roll imperiled civilization! Rock music was degenerate, emblematic of the decline of morals. Where there is rock 'n' roll, young people are lazy, unmotivated and disrespectful of authority.

Marwee stated that its very beat, the syncopated, irregular rhythm endlessly repeated, was capable of damaging the human nervous system. The music could even be the vehicle whereby dangerous men such as John Lennon (who was singing about peace) or Bob Dylan (who later became a Christian) might try to give a secret "signal" to their young followers to suddenly attack their parents!

It wasn't the Communists, the black people or the music. It was the fear. Mendel and Marwee succumbed to it. It affected their home life, their marriage, their politics, everything. Fear was one of their core values.

Mendel feared losing his power. He feared Negroes, Communists and students. Marwee feared the intruders who might enter her home. She also feared walking alone after dark, not having an escort and aging.

They came of age in the Great Depression. They were steeped in the ethos of poverty, the peculiar concept that poverty is the natural state of human beings and that any person who isn't poor is temporarily lucky. In economics, they valued little things, like the last dollop of honey in the bottom of a plastic honey jar. They would rather soak the jar in hot water and spend ten minutes fighting to get the last drop of honey out of the jar, than just buy more honey. Marwee believed that another Great Depression would return in her lifetime and expected it any day.

The threat of world Communism permeated the universe of Mendel and Marwee like an untreated infection. They worried about nothing quite like the threat of world Communism. It was everywhere, progressive and virtually unstoppable. They were not alone in that obsession, but they clung to it as firmly as anyone. To Mendel and Marwee, Communism was not just a group of opposing people. Communism was evil itself, a manifestation of the worst human impulses, a sort of creeping darkness.

Mendel and Marwee were shocked by the culture change of the late 1960s. They expected a cultural correction the other way. They had been disgusted by the leftward thrust of the 1950s, what with beatniks, the blackboard jungle and urban gangs, and they fully expected that the 1960s would produce a rightward shift back to "normal" times, times like the world they grew up in, the 1930s.

When the 1960s veered—not back to the right, but sharply leftward—Mendel and Marwee felt betrayed. The country was already too far to the left! How much more could we take before collapse? The country was passing them by. Mendel would give speeches criticizing long hair and short skirts. Marwee learned to utter the words "liberal" and "homosexual" with a sort of drawn-out slur, wrinkling her nose and stretching out the syllables as if she had just detected a foul odor.

Mendel didn't live to see how wrong he was about the Communists, but Marwee did. She admitted no error. I asked her in 1989, when the Berlin Wall was crashing down, how she felt about seeing her archenemy vanquished. She smiled slowly. "I'm not at all sure the Communists aren't behind all this. They're probably controlling this whole charade."

That was it! That was Marwee's sole comment on seeing the most terrible scourge that humanity had ever faced, destroyed forever: they're probably behind this. After the Wall fell, she lost interest in the Communist threat. In fact, I never heard her discuss it again. She directed her fearmonger probe toward liberals and homosexuals and discovered she was very, very afraid of them. The Communists were gone, but the fear remained.

They misjudged black people just as much. They predicted violence, decline and mayhem if black people were admitted into the white man's world. The mayhem never arrived. There were some confrontations, and there was some violence. But black Americans demonstrated remarkable restraint upon entering previously white-only society. They did not pillage and assault. Most were grateful for the chance to taste a better life. They simply behaved as all other immigrant groups in America have, and they struggled to better themselves. Segregation, not civilization, ended.

But fear is not the entire story. Marwee and Mendel may have given in to their fears, but I believe some part of them knew how foolish all that fear was and longed to overcome it. And they showed my sisters and me the only pathway out: free inquiry and free expression.

I am indebted to them for that. Mendel told young Peggy: "Don't just quote me. Think for yourself." Marwee could display great independence of thought: She questioned the wisdom of drug laws and indeed all victimless crime laws as far back as the 1950s, far ahead of her time. She supported abortion rights because she believed young women should have the right to be as sexual as young men and admitted in her later years that a terrible injustice had been visited upon the black race, an injustice she would have to help redress.

While neither of them requested constructive criticism, they endured it, even Mendel. He allowed his children to think independent thoughts. Some part of him realized he would be gone someday and they would need those independent thoughts, to survive.

They both loved the written word, and they both wrote. He wrote his own speeches, and she wrote poetry. They may have been frustrated, angry and afraid, but they were not silent. They expressed their frustrations sometimes through elegant prose and elevated poetry, and sometimes through angry invective and hysterical posturing. But at least they expressed themselves, and they taught their children to speak out, to take a position and to accept the consequences. They taught us that our opinions matter and that the deeds of little people can change the world. They taught us there is a battle raging out there, and we are fit for the struggle.

Marwee and Mendel stood for something. In hindsight, it was not always the "right" side. But life is complicated, and there isn't always a right side. There are simply opposing sides, men and women who stake out a position and defend it with their honor. Marwee and Mendel tried to be persons of honor. They believed deeply, they spoke clearly and they fought the good fight passionately. If they were in fact "wrong," then they still stand out as beacons to learn by, teaching us as much by their folly as by their wisdom.

Struggling on day by day, when all seems lost, doing the daily unheroic work of life and of civilization. when the world is spiraling out of control, requires courage and strength. From the safe vantage point of hindsight, we can laugh at the fears that made Mendel and Marwee worry so, but we cannot laugh at their courage and strength. Those are their attributes I want to remember—more than the fear, the pessimism and their strange, selective view of history.

That courage and strength is our inheritance. May we be worthy of it.

Bibliography

"At Last, MacArthur Gets Gratitude of the Nation." *New York Herald Tribune*, July 31, 1962.

Baptist Courier. Charleston, December 5, 1968.

Berkeley County (South Carolina) Clerk of Court MF File # CP-08-A86-020, suit captioned "Margaret R. McCay; Annie E. Andrews, Individually and as Trustee; Henrietta M. Rivers; C.H. McCay and Fannie D. Upham vs. Marion R. Kinard, Margaret M. Kinard, Thomas A. Kinard, Annie Mae Kinard and Joseph I. Kinard," filed February 10, 1917, L.D. Jennings, Plaintiffs' attorney. Suit to confirm sale of timber on behalf of minors.

Berkeley County (South Carolina) Clerk of Court MF File # CP-08-A87-001, suit captioned "Ella G. Wren, Laura E. Pipkin, Henrietta Rivers, Fannie Johnson, A.W. McCay, Jr., Carrie M. Wren and Minnie M. McCay vs. Margaret R. McCay; Charles H. McCay; Frances D. Upman and Annie E. Andrews, in their own respective rights and as Executor and Executrices and as Trustees of and under the Will of Thomas A. McCay, deceased; Marion R. Kinard; Margaret Kinard; Arthena J. McCay; Atlantic Coast Lumber Corporation; E.P. Burton Lumber Company; A.C. Tuxbury Lumber Cumpany; R.L. Montague; R.P. Tucker; Thomas A. Kinard; Mae Kinard and Joseph Kinard," filed November 6, 1917, Edward J. Dennis, Plaintiffs' attorney. Suit for accounting and to partition remaining lands of C.G. McCay.

Charleston News and Courier, April 4 and 5, 1879. Re: C.G. McCay.

———. February 24, 1971, and April 28, 1971. Re: Mendel Davis.

"Congress Hands Accolade to 'Old Soldier' M'Arthur." *Washington Post*, August 17, 1962.

Dikerman, G.S. *House of Plant*. New Haven, CT: Tuttle, Morehouse & Taylor Company, 1900.

"Family Letters of My Great Grandfather." *Bermuda Historical Quarterly* 28, no. 4 (Winter 1971).

Gaillard, J. Palmer, Jr. *Boards to Boardrooms: The Life and Memoirs of J. Palmer Gaillard, Jr.* Charleston: J. Palmer Gaillard Jr., 2004.

Gibbes, A. Mason. "Distinguished Richlander: James Hopkins Adams, 1812–1861: A Paper to be Read to the Forum Club, Columbia, SC, March 7, 1968." Rivers Family Collection, College of Charleston Special Collections Library.

Hamrick, John A. "Eulogy to L. Mendel Rivers." Charleston, January 31, 1971.

Hasell, Annie Baynard Simons. *Baynard: An Ancient Family Bearing Arms*. Columbia, SC: R.L. Bryan, Company, 1970.

McCay, C.G. Will. Charleston County Probate Court, Case # 255-23.

McCay, Timothy S. *Charles Greenland McCay (1807–1879), South Carolina Timber Baron, and His Descendants*, Hamilton, NY, 2003. Rivers Family Collection, College of Charleston Special Collections Library.

Middleton, Margaret Simons. *Live Oak Plantation*. Charleston: Nelsons' Southern Printing and Publishing Company, 1956.

Ravenel, Marion Rivers. *Rivers Delivers*. Charleston: Wyrick & Company, 1995. Source papers at the South Carolina Historical Society, Charleston.

Rivers Papers. Rivers Family Collection. College of Charleston Special Collections Library, Charleston.

Rivers, Margaret M. *Diaries*. Rivers Family Collection, College of Charleston Special Collections Library.

———. *Fanfan*. Charleston: Nelson Printing Corporation, 1984.

———. *Verses by Marwee*. Charleston: J.R. Rowell Printing Company, 2004.

Rivers, Margaret M., Margaret M.R. Eastman and L. Mendel Rivers Jr. *Mendel*. Charleston: Quinn Press, 2000.

Stern, Theodore S. *No Problems, Only Challenges*. Charleston: McNaughton & Gunn for the College of Charleston, 2001.

Stevens, Margaret. "McCay 'Stole' His Bride; Many Tracts Traced to Will." *News and Courier*, Charleston, May 18, 1972.

St. Stephen Episcopal Church Register, St. Stephen, South Carolina.

Von Kolnitz for Congress Committee. *Alfred H. von Kolnitz, Candidate for Congress, First District, South Carolina, 5158*. Campaign literature, 1940.

White, John. "'Straddling the Fence': South Carolina Congressman L. Mendel Rivers in the Second Reconstruction, 1941–1971." Master's thesis, University of Charleston and The Citadel, 1999.

Additional L. Mendel Rivers papers are located at The Citadel, Charleston, South Carolina.

About the Authors

Margaret Middleton Rivers, better known as Marwee, was a descendant of some of the most distinguished families in South Carolina. She was a relentless chronicler all her life, scribbling out diaries, poems, commentary, lists and even statistics—just about anything that could be recorded. These are her memoirs.

Marwee's children—Margaret Rivers Eastman, known as Peg, and L. Mendel Rivers Jr.—compiled this collection after her death using her memoirs and their own research. Peg is a consultant who teaches job documentation techniques for regulatory compliance in highly hazardous industries. She lives in Charleston, South Carolina. Mendel is a retired Family Court Judge, South Carolina State Representative and attorney who now resides in Portland, Oregon.